Full Belly

Good Eats for a Healthy Pregnancy

• • •

TARA MATARAZA DESMOND

with Shirley Fan, MS, RD

RUNNING PRESS
PHILADELPHIA · LONDON

To my children,

Abigail, Timothy, and Miles,

who inspire me to eat better and
be better every day

• • •

Copyright © 2014 by Tara Mataraza Desmond
Published by Running Press,
A Member of the Perseus Books Group

Printed in China

Books published by Running Press are available at special discounts for bulk purchases in the United States by corporations, institutions, and other organizations. For more information, please contact the Special Markets Department at the Perseus Books Group, 2300 Chestnut Street, Suite 200, Philadelphia, PA 19103, or call (800) 810-4145, ext. 5000, or e-mail special.markets@perseusbooks.com.

ISBN 978-0-7624-4935-4

Library of Congress Control Number: 2013951597

E-book ISBN 978-0-7624-5530-0

9 8 7 6 5 4 3 2 1
Digit on the right indicates the number of this printing

Designed by Frances J. Soo Ping Chow
Edited by Kristen Green Wiewora
Food Stylist: Carrie Purcell
Assistant Food Stylist: Monica Pierini
Prop Stylist: Mariellen Melker
Typography: Avenir, Maxwell Slab, The Carpenter, and Univers

Running Press Book Publishers
2300 Chestnut Street
Philadelphia, PA 19103-4371

Visit us on the web!
www.offthemenublog.com

Contents

Acknowledgments

I t takes a village to raise a baby *and* to write a book. I am endlessly grateful for my village for helping me birth *Full Belly*.

Clare Pelino, my agent who ushered this book along. My editor, Kristen Green Wiewora, whose practical nature made it easy to talk through the details, from concept to design, and who brought my family homemade burritos in the dizzying days after our twins were born. The burritos were so good I included them in this book (Baby Bundle Burritos, page 188). Photographer Steve Legato for his artistic talent and easy-going temperament that made me feel like less of a weirdo while he snapped pictures of me cooking and eating at six months pregnant with twins. Food stylists Carrie Purcell and Monica Pierini for making the food as photogenic as a sweet new baby. Frances Soo Ping Chow for designing a book to catch the attention of overwhelmed moms-to-be who could use something good to eat.

Shirley Fan for balancing her professional contributions as a registered dietitian with her personal experience as a mother and cookbook author herself. Her down-to-earth demeanor made complex nutrition issues understandable and translatable to an important population of expectant mothers. Thanks, too, to Chad Borkenhagen for guiding us through a few snafus with his technical aptitude, saving us from pain worse than pregnancy heartburn.

Clare Leschin-Hoar, Sam Beebe, and Rebecca and Fred Gerendasy for helpful guidance navigating the murky waters of safe fish consumption. Hannah Holena for suggestions and particulars from the world of midwifery.

Allyson Evans and Craig Line, who worked tirelessly and enthusiastically with me to perfect several recipes in this book, especially Seven-Grain Pancakes (page 59) and Maple Pecan Popcorn (page 93). Cheryl Sternman Rule for support that can only come from someone who knows firsthand the professional and also deeply personal ins and outs of this business. Liz Pollitt Paisner and Maureen Petrosky, whose empathetic correspondence lifted me up out of the misery of the sick start of my second pregnancy. Jennifer Lindner McGlinn, whose gift of homemade gingersnaps during my first pregnancy spurred the idea for the ginger cookies in this book.

Full Belly survey participants, who shared their stories, often deeply personal and frequently very funny. They helped make this book even more personable through the Belly-to-Belly sections.

The recipe testers who went to work in their kitchens to make *Full Belly* dependable and satisfying for moms, their growing babies, and their families. They include: Cathy Baglieri, Caoimhe Beil, Deacon and Erika Chapin, Denise Downing, Allyson Evans, Gina Fenton, Tara Hoey, Craig Line, Jennifer Mataraza, Paula Mataraza, Kris Nelson, and Julie Solomon. Special thanks to Liz Tarpy for donating her professional competency in recipe development, which always helps me deliver something better. Also to Matt Grande, who helped with the administrative details of book-writing and whose commitment to testing recipes for pregnant women never wavered, despite being a man who will never become pregnant himself.

Thanks to my parents, Paula and John Mataraza, for taking care of my family and me when I was struggling through pregnancy and treading frantically after.

Collective thanks to my three kiddos, Abby, Tim, and Miles, whose smiles and giggles make every rough part of pregnancy worth it, and whose hugs confirm what a blessing and privilege pregnancy is in the first place.

My husband, Topher, for scooping the ice cream in celebration of good marks at pre-natal checkups when we were expecting Abby; for buoying me with support and positivity through the months of the twin pregnancy when I could barely eat or function; and for being an example of everything good that I want our kids to be.

• • •

A cookbook for pregnant women is a brilliant idea, and *Full Belly: Good Eats for a Healthy Pregnancy* is a nourishing survival guide for moms-to-be. During pregnancy, nutrition is crucial and affects mothers and babies more than you probably think. I am an obstetrician/gynecologist with a master's degree in clinical nutrition. As the founder of a large ob/gyn group and a national weight-loss franchise, I practice obstetrics and weight-loss medicine simultaneously. I have firsthand experience with problems stemming from poor nutrition during pregnancy as well as the medical problems that perpetuate afterward. And I know the good that comes to mothers and babies from a well-nourished pregnancy.

There is a lack of education and knowledge about the health benefits of good, fresh food to our bodies and our unborn children. In fact, this cookbook reminds me to spend more time in my practice on nutritional counseling with my pregnant patients so they'll understand and embrace a lifestyle of eating well, not just for these forty weeks but for the years to come.

Full Belly offers tips and tricks for making healthful cooking and eating an easy priority. I am genuinely excited about this cookbook because, through both of my professions, I see that many young people are not equipped with the tools and know-how to prepare food and eat properly for themselves or their families. These months of pregnancy are bursting with inspiration and motivation to start fresh or to continue a commitment to making good food choices for your growing baby, yourself, and your brand new family.

Opting for fresh foods instead of processed ones and cooking for yourself will promote healthy weight gain and maximize the nutritional worth of a day's intake. What's more, these simple acts can prevent many of the nutrition and weight-related problems that plague our country, our mothers and children included. Lots of us eat too many meals at restaurants or on the go from fast food drive-throughs. Cooking skills that used to be passed from generation to generation are getting lost. Today, the time-honored home-cooked family meal is no longer the rule but the exception. This cookbook provides approachable, realistic ideas for healthy eating during pregnancy and beyond. *Full Belly* encourages parents to make the time to take care and provides hope for the return of the homemade family meal.

The Full Kitchen: Stocking Up for a Pregnancy Appetite (page 32) is especially for moms-to-be who tend to hurry through the day without taking the time to plan ahead for meals. There is nothing worse than being pregnant, exhausted, and feeling like you have nothing in the house. *Full Belly* shows you how simple it is to eat healthy, wholesome food without spending hours in the kitchen. Plus, mastering the art of planning to eat well is terrific practice for parenthood's most hectic days!

Full Belly also gives important tips for different stages of pregnancy. The nausea of the first trimester leaves many pregnant women reaching for whatever will stay down. These initial twelve weeks are a crucial time for the developing fetus, and the suggestions for muddling through morning sickness in What to Eat When You Don't Want to Eat (page 27) are invaluable. Later, when your growing baby starts to encroach on your own digestive space, recipes for lighter meals and ideas for smaller servings in all six chapters will help you stay comfortable and still well-fed.

Sections throughout the book offer very clear explanations of why certain foods and nutrients are necessary for fetal development. Sometimes doctors and practitioners are rushed and offer explanations that don't have practical meaning for patients. Sections like Major Nutrients for Pregnancy (page 20) and sidebars about foods to seek out or avoid are fantastic supplements to conversations between moms-to-be and their healthcare providers.

When I was pregnant with my daughter, despite good intentions, I gained too much weight and developed high blood pressure and type 2 diabetes. I had a lot of knowledge about nutrition, but it still happened. I knew that if I didn't change my habits I would have these medical problems and the excess weight for the rest of my life. Obese women and those whose diet choices neglect wellness are predisposed to many serious pregnancy complications, including higher risk of miscarriage, maternal diabetes, hypertension, heart failure, increased incidence of cesarean section and stillbirth, and lifelong issues for the unborn children to name only a few. This cookbook offers what I really could have used in my pregnancy—suggestions for healthy food (that will stay down!) for mother's well-being and baby's growth and development.

As a mom, your commitment to seeking out good eats for a healthy pregnancy is a major first step in caring for your baby before he or she (or they!) is even born. Start with dinner, or go all in from breakfast to bedtime snacks. No matter how you approach it, this cookbook will be indispensable. *Full Belly* should truly be in every pregnant mom's kitchen and in the waiting room of every obstetric practitioner. I know it will be in mine!

Rebecca Cipriano, MD, FACOG
MS Clinical Nutrition
Cofounder: Healthy Woman Ob/Gyn, Freehold, NJ
Founder: Pop Weight Loss, corporate headquarters, Freehold, NJ
Author: *Pop: Burst the Diet Bubble and Finally Lose Weight*

Introduction

When the infamous pink plus sign showed up, confirming my first pregnancy, I was immediately nervous about a lot of things. Parenthood and its complexities scared me. Picking out a paint color for the baby's room overwhelmed me. The thought of walking into a baby superstore exhausted me. Stretch marks, split abdominal muscles, ever-expanding boobs, and baby weight made me cringe. I started worrying about modern-day kid issues—the stuff of morning show interviews with child psychologists. "Sexting," bullying, and 'tween angst were all years away, but they rushed my brand-new mom-to-be brain.

The one thing I figured I had in the bag was nutrition for pregnancy. I cook and write about food for a living, with an emphasis on eating for wellness. I eat consciously, make healthy, from-scratch meals for my family almost every day, and thought I wouldn't have to think much about eating for two, save for battles with inexplicable cravings and aversions that everyone talks about. I'm a professional, and that was one thing pregnancy wasn't going to challenge.

I was wrong.

During that first pregnancy, I was part of the culinary crew on the set of a Food Network production. I was surrounded by food thirteen hours a day with access to some of the best ingredients in New York City. We cooked all day, turning out pots, pans, and plates of beautifully steamy, sizzling, saucy recipes that posed for the cameras with the sex appeal of a supermodel strutting down a runway. Yet there I was, feeling stuffed into my regular jeans, my growing baby belly hidden beneath an oversized chef's coat, skeptical of every dish that went to set. I was surrounded by mouthwatering food made by pros, and I didn't want any of it. I was anxious to be home, where I could cook what I wanted and what I knew was really good for the brand-new person for whom I was responsible.

Like most expectant mothers, I had the best intentions from the very beginning to live and eat as healthfully as possible. But even for me, a cookbook author and recipe developer, the responsibility of eating right for pregnancy felt daunting. As I listened to the celebrity chef chatter on about the virtues of his handsome meal, I thought about all of my fellow pregnant women who could use a food professional to translate prenatal nutritional requirements into meals as deliciously appealing as the ones that make great food television.

At home, my nightstand was stacked with pregnancy books filled with indispensable information about what to expect over those forty weeks. The first sections I read were the ones about nutrition. I expected they would validate my command on the topic of food for baby-growing. But the chapter was sodden with dos and don'ts and clunky with scientific measures and nutrient lists. The "guidelines" felt as constricting as the waistline of my pants against my growing midsection. Even for someone professionally fluent in the language of food, the details made me want to surrender to a sleeve of Oreos.

Most of the books offered a chapter about "diet," including exhaustive lists of nutrients singled out as those that will foster the baby's brain development, strong bones, and sturdy musculoskeletal system. "Be sure to get enough folate, especially in the first trimester"; "Don't skimp on the B vitamins"; "If you're running low on iron-rich foods, you run the risk of developing anemia." Though I was a voracious reader of the science, I saw a significant gap between the information offered by the medical community and practical guidance on how pregnant women should translate it to breakfast, snacks, lunch, dinner, and, of course, dessert. Eventually I found my way, reading the nutrient lists in reference books and using the information to create appetizing recipes that delivered what's advised.

When my second pregnancy proved to be twins, however, the confidence gained from navigating and cooking through my first pregnancy evaporated. Aside from the news of twins being a complete game changer across life's board, I was writhing with life-sucking nausea nearly all day every day for two months. The sickness made it close to impossible to eat the way I knew how, and I subsisted on a diet that made me question my identity, eating quirky things I had abandoned after childhood. During the rare and unpredictable windows of appetite revival, I desperately tried to consume something with redeeming qualities to save the twins and me from my one-dimensional diet of things such as Cheerios and mint chocolate chip ice cream. I worried constantly about getting enough to sustain the growth of two babies when all I wanted to do was sleep until the misery lifted.

If I felt intimidated by all the rules about what to eat, I was certain that women who don't cook and eat for hire must be especially tentative. The ones I talked to admitted to glazing over while reading nutrition advice and daydreaming about glazed donuts instead. While most understood the importance of eating well for baby's sake, the clinical bent of much of the advice didn't translate into practical direction in the kitchen. The tendency for information to center on what pregnant women *shouldn't* eat frustrated moms-to-be, who were already quietly worried enough about other things. Women I surveyed told me they would buy a book that goes easy on the academic and medical details and offers quick, approachable recipes that are good for them, their baby, and their family. Most admitted that they just want to be told what to eat and how to prepare it so they could enjoy it, knowing they're doing right by their baby, and then get on with managing the registry and decorating the nursery.

Full Belly: Good Eats for a Healthy Pregnancy translates recommendations by experts in the medical and nutrition science communities into a cookbook full of approachable and appealing recipes that deliver the nutrients pregnant women need. I collaborated with nutrition expert Shirley Fan, MS, RD, to take the guesswork out of cooking for pregnancy, so you can rest assured knowing the recipes will keep you covered nutritionally. *Full Belly* is a cookbook for a generation of mothers who are concerned with and participating in discussions about food safety, child nutrition, and food and cooking as drivers of good health. It pays heed to scientific research that proves that smart food choices throughout pregnancy foster the well-being of mother and baby. It is written with the ideas put forth by the fetal origins hypothesis, which asserts that maternal lifestyle during pregnancy, including diet, has a direct impact on development long after birth.

Though my principal goal in writing this book is to foster healthy, happy pregnancies by promoting eating well, I must admit an ulterior motive: I am using you to access and influence a new generation of better, more balanced eaters. If I can encourage you to cook well for yourself now (or have someone else do the cooking for you), during these precious, critical months when you are acutely aware that your choices have such important implications, then you are more likely to continue living and eating this way after your baby is born. If your child is born to a mother who cooks and eats mindfully, the odds are much better that she will grow up to be a good eater and a healthier person. Training yourself to tune into food and its tremendous impact on health while your motivation to take good care is at an all-time high means you will probably be determined to teach your family the same. You'll also be fit to endure the fickle palate of toddlerhood that may be up ahead, and to remain steadfast against the fallacy of "kid food" like chicken nuggets, hot dogs, and hoards of brightly packaged, strategically marketed processed products that aren't doing our kids any favors. If you relish your food, mealtime will become an important fixture in your family's life and memories, and your child will likely pass that on to his own someday.

This book is for women who have every intention of eating well throughout pregnancy without obsessing over the details, counting calories, feeling deprived, or misinterpreting the real meaning of "eating for two." It's for those who believe that good food is strong medicine. It's for mothers-to-be who know that one of the easiest ways to give babies a healthy leg up on life is by choosing great food during all three trimesters. *Full Belly* isn't intended for that stack of reference books on every pregnant woman's nightstand. It is meant to stay in the kitchen, with the food, where every pregnant woman spends plenty of time!

Full Belly is written with the belief that food is one of life's greatest pleasures and a healthy pregnancy is one of life's biggest joys. Here's to enjoying both.

How to Use This Book

I wrote this book from my kitchen, which is where I hope you will use it most. My goal is to empower you to eat for your health and that of your growing baby without it feeling like any kind of effort, but rather a true pleasure peppered with a bit of discovery. I know that the energy shifts of pregnancy dictate productivity and the complexity of meals. Aversions, nausea, and exhaustion often drive mothers-to-be from the kitchen. I set out to create practical recipes for moms-in-the-making that will become favorites long after the little one is born.

When I was pregnant, I coupled my professional base with what I learned from researching pregnancy reference books to decide what to eat. I knew to look to leafy greens as a vibrant source of folate, a nutrient that plays an important role in neural tube development; that animal proteins are the only whole food source of vitamin B12, which helps guard against preterm labor; and that seafood, beans, and vegetables are excellent nondairy sources of calcium, which the growing baby's bones need. But if your profession or personal interests don't foster fluency in nutrition and cooking, you might feel overwhelmed by scientific direction that doesn't translate into relatable advice for eating. Instead of giving yourself over to fast food and candy bars, use this book to help build a balanced diet and make your pregnancy the best it can be.

THE RECIPES

The book's recipes are categorized by the course of the day, from breakfast through dessert, with snacks and different types of meals in between. I tried to include something for everyone and every appetite. Chapter 5, "For Now and Later," is composed of bigger-batch recipes that freeze terrifically or keep well for several days, promising from-scratch meals when you need them most.

Nutritional calculations and features offer a cursory look at why each recipe qualifies for your ongoing pregnancy menu. We've included dependable nutritional information, including calorie totals, if you're interested or concerned. The Belly Bonus notes are succinct highlights of each recipe's nutritional assets and how they apply to pregnancy.

I limit the depths to which I dive into science, nutrition, and medical information and instead defer to the scientists, doctors, nurses, midwives, dietitians, and nutritionists on comprehensive exploration of the topics in which they specialize. There are loads of wonderful books authored by pregnancy experts about proper nutrition during these nine months, or any other of the amazing facets of pregnancy. I read many cover-to-cover and I recommend you do, too, if you are inclined, and whilst reclined! I left those books on my nightstand or next to the couch, where I propped up my feet and took a load off.

The Nutrients

Refer to the Major Nutrients for Pregnancy descriptions on page 20 for an overview of nutrients that are especially important for you and your baby. Want to bulk up on folate? Need some extra iron? Looking for something tasty with a bonus dose of choline? Peruse the recipes and nutrients chart after the introduction of each chapter to find recipes that are good sources of a particular vitamin or mineral, fiber or fat.

If you have no urges other than the burning desire to avoid nearly everything edible, courtesy of the dismal right of passage called morning sickness, check out "The Misery of Morning Sickness and NVP" (page 24) and "What to Eat When You Don't Want to Eat" (page 27) chapters. I offer commiseration and suggestions for finding important nutrients in things that you might be able to stomach during your stomach's strike.

Sidebars

Sidebars throughout the book address issues ranging from progesterone-induced constipation and tips for staying hydrated, to reeling in the facts about eating fish and why you've been advised to steer clear of certain food and drink for these nine months. You'll find overviews of complications like gestational diabetes and iron deficiency to supplement discussions with your medical advisor.

Belly-to-Belly

This cookbook celebrates the communal nature of women through anecdotes about pregnancy from mothers who have experienced it. Belly-to-Belly blurbs throughout the book feature empathetic quotes about cravings and aversions, morning sickness, and the ups and downs of pregnancy. Read them while something simmers or bakes. They are intended to remind you that this has been done before, that the ride can be a little wild, and that you're not the only one who has eaten or done X, Y, or Z while donning full-panel maternity pants.

General Pregnancy Guidelines

Getting great food into your body and to your baby is my goal for this book. In fact, I hope that you'll continue to use these recipes long after your pregnancy. Good eats that contribute to a healthy, happy pregnancy are the same good eats that contribute to a healthy, happy life. Learning how to choose and cook healthfully will spare you, and your child, from having to fiddle around with "diets" or struggle with abstention. Filling your life with a variety of whole foods, complete with treats and indulgences, is the least complicated and most pleasurable way to be well and stay well.

Prenatal Vitamins

Food is the most direct line to the nutrients we need, whether we are pregnant or not. During pregnancy, prenatal vitamins are insurance that we are wise to include as part of an overall plan to fuel our bodies right. But they can't replace eating well, so popping them and hoping for the best while you wash down a bag of cheese curls with a diet cola isn't going to cover you. Take your prenatal vitamin for what it is: a supplement to a good diet. Your doctor or midwife can point you to an over-the-counter option or prescribe one to you. Discuss any other types of supplements, especially herbal, before you take them. Some are not safe during pregnancy.

"Eating for Two" and Extra Calories

You are eating for two, and that means choosing foods that nourish you and your baby both. It doesn't mean mowing down the equivalent of what two grown people eat, or wrapping up every single day with the excavation of a pint of ice cream balanced on your baby bump. That's going to leave you with a whole lot to sort out, and off, after the baby arrives. Seek out nutrient-dense food most of the time rather than junk, and you will be on the right track. Aim for a week of eating well overall. If you succumb to a cupcake or three at a birthday party, but you've stuck with nutritious meals and snacks otherwise over the last seven days, then don't fret about it. (This attitude comes in very handy when your two-year-old goes on an indiscriminate hunger strike, refusing everything you offer and insisting on only crackers.) Every recipe in this book, from the egg sandwich to the cookies and the salads in between, offers nutritional bonuses for your baby and your belly.

I'm going to shoot it completely straight with you. I've never counted calories in my life, including during the combined seventy-seven weeks I've spent pregnant. I think it's an unrealistic and unfair expectation for a woman who has to find a new bra every other month to fit a mind-boggling breast expansion, shop for a wardrobe of clothes she'll wear for half a year, think of a name (or a couple of names) for a brand-new human, remember all those prenatal appointments, get up multiple times during the night to pee, and contemplate the enormous impending life change that is parenthood. When I asked Shirley her professional opinion about this, she doled out a suggestion I can get behind: women should be less concerned about caloric totals and more cognizant of excessive weight gain. She makes this recommendation as a dietitian and as a woman who has experienced the journey of pregnancy, and I think it's perfect guidance. A normal range of weight gain for healthy pregnant women of normal pre-pregnancy weight is between twenty-five and thirty-five pounds. Your healthcare provider will help keep you on track.

Still, it's smart to at least acknowledge some general parameters for caloric intake.

It's typically suggested that healthy pregnant women who were neither overweight nor underweight prior to pregnancy take in an extra 300 calories per day. That doesn't equate to a ton of food. It's about an apple, a cup of whole milk yogurt, and a granola bar, not a cheesesteak and a milkshake, which can compute to upward of 1,100 calories total.

Recommendations also vary per trimester. Some experts propose no extra calories in the first trimester, bulking up a bit for your second, and adding even more in your third. Suggested daily caloric tallies range from 2,000 to 2,900, depending on your weight pre-pregnancy, and your lifestyle (are you still training for that half-marathon?). Of course, if you're carrying multiples, those totals will increase. Ultimately, conversations with your medical provider should lead you to a personal target that's right for your pregnancy.

CRAVINGS AND AVERSIONS

Your tastes under the influence of pregnancy are utterly unpredictable. There were a few days during my first pregnancy when I could only ingest things that were either white or beige (baked potatoes, tortillas with melted mozzarella, hummus and pretzels), but the second time around, I spent two months hiding from most food. When I was expecting our daughter, I had to have an apple or an orange almost every day. Both tasted like the best stuff on earth to me. Two years later, when I was pregnant with our twin sons, the smell or taste of oranges was a violent assault on my senses. I couldn't bear it. I also couldn't manage any kind of leafy green for the first trimester. Under normal circumstances, I could eat them all day, every day. But save for the three days when I suddenly had to have iceberg lettuce doused with bottled Italian dressing, I could hardly look at salads for weeks on end.

There is only supposition to why cravings and aversions happen. Some suggest it's a defense mechanism or the body's way of signaling a need for a specific nutrient. Others assert cravings are spurred by the psyche. But no science has definitively uncovered why pregnant women feel such strong urges for or against certain foods, and why the subjectivity of tastes can swing wildly throughout the nine months. If you find yourself loathing the idea of an old favorite or simply are unable to eat a food you're sure you should for its nutritional worth, try not to worry about it. It will most likely pass, and plenty else can stand in its place until your tastes come back around. Morning sickness is another beast altogether, and I talk about that on page 24.

WATER

If I collected a dollar every time someone told me to drink enough water while I was pregnant, I could pay our kids' college tuitions in cash. (Maybe.) People dole out a lot of advice (often unsolicited) to pregnant women, and some of it is silly. But the decree to drink up is warranted, especially if you are pregnant during the consistent heat of summertime. I got wicked headaches during both pregnancies, and water was always the first line of defense. It helps the body materialize all that extra blood needed to build a baby, it does its best to keep things moving when progesterone slows down the digestive system to a snail's pace (see "Belly Woes: Digestive Troubles during Pregnancy" on page 38), and it keeps hydration and electrolytes in check. Recommended totals are a little bit more than when you're not pregnant—at least three liters, or about twelve eight-ounce glasses daily—but skimping is more troublesome than it is when you're not with child. Dehydration can thwart amniotic fluid production and prompt uterine contractions, heart palpitations, and other complications. If you're having a tough time guzzling enough, see the sidebar "Drink to That: Getting Enough Water" on page 85 for ideas on how to make water more appealing.

DOS AND DON'TS

My professional familiarity with food usually overrides food-related paranoia, but during pregnancy I erred on the side of caution. Even if my gut told me something was probably safe, if it fell into a questionable category at all, I decided to skip it and choose something else. Some women aren't convinced that certain items should be included on the list of foods to avoid, either because it seems overly cautious or because their pregnant counterparts in other countries are eating the same things without flinching. That comparison gave me pause, too. But often, women misunderstand why they shouldn't eat something and make a misinformed decision to consume it anyway. For example, pregnant women shouldn't eat deli meats not because they're not very nutritious (which they're not), but because they have the potential for harboring *Listeria monocytogenes*, the bacteria that cause listeriosis, which can seriously harm you and your baby in utero. The "everything in moderation" rule of thumb isn't an applicable defense where harmful bacteria are concerned, especially while you are in an immune-suppressed state and extra-vulnerable to food-borne illnesses. The good news is that when it's set against the list of things pregnant women *can* eat, the "can't" side is reasonably short. So is the amount of time you need to abstain. Acquaint yourself with what's not recommended and why ("What to Avoid: A Very Short List," page 30), and when in doubt, pick something else.

Eat Smaller Meals More Often

Things can get pretty uncomfortable as your digestive system loses real estate to your uterus! Eating meals constructed of smaller portions or lighter fare is usually the ticket to comfort (or at least less discomfort) and provides the variety that ensures you're able to pack in as many nutrients as you can, as contentedly as you can. Chapters 2 and 4, "Snacks and Sips" (page 74) and "Salads and Soups" (page 148), will come in especially handy for good eats that don't stuff you too full when you feel like you're running out of room.

And in the End...

The moment your baby is born is the instant you are no longer pregnant. Semantically, it shifts just like that. Weird, right? But you are still a version of you that's far from your pre-pregnancy self, so keep taking care of yourself with extra attention. That's not easy, I know. But it's important for your family and for your sanity! You are now in recovery, and healing from that forty-week journey is a slow—and I mean slow—process. We tend to rush this phase, minimizing what the body is going through. Society definitely hurries it along, shifting the attention off you, onto the baby, and back toward getting on with the rest of life. You need to eat food that's good for you, and you need to do it sitting down at least sometimes! You need to stay well hydrated. And you need help doing both. If friends and family ask what they can do for you, tell them they can bring you a meal and nutritious snacks. Ask your partner to fill up water bottles and leave them around the house so you find them and are reminded to drink up. Prompt yourself to have something other than tortilla chips eaten out of one hand while you bounce your newborn up and down.

When I assess my personal story with 20/20 hindsight, I see that I should have paid even more attention to nutrition's impact on my wellness after our twins were born. I would have sought out more DHA, choline, fat, and iron, which studies say may help conquer the depressive dips and swift mood swings some women (including this one) experience as their hormones and bodies recalibrate post-pregnancy. If your bout of baby blues stretches longer than you're sure it should, speak up about it to your partner and your practitioner, and consider investigating dietary enhancements or tweaks that may help.

After you've recovered and adapted to your life with this new life, keep seeking out good eats for you and your child.

Major Nutrients for Pregnancy

Your body is going through an incredible metamorphosis. Among the things that are happening: organs shifting, digestive system slowing, hormones spiking and dipping, blood volume doubling, body parts moving, metabolism changing, life-sustaining placenta materializing, and brand-new person growing inside you. The way you eat plays a role in every single thing happening to you and your body. The science of nutrition is complex and often befuddling, but over time reliable studies have pointed consistently toward a handful of specific nutrients that are important for this extraordinary time. My overarching advice to pregnant women is to aim for balance and a mostly whole foods diet without too much emphasis on processed foods. Homemade meals are usually the most direct and nutritious route to the vitamins and minerals your body needs.

These are the nutrients your pregnant body relies upon heavily to do its magic.* After the introduction to each chapter, an index chart will help you find recipes that are particularly good sources of a certain nutrient. If a serving of a recipe offers 10% to 19% of the daily recommendation for a nutrient, we say it's a good source of that nutrient. If the recipe offers 20% or more of the daily recommendation for a nutrient, we say it's an excellent source of that nutrient. So if you're in the mood for soup or a salad and you could use a little extra iron, flip to the chart that follows the introduction in chapter 4 and scan down the recipes to find those that promise a dose.

---

* Unless otherwise noted, daily recommendations are based on Dietary Reference Intakes (DRIs) developed by the Food and Nutrition Board at the Institute of Medicine of the National Academies.

VITAMINS

A
770 mcg daily
Promotes healthy skin and eyesight and helps with bone growth
Sources: carrots, broccoli, yellow and orange bell peppers, leafy greens, sweet potatoes, tomatoes, milk, eggs

D

600 IU daily

Aids in the absorption of calcium and helps build healthy bones and teeth

Sources: salmon, tuna, fortified milk and juice, asparagus, eggs

C

85 mg daily

Enhances the absorption of iron and maintains healthy teeth, bones, and gums

Sources: bell peppers, citrus, strawberries

B6

1.9 mg daily

Helps form red blood cells and is useful in stress management

Sources: salmon, tuna, poultry, beef, potatoes, sweet potatoes, bananas, spinach, sunflower seeds, chickpeas

B12

2.6 mcg daily

Maintains nervous system and assists in the production of red blood cells

Sources: beef, milk, fish and seafood (salmon, scallops, sardines, tuna)

Folate/Folic acid

600 mcg daily

One of the B vitamins, folate makes healthy cells and helps prevent neural tube defects, specifically spina bifida. Folic acid is the synthetic version of folate and used to fortify food and vitamins.

Sources for folate: dark leafy greens, dried beans and peas, lentils, edamame, citrus, poultry, eggs, liver

Sources for folic acid: fortified cereals, pasta, rice, bread

Choline

450 mg daily

Integral in the development of brain cells and helps prevent birth defects; may also be helpful in warding off postpartum depression

Sources: eggs, cauliflower, wheat germ

Calcium

1,000 mg daily

Builds strong bones and teeth and is used for muscles, nerve transmission, and cell signaling

Sources: dairy products, dark leafy greens, beans, fortified juices and cereals, salmon, shellfish

Also see "We All Scream for Ice Cream" on page 250

Iron

27 mg daily

Prevents anemia and assists in making more red blood cells that carry oxygen to you and your baby. Helps prevent premature delivery. Your need for iron doubles during pregnancy as your blood volume doubles, too! Vitamin C helps absorption of iron, and calcium can prevent it.

Sources: lean red meat, poultry, fish, nuts, legumes, dried fruit, fortified cereals

Also see "Iron Deficiency" on page 194

Fat

Pregnancy is not the time to be restrictive of fat. Instead focus on getting good fats into your system, which your body will use to maintain itself and your baby will use to grow. Of particular importance are essential fatty acids, which we have to source from food since our bodies can't make them. Omega-3 fatty acids, especially DHA (docosahexaenoic acid), are critical for the development and health of a baby's brain and eyes. DHA may also help guard against postpartum depression. It is recommended that pregnant women get at least 200 to 300 mg of DHA a day. Great sources include wild salmon, sardines, tuna, shrimp, and eggs from chickens whose diet was fortified with DHA. Some studies suggest that eating full-fat dairy products is beneficial for pregnant moms and their babies. That's not a prescription for daily triple-scoop ice cream sundaes, but whole milk and whole milk products shouldn't be vilified. Fat-intake guidelines for pregnant women are the same as they are for healthy women who are not pregnant: 20% to 35% of daily calories. As is the case with a normal healthy diet, unsaturated fats should outnumber saturated fats.

Fiber

28 g daily

Prevents constipation and helps digestion

Sources: whole grains, fruits, vegetables, beans, legumes

Protein

71 g daily

Helps support a baby's growth, especially in second and third trimesters

Sources: chicken, turkey, lean meat, fish and seafood, eggs, beans and legumes, nuts, dairy products. If you are vegetarian or vegan, work with your health advisor to devise a plan that covers the bases of plant-based proteins to puzzle together all the amino acids needed for coverage. You may be monitored for protein deficiency if you are vegan.

Calories

Energy sustenance for functioning

While pregnant you'll need about 300 extra calories on top of your usual intake, which depends on your body and your lifestyle. See "General Pregnancy Guidelines" on page 15 for more about extra calories.

Fluid

At least 3 liters/101 ounces (about twelve 8-ounce glasses), preferably of water

Hydrates, prevents constipation, helps your body make and maintain the extra blood it needs to sustain pregnancy

Sources: Your best bet is water, water, water. Coffee, tea, other beverages, soups, and water in fruits and vegetables count toward your daily tallies, but remember that high-calorie and sugary drinks aren't beneficial, and fruit juice consumption should be minimal.

The Misery of Morning Sickness and NVP

I had all-day "morning sickness" or "nausea and vomiting of pregnancy (NVP)" for over twelve of the thirty-seven weeks I was pregnant with our twins. I was endlessly gripped with the breathtaking dread that happens the moment before vomiting. The nausea settled deep down in my gut and radiated up to my mouth in a way that made it involuntarily hang open, almost in waiting; or it made me continuously grit my teeth against the threat of eruption. I grew powerless against it quickly, my body reaching an exhausted, depressed state where moving around much was too cumbersome. Enthusiasm was hard to come by, including enthusiasm for pregnancy, which made me feel guilty and self-centered. The part of the day I looked forward to most was the end of it, when I could crawl into bed and hide away in sleep.

My norms took a hit. I couldn't exercise because I had no energy, and the act of moving with vigor would agitate the slow simmer of sick. I couldn't eat because nothing was palatable, and I couldn't muster an appetite no matter how I tried. My kitchen, the most active room in our house, went dark. I didn't cook for weeks. It was difficult to remain attentive to my two-year-old daughter, and I grew dependent upon a twenty-five-minute cartoon music DVD that she loved. I would get her cozy on the couch and push play, and then I would splay out on the floor and close my eyes and try not to cry in front of her. Still today, when I hear the songs from that DVD, I think my subconscious goes on the defensive, expecting the physical revulsion like some kind of Pavlovian experiment.

I was a few weeks into the 24/7 misery when I begged my husband to wake me at the twelve-week mark when, "on average," mercy is usually bestowed as hormone levels in pregnant bodies even out. But that was only if he could promise the wretchedness would lift. What if I was among the small percentage of women paralyzed by sickness so severe that it lands them in the hospital repeatedly over the course of the entire pregnancy? Hyperemesis gravidarum is a dangerously debilitating condition of nausea and vomiting that leads to excessive weight loss and dehydration, and it requires medical intervention for mother and baby.

Thankfully, I didn't have HG, but the round-the-clock nausea was incapacitating nonetheless. I was the antithesis of myself. It was difficult to be social, and I felt terribly isolated because of it. I was hardly productive at all. Often the best I could do was accomplishing one or two tasks a day, and I was lucky if either of those was eating something nutritious. My husband would assure me that it would be over soon, and I'd feel miffed because when you're moving around in the world with what feels like a stomach virus for weeks and weeks, "soon" isn't soon enough.

I worried that my inability to eat the way I knew I should for my health and that of the babies' was going to be detrimental. I raised the topic with my obstetrician several times, and she always waved it off with no concern at all. I wasn't gaining weight, but I wasn't losing it. And though I wasn't eating much lunch, I wasn't losing that either. By her measures, the babies would rob me of whatever they needed, and I would rebound once I started feeling better. Of course, this alleviated some of my anxiety. But I still wondered if I was gestating gummy bears instead of babies because of my out-of-character consumption of excessively sugary items like cola and chewy candy, some of the few things that tamed my stomach for short spurts of time.

So why am I droning on about feeling too sick to eat in a cookbook? Because when I flipped desperately through reference books and magazines to the paragraphs titled "morning sickness," I only found suggestions that I'd already tried and no solace in commiseration. Empathetic support is what I credit most with buoying me through those very difficult months. Email exchanges with a dear friend who had been through it herself propped me up on the worst days. She couldn't offer a secret weapon against the physical assault, but her recognition of the mental and emotional side effects made me feel less alone and confirmed that I wasn't fabricating any of it in my head. This kind of sickness is so common in pregnancy that it doesn't get much more than a sympathetic nod and a couple of ginger chews thrown at it. I'm including my own crummy details here with the hope of offering a knowing pat on the back and an extended hand through words to pull a fellow sufferer through to the other side, where good food and good feelings await.

One evening, after a couple of months of feeling like I might never enjoy food again such that I wondered if I should consider a career change, I was back in my kitchen. It was a bumpy start: I had to fight back gagging when the garlic hit the hot oil and the aroma that I usually love wafted up into my nostrils. I gripped the counter for a minute and then kept at it. Soon I was stirring a big pot of nourishing vegetable noodle soup that I'd prepared myself. When my husband got home, he walked into the kitchen, almost guarded, eyes wide as if he expected to come upon an intruder who had stopped to make dinner before sneaking away. Instead it was me at my post. The relief washed over his face, and mine.

Sickness eventually lifted altogether, and I went on to eat with fervor through the rest of my pregnancy. There were holdover aversions from the days when everything offended my senses, and there were peculiar preferences right up until the boys were born, both healthy and weighty enough for twins. But the paralyzing nausea had ceased, and every day that it was gone from me I felt liberated.

Later, when a friend's husband called to ask me what he could do to help his wife manage her pregnancy nausea, my heart sank knowing I could run down the litany of suggested aids, but none would be a sure cure. I said instead, "Tell her to call me whenever she needs to vent or cry." If the most honest and realistic prescription for morning sickness is just to muddle through it, we shouldn't have to go it alone.

What to Eat When You Don't Want to Eat

NVP is still a mystery in the medical and science fields. Suppositions point most to the hormonal barrage of pregnancy, especially during the first trimester, when NVP is typically the most intense. Some suggest that it's a good sign that the pregnancy is progressing. But there is no certainty around why it happens.

There's also no surefire way to manage or quell it because every woman's body is processing her pregnancy differently than the next. I tried almost every suggestion. Some didn't work at all and some worked occasionally. I didn't find anything I could depend upon to consistently alleviate the nausea, and I had to wait for unpredictable windows of opportunity during which I could stomach something substantial and nutritious.

Here is a list of NVP remedies and food that might be palatable while you're under the weather. Chances are you'll have to toil through many trials and errors to find what works for you. Try to keep that faith and know that you will eventually feel better.

STRATEGIES

- Call a friend who has lived through it for mental and emotional support.
- Schedule acupuncture with a practitioner who specializes in women's health and pregnancy.
- Wear motion-sickness bracelets (such as Sea-Bands).
- Eat small meals often to suppress queasiness and maintain blood sugar levels, since dips can contribute to nausea.
- Take vitamin B6 supplements with guidance from your healthcare provider.
- Talk to your obstetrician about prescription anti-nausea medication.
- Have someone else cook for you. My friend summed it up best when she said, "When you eat something that you don't have to prepare, you can be very business-like about it and just get it done with." The less time I spent with the food before I ate it, including seeing it and smelling it, the better off I was.
- Do the best you can under extenuating circumstances. When I was sick, the things that I could manage to eat were a nonsensical combination of stuff I almost never eat and other food I'd get a taste for out of the blue. Boxed macaroni and cheese, bright-pink strawberry kiwi-flavored water, soda, Cheerios, mint chocolate chip ice cream, roasted

turkey, tuna sandwiches. If I felt even a vague urge to eat something, I usually did it just in the name of eating at all.

FOODS WORTH TRYING

• Chicken soup or even barebones chicken stock (page 174 and page 214, respectively)

• Plain rice. If you can make it brown rice, that's a bonus.

• Tortillas. Flour or corn. Soft or toasted. Plain or adorned.

• Hummus (page 89)

• Yogurt

• Cereal

• Pineapple: My mother-in-law heard that it might help. It didn't make me feel better, but it tasted good, and it was a relief to eat something candy sweet that was nutritious, not garbage candy!

• Ginger: There are a number of recipes throughout the book that call on the soothing power of ginger (Citrus Ginger Pops, page 81; Ginger Bok Choy Stir-Fry, page 117; Golden Split Pea and Pumpkin Stew, page 202; Ginger Cookies, page 255), but if your tummy is especially tentative, a simple ginger tea or sliced ginger coins in seltzer might be a safer place to start. Be cautious about consuming it in large amounts or in supplement form. Check with your physician if you have questions or concerns about ginger.

• Protein bars: My friend and morning sickness confidante, Liz, tipped me off to protein bars as a possibility for offering some relief. They are never on my grocery list otherwise (I prefer homemades such as Mama Nature's Candy Bars, page 96, or Trail Mix (Bars), page 103), but in the days of desperation, I was able to get these down and sometimes felt stable for a few hours after.

• Roasted turkey: The protein and plainness helped. Plus, roasted turkey reminds me of my grandmother and my mother, so I think there may have been something psychologically comforting about it, too (see Roasted Turkey, page 216).

• Lollipops or hard candy: I had mixed results here because having something in my mouth, especially a lollipop, sometimes made me gag (more). But lots of women swear by preoccupying your mouth with candy or gum.

• Ice pops: As with lollipops, this can be hit or miss depending on a sensitive gag reflex. But the cold sweetness can be helpful (see Citrus Ginger Pops, page 81).

• Lemon: The scent and the tartness can be refreshing. I liked it in my water, and I went through a phase in both pregnancies when I wanted lemonade or iced tea with lemon or lime.

• Crackers: Pick your pleasure from the variety available, but the plainest among them is usually most popular. Some women keep their bedside table and purses stocked at all times, in case of emergency!

• Plain Cheerios: If you can handle milk or yogurt with them, that's a bonus.

Belly-to-Belly

On morning sickness, NVP, heartburn, constipation, and attempted remedies.

Karin M: "Ginger ale, ginger ale, and did I say ginger ale? And no, it did not help!"

Adelaide L: "I lived on avocado on white toast. I tried ginger ale and saltines. I think it just made me gain more weight!"

Cathy B: "My aunt swore I should eat papaya. Not only did it not work, the smell, texture, and taste made it even worse. What worked was hitting that beautiful second trimester."

Alison G: "I did make my husband run out from the hospital and get a burrito for me as soon as I had my second baby because I was so happy to not worry about heartburn anymore."

Dina V: "I drank orange juice every morning as soon as I got out of bed. Once, my husband drank the rest of my orange juice and was planning to replenish it. I screamed at him, 'Well, that doesn't help me now, does it? Buy your own orange juice! How can you finish someone's orange juice??' He never touched it again—but he still thinks I'm nuts."

Laurie F: "For constipation, I did yoga poses (deep squats) and some self-acupressure techniques. And I drank a ton of water and ate prunes or the yogurt with prunes in it."

Jessica P: "If I never see prune juice again, I will be one happy girl."

Jess T: "I was comforted by the feeling of morning sickness. I was told it would be hard for me to hold on to a pregnancy, and the sickness meant things were going in the right direction."

Kat B: "Nothing sounded good, even when I was really hungry. I was afraid to go to friends' houses for dinner because even if they asked me what I would prefer, I couldn't guarantee that I would be able to eat it. We didn't eat out because by the time my order arrived I would often be turned off by whatever I had chosen."

Lari R: "I had constant nausea. It was the worst of a heavy night of drinking with no drinking. Hardly seems fair."

Jill R: "For morning sickness, lemonade was the remedy. It worked sort of, but when it didn't . . . man it burns your nose when you vomit."

Joelle G: "For constipation, my yoga teacher taught me a mudra where you press your thumb at the base of your ring finger. It works. I will leave it at that."

Stephanie V: "I was so ill with all-day morning sickness it was debilitating. I felt like I was suffering from a chronic illness that wasn't ever going to end."

Lauren K: "During the first few months of pregnancy, I sucked on Jolly Ranchers. I think the strength of the flavors helped me to tune out any smells that might have otherwise made me queasy."

What to Avoid: A Very Short List

There are certain foods that we are instructed to avoid during pregnancy. These advisories are different from, say, "Don't eat half a chocolate cake every night." The "everything in moderation" rule doesn't apply to a short list of food and drink because of inherent danger. When you are pregnant, even if you are in excellent health, your immune system is considered compromised because of all of the attention deflected toward the safekeeping of new life, making you susceptible to serious illness. And a rapidly developing fetus is exceptionally vulnerable to outside threat. All it takes is one run-in with nasty bacteria to put your baby's health in jeopardy. I couldn't fit into one book everything that's fine to eat during your pregnancy, but the very few things you really should avoid nearly fit on a single page. That's pretty painless considering we're talking about abstaining for the sake of your kiddo. Here's a list of what you should avoid and why. If you truly spend nine months desperate for any or all of these things, then on your way to the hospital to give birth, tear out this page and hand it to your partner with instructions for procurement as soon as the baby arrives.

Take a look at the chart and then go forth and enjoy something else, including any of the other delicious options in the book. You could birth more babies than the stuff of reality TV before you ran out of alternatives to the short list of "don'ts."

What to skip for now:

SKIP	WHY	OPT FOR
Unpasteurized juices	Organisms that cause listeriosis and other dangerous illnesses can be found in unpasteurized juices.	Pasteurized juices or juices you've squeezed yourself for immediate consumption
Raw milk and raw milk products, including unpasteurized cheese	These carry the risk of *Listeria* infection, which can have serious consequences for pregnant women and their babies.	Any cheese made with "pasteurized milk," even "soft" cheeses (such as feta, goat cheese, Brie, cream cheese, and ricotta), are safe to eat. Confirm before purchasing or eating and ask restaurants to check their labels.
Undercooked and raw eggs	Risk of infection from the bacteria *Salmonella*, which can be killed by cooking and pasteurization.	Eggs cooked until just set are a great choice.

SKIP	WHY	OPT FOR
Deli meats or uncooked cured meats (like prosciutto or soppressata) and fish	High risk for *Listeria*, a bacteria that causes the serious foodborne illness listeriosis, which can harm your baby.	Roasted turkey and chicken sandwiches; veggie, tuna, and salmon salad sandwiches
Raw or undercooked meat or fish, including sushi, ceviche, raw shellfish, and pâté	Parasites and bacteria that cause illness may be harbored in this type of food (either naturally or because of improper handling).	Vegetable or cooked fish sushi rolls and steamed, poached, or sautéed seafood
Alfalfa sprouts and other sprouts	Bacteria lurking in cracked sprout seeds that isn't rinsed away with thorough washing and that can cause foodborne illness	Microgreens and finely shredded lettuce or cabbage
Caffeine	Limit to one twelve-ounce serving of coffee (under 300 mg per day of caffeine): that's a tall Starbucks cup. Caffeine passes through the placenta, and your fetus can't metabolize it. Some studies link high caffeine exposure to preterm labor, low-birth-weight babies, and miscarriage.	Decaffeinated coffee and tea, hot chocolate
Alcohol	Alcohol passes uninhibited through the placenta to your baby. Your baby's tiny system is not prepared to metabolize alcohol. Fetal alcohol syndrome is caused by high levels of exposure.	Ask your bartender to mix you something sans booze: you might not even miss it.
Some herbal teas	Certain herbs used in teas and tinctures are suspected to cause problems during pregnancy, including miscarriage.	Ask your healthcare provider for a list of herbs that are considered safe.
Artificial sweeteners	The jury is still out on chemicals' impact on our bodies and developing babies. Now is not the time to be a lab rat.	Sugar and other natural sweeteners such as honey, maple syrup, and molasses
Seafood with too much mercury, methylmercury, and other contaminants, especially swordfish, tilefish, king mackerel, and shark (see "Safe Fish: What's the Catch?" on page 130)	Mercury and other prevalent environmental contaminants can cause developmental delays and interfere with organ growth.	Countless other varieties of fish

*Visit the Centers for Disease Control and Prevention at www.cdc.gov
for more information on eating safely during pregnancy.*

Full Kitchen: Stocking Up for a Pregnancy Appetite

The first step toward eating well for pregnancy (and life) is to stock your kitchen (and purse, car, desk, and nightstand) with nutritious food that ensures something good, fast. Pick nutrient-dense foods that appeal to you in an effort to make more bites count. If there's a period of many weeks when you can't even stand to look at the words that make up this list (see "The Misery of Morning Sickness and NVP" on page 24 and "What to Eat When You Don't Want to Eat" on page 27), try not to worry too deeply and assume that you will feel better and will be able to eat better in the days ahead.

On a cash register receipt, eating well might look kind of expensive. Fresh, unprocessed ingredients generally cost more than processed, packaged foods. Organic options usually have a bigger price tag than their conventional counterparts (see the sidebar "Organic or Panic?" on page 154 for more on organic choices). But in the long run of life, and in the short run of creating and fostering a new life, it's an investment that returns in spades. Plus, cooking at home is much less costly than eating out often or otherwise paying someone else to cook for you. The more familiar you become with buying and handling good ingredients, the more cost efficient you can be, too.

Take advantage of the bulk foods department of your grocery store if it includes one. You can buy only what you need and won't pay for packaging and marketing expenses built into the cost of other products on the shelves. Farmers' markets, buying clubs, and community supported agriculture (CSA) programs give you access to reliable sources of quality food, for which you will sometimes pay less than you would for the same items in a conventional supermarket.

Stock your freezer to sustain you through the first few months after your baby arrives, when cooking is quick to drop out of the juggle of caring for a newborn. (Refer to chapter 5, "For Now and Later," for more.)

Belly-to-Belly

"What's the very first word or thought that comes to mind
when you think food and pregnancy?"

Amy M: "Enjoy!"

Karin M: "Eat well!"

Adelaide L: "My relationship to food during pregnancy generally progresses like this: 'Yuck, ugh' (as in, do I really have to feed myself or others?), and then 'More please.'"

Alison G: "Ugh. (I'm eight months pregnant with terrible heartburn right now!)"

Carrie S: "Be realistic, don't throw caution to the wind."

Cathy B: "First word: indulgence. And then second is: healthy."

Danielle M: "Cheese. Yes, cheese."

Dina V: "Balance (or clementines and Snickers bars)"

Grace R: "Nausea."

Jess T: "Lots."

Kat B: "Grilled cheese."

Nicole R: "Was I really hungry all the time?!?!?!"

Tara H: "Comfort. I wanted my babies to be comforted in the womb, with foods that I loved and that comforted me."

Joelle G: "Crock pot."

Carita G: "Lifeline."

CHAPTER 1

Breakfast

Pregnant or not, a good breakfast is like the key to your body's ignition. Without it, you'll advance sluggishly through the morning, and your metabolism will idle until something finally prompts it to get going. When you're expecting, a nutritious meal first thing is more important than ever because it's fuel for your usual daily duties, and for your latest priority, building a baby. Breakfast recalibrates blood sugar after hours of rest, which helps ward off nausea, crankiness, headaches, and lethargy.

Some pregnant women start with breakfast in bed, and not the fancy kind complete with a tiny vase and a pretty flower on a gilded tray. I'm talking about plain crackers straight from the package that stands sentry on a bedside table, ready to squelch morning sickness as soon as it wakes. If you're in that phase of pregnancy, hang in there until you feel better, and you can really get the morning off to an energetic start.

The recipes in this chapter range from breakfast of the hardiest kind (Seven-Grain Pancakes, page 59, and Molasses Waffles with Cinnamon Pears, page 54) to smaller servings meant to be part of a complete breakfast, or for women who go about their days eating little meals more frequently (Honey Peanut Banana Muffins, page 48, and Lemon-Berry Barley Scones, page 51). Plenty are perfectly portable for commuter or at-the-office breakfasts, too.

Whatever your strategy for starting each morning, don't leave out the nutrients and energy that come from the most important meal of the day.

RECIPE	VITAMIN A	VITAMIN C	VITAMIN D	B6	B12	FOLATE	CHOLINE	CALCIUM	IRON	DHA	FIBER	PROTEIN
Blueberry Kefir Smoothie								*				
Cheddar Rye Drop Biscuits												
Chive Fried Egg and Bacon Sandwich	*			**	**	*	**	**		*	**	**
Cinnamon Raisin Bread											*	
Coffee Thickshake	*		*		**			**				*
Frittata Florentine	*		*		**		**			**		*
Honey Peanut Banana Muffins											*	
Lemon-Berry Barley Scones								**			*	
Molasses Waffles with Cinnamon Pears					*		*	**	*		**	**
Nectarine Pecan Baked Oatmeal					*			*			*	
Seven-Grain Pancakes Make-Ahead Mix			*	*	**	*	*	**	*		**	*
Steel-Cut Oats Breakfast Buffet	**		*		**			**			*	**
Sweet and Toasty Granola											*	
Sweet Potato Bran Muffins	**										*	
Toasted Millet and Coconut Porridge											*	
Tomato and Swiss Baked Egg Muffins	*				**		**	*		*		*
Yogurt Muesli Parfait with Strawberry Sauce		**			**			**			*	*

Key:
* = Good Source (10 to 19%)   ** = Excellent Source (>20%)
Note: DHA is based on 200 mg recommendation

Blueberry Kefir Smoothie

Saddled with the infamous pregnancy affliction, constipation, I embraced a high-fiber diet more than ever. Still, things were slow going and terribly uncomfortable. Finally, I discovered a regimen that offered some relief. A daily dose of prune juice and probiotic-rich kefir helped give my sluggish system a nudge. Though prunes are fiber filled, their juice is virtually void of it. Prune juice's regulating potion is actually sorbitol, a sugar, which retains water and, in turn, softens stool. Kefir, a cultured milk product similar to yogurt, contains good bacteria that help keep the digestive tract balanced and healthy.

Makes 4 servings

2 cups/473 ml plain kefir

2 cups/280 g fresh or frozen blueberries

1 cup/237 ml prune juice

Combine the kefir, blueberries, and prune juice in a blender. Blend on high speed for about 30 seconds into a smooth, purpley liquid speckled with blueberry skins. Serve immediately. Cover and refrigerate leftovers up to 3 days; stir well or quickly blend again before serving.

BELLY BONUS: In addition to the cleansing effect of prune juice, it is also a good source of potassium, an electrolyte credited with warding off muscle cramps and irregular heart rhythms. Electrolyte imbalance is fairly common during pregnancy and can be avoided with a balanced diet and healthful choices like this smoothie.

NUTRITION PER SERVING (ONE 10-OUNCE/296 ML GLASS)

Calories 160 | Total fat 4 g (Saturated 3 g, Poly 0 g, Omega-3 0.04 g, DHA 0.00 g, EPA 0.00 g, Mono 0 g), Cholesterol 15 mg | Protein 5 g | Sodium 72 mg | Carbohydrates 27 g | Fiber 3 g | Sugars 17 g | Vitamin A 3 mcg | Vitamin B6 0 mg | Vitamin B12 0 mcg | Vitamin C 7 mg | Vitamin D 50 IU | Choline 4 mg | Folate 4 mcg | Calcium 159 mg | Iron 1 mg

Belly Woes: Digestive Troubles during Pregnancy

DURING BOTH PREGNANCIES, BUT ESPECIALLY THE FIRST, I WAS WEIGHED DOWN HEAVILY BY CONSTI-pation, a pregnancy-induced digestive snafu. I would go days staring longingly at the toilet and watch enviously as my husband would emerge from the bathroom with a lighter lilt in his step. Accusatory fingers are most often pointed at progesterone, a hormone that plays a critical role in readying the uterus for the rigors of pregnancy. It is notorious for slowing down the works of the digestive system. You can try to override its traffic-jamming effects by drinking lots of water (which you should be doing anyway), getting plenty of fiber (again, already on your to-do list), and sneaking in substances like sorbitol, which may be helpful in loosening things up. For some women, constipation is a major problem that is especially annoying in the first trimester, when progesterone is really ruling the roost.

Tying constipation for misery points is heartburn! There are theories from every direc-tion, including old wives' tales about hairy babies, that attempt to explain or prevent the pain of heartburn, but the dependability of any one in particular is hit or miss. From my own per-sonal experience I can confirm that it helps a little to avoid acidic or spicy foods that might aggravate things, but I also ate pizza on occasion with no ill effects and, later, seemingly benign things like plain rice that resulted in five-alarm fires in my chest. I tried to eat less and eat earlier before bedtime. Sometimes that helped. Sometimes it didn't. When the heartburn was at its worst, I tried a shot of unfiltered apple cider vinegar, which I heard was a cure-all. In my experience, it stung going down and may have taken the edge off the heartburn some, but I didn't make it a part of my regular routine for addressing the discomfort. I know I'm not the only woman who developed an intimate relationship with her bottle of antacids while pregnant. (Double-check your brand of antacid with your healthcare provider.)

I had the same inconsistent results with preventing the ever-so-ladylike gassiness of preg-nancy. Beans or no beans, fiber or not, the musical stylings of pregnancy are an inevitable passing (no pun intended) phase that can be chalked up to the beautiful havoc being wreaked on your system. Laugh, embrace it, and shrug it off.

Cheddar Rye Drop Biscuits

A mix of whole grain flours tempered with a puff of all-purpose flour yields chewy little bumps of biscuits that are sharp with strips of Cheddar and pleasantly sour from buttermilk. They're a nice savory addition to the roundup of sweeter morning breakfast breads. These also make petite sandwiches perfect for the kind of mindful midday pick-me-up pregnant women need. Try a folded-up single-egg omelet sandwiched between the top and bottom, slices of roasted turkey (page 216), and a piece of cheese; shredded chicken with apple; beef brisket (page 225); or a small scoop of salmon and quinoa salad (page 133). (Take note for future reference: little sandwiches made with these biscuits are enthusiastically welcomed in the lunch boxes of preschoolers!)

Makes 12 biscuits

¾ cup/84 g rye flour	¼ teaspoon baking soda
½ cup/67 g all-purpose flour	¼ teaspoon fine sea salt
¼ cup/28 g white whole wheat flour	½ cup/56 g shredded sharp Cheddar cheese
1½ teaspoons baking powder	1 cup/237 ml regular or low-fat buttermilk

Preheat the oven to 400°F/200°C/Gas 6. Line a baking sheet with parchment paper.

Whisk together the rye flour, all-purpose flour, white whole wheat flour, baking powder, baking soda, and sea salt. Scatter the cheese over the flours and use your fingers to disperse it throughout the mix.

Drizzle half of the buttermilk over the dry ingredients and use a large rubber spatula to fold the ingredients together, dampening the mix as you go. Drizzle the remaining buttermilk and fold gently and continuously until a sticky dough forms. Be sure there are no pockets of dry ingredients at the bottom of the bowl or in the moistened dough.

Scoop up a dozen heaps (about 3 tablespoons each) of the sticky dough, pushing them onto the prepared baking sheet one at a time, about 2 inches/5 cm apart. Bake the biscuits for 25 minutes, or until their tops are tanned and craggy and their bottoms are light brown. Move them to a rack to cool, but definitely enjoy one while it's warm.

Store the biscuits in an airtight container for up to 5 days. Warm them in a 350°F/175°C/Gas 4 oven for 10 minutes, or use a toaster oven.

BELLY BONUS: Compared to a Cheddar biscuit you might find at a well-known restaurant chain, these biscuits supply half the calories and sodium and 6 fewer grams of fat, including 1.5 fewer grams of saturated fat.

NUTRITION PER SERVING (1 BISCUIT)

Calories 81 | Total fat 2 g (Saturated 1 g, Poly 0 g, Omega-3 0.01 g, DHA 0.00 g, EPA 0.00 g, Mono 0 g) | Cholesterol 5 mg | Protein 3 g | Sodium 183 mg | Carbohydrates 13 g | Fiber 1 g | Sugars 1 g | Vitamin A 3 mcg | Vitamin B6 0 mg | Vitamin B12 0 mcg | Vitamin C 0 mg | Vitamin D 0 IU | Choline 5 mg | Folate 14 mcg | Calcium 92 mg | Iron 1 mg

Chive Fried Egg and
Bacon Sandwich

Oversized egg sandwiches from greasy spoons, oozing with cheese and piled high with bacon, are more problematic than virtuous and have earned a bad name for what could otherwise be a very sensible breakfast option. Eggs are a great source of choline (about 125 mg per egg), a vitamin that can boost your memory, assist in fetal brain development, and help prevent birth defects. Pregnant women should consume about 450 mg per day (it goes up to 550 mg if you're lactating). If you love bacon, indulging in it a little will do no harm. This recipe aims to arrange bacon and eggs in a way that doesn't smother the duo's nutritious worth, including protein, which is often associated with helping keep pregnancy-induced nausea at bay.

Makes 4 sandwiches

6 strips thick-cut bacon (about 6 ounces/170 g)	1 heaping tablespoon finely chopped fresh chives
2 teaspoons unsalted butter, divided	8 slices artisan whole grain bread, toasted
4 large eggs	Sea salt and freshly ground black pepper

Preheat the oven to 400°F/200°C/Gas 6.

Line a baking sheet with parchment paper and arrange the bacon slices on it, spacing them ½ inch/1.3 cm apart. Bake the bacon for 10 to 12 minutes, flipping the strips over halfway through, until they are visibly crisp. Transfer the cooked bacon to a paper towel–lined plate and let it cool slightly.

While the bacon cooks, heat a large frying pan over medium heat. Add half of the butter and swirl it around as it melts to coat the bottom of the pan. When the pan is hot, crack two eggs into the pan. Sprinkle fresh chives around each egg white. Cook for 30 seconds, letting the translucent egg white start to set into a firm, stark white. Using a fork or a sharp knife, poke the egg yolk, letting it flatten and run a little bit out over the white. Cook an additional 30 seconds to 1 minute, or until the white is completely set and the yolk is starting to cook through. Using a spatula, flip each egg over and continue to cook an additional 1 to 2 minutes, or until the egg yolk is completely set and light yellow. Place each egg atop a piece of toast and repeat with the remaining two eggs, using the remaining teaspoon of butter for the pan before dropping in the eggs. Season to taste with salt and pepper.

Break the bacon strips in half and add three halves on top of each egg. Finish the sandwich with another piece of toast and enjoy immediately.

BELLY BONUS: Researchers are looking into the effect that the essential nutrient choline has on cognitive function, Down syndrome, diabetes, and depression, and the results seem promising. Plus, depending on the kind you purchase, eggs can also be a source of DHA, a type of omega-3 fatty acid. Check the label to confirm the hens were supplemented with the brain-boosting fat.

Calories 379 | Total fat 22 g (Saturated 10 g, Poly 1 g, Omega-3 0.06 g, DHA 0.03 g, EPA 0.00 g, Mono 2 g) | Cholesterol 234 mg | Protein 30 g | Sodium 1,365 mg | Carbohydrates 28 g | Fiber 10 g | Sugars 2 g | Vitamin A 98 mcg | Vitamin B6 1 mg | Vitamin B12 1 mcg | Vitamin C 1 mg | Vitamin D 42 IU | Choline 147 mg | Folate 105 mcg | Calcium 229 mg | Iron 3 mg

Calling in Reinforcements

REGISTERED DIETITIANS (RDS OR RDNS) ARE TRAINED AND CREDENTIALED PROFESSIONALS WHO ARE experts in food and nutrition. They can advise people on healthier diets or help people achieve specific health-related goals through eating. Since many women don't pay attention to specific nutrients or foods until they are pregnant, they could benefit from a consultation with a dietitian to help answer questions about proper nutrition, weight gain, and food safety. RDs can also help create individualized eating plans and monitor your progress throughout the pregnancy.

If you have a health condition, food allergies, or pregnancy-induced problems such as iron deficiency or gestational diabetes, or if you follow a restrictive diet, a healthcare provider may refer you to a dietitian for help.

If you're unable to see a dietitian, there are plenty of reputable resources to consult. Check out the USDA's Health & Nutrition Information for Pregnant & Breastfeeding Women (www.choosemyplate.gov/pregnancy-breastfeeding.html) or the Mayo Clinic's pregnancy guidelines (www.mayoclinic.org). You can also talk to your healthcare provider about recommended resources. Many insurance companies will cover consultations, but they may require preapprovals or authorizations. Check with your insurance company about coverage before scheduling an appointment.

Cinnamon Raisin Bread

After you wait impatiently through the baking, when your kitchen slowly fills with the smell of sweet cinnamon, frost a thick slice of this quick bread with softened cream cheese or a liberal spread of salted butter. Fix a mug of milky tea, hot chocolate (page 257), or your coveted cup of coffee if you're sneaking in your daily caffeine allowance. Prop your feet up and enjoy—the bump of folic acid and fiber from whole grains and raisins will be an added bonus. If you're having trouble getting in that extra 300 calories a day, a slice of this bread will get you there. It's also packed with fiber, calcium, iron, protein, and folate (more than half of which comes from wheat germ here), all key nutrients during pregnancy.

Makes 1 loaf (12 slices total)

2 cups/473 ml regular or low-fat buttermilk	½ cup/113 g turbinado sugar, divided
1 large egg, beaten	2 cups/238 g white whole wheat flour
3 tablespoons molasses	1 cup/58 g all-purpose flour
¼ cup/47 g dark brown sugar	½ cup/58 g wheat germ
3 tablespoons extra-virgin olive oil, plus more for the pan	2 teaspoons baking soda
½ cup/58 g old-fashioned rolled oats	1 teaspoon fine sea salt
	1 tablespoon ground cinnamon
	½ cup/83 g raisins

Preheat the oven to 375°F/190°C/Gas 5. Lightly grease a 9 x 5-inch/23 x 13 cm loaf pan with extra-virgin olive oil.

In a large, spouted measuring cup or a medium mixing bowl, whisk together the buttermilk, egg, molasses, brown sugar, and olive oil. Stir in the oats and set aside.

Reserve 1 tablespoon of the turbinado sugar for the top of the bread. Add the rest to a large mixing bowl along with the white whole wheat flour, all-purpose flour, wheat germ, baking soda, salt, and cinnamon. Whisk thoroughly. Stir in the raisins.

Pour half of the buttermilk mixture over the surface of the dry ingredients. Using a large rubber spatula, fold the wet ingredients into the dry about ten times, or until things turn crumbly in the bowl. Add the remaining liquid ingredients and continue to fold to make a smooth batter dotted with raisins. Be sure no pockets of dry ingredients are hiding at the bottom of the bowl or throughout the batter.

Scrape the batter into the prepared loaf pan. Sprinkle the reserved tablespoon of turbinado sugar across the top. Set the pan on the center rack in the oven and bake for 50 to 55 minutes, or until a toothpick or fork poked into two or three spots toward the center of the loaf comes out clean and a sparkly dark brown crust from the sugar forms.

Let the loaf cool slightly, about 10 minutes, and then invert it out of the pan to continue cooling on a rack. Don't hesitate to slice when it's still warm.

Wrap the cooled loaf tightly in foil. Eat slices at room temperature or toasted. Refrigerate the bread during warmer weather to prevent molding. To freeze up to 3 months, wrap the bread tightly in plastic wrap and then again in foil.

BELLY BONUS: Buttermilk is naturally low in fat and is an excellent source of calcium, which is essential for building strong bones and teeth. Per cup, it has about 8 g of protein. Because it's cultured, it has a creamy texture and a tangy flavor that's great for baked goods. Try it in your oatmeal (Steel-Cut Oats Breakfast Buffet, page 61), swapped in for milk in pancake recipes (Seven-Grain Pancakes, page 59), or even instead of yogurt or milk in your smoothies.

NUTRITION PER SERVING (1 SLICE)

Calories 271 | Total fat 6 g (Saturated 1 g, Poly 1 g, Omega-3 0.04 g, DHA 0.00 g, EPA 0.00 g, Mono 3 g) | Cholesterol 17 mg | Protein 7 g | Sodium 442 mg | Carbohydrates 51 g | Fiber 5 g | Sugars 23 g | Vitamin A 13 mcg | Vitamin B6 0 mg | Vitamin B12 0 mcg | Vitamin C 1 mg | Vitamin D 4 IU | Choline 21 mg | Folate 45 mcg | Calcium 82 mg | Iron 3 mg

Coffee Thickshake

If you're a lover of coffee drinks left cold by the notion of abandoning them for nine months, treat yourself to this concoction, which delivers the flavor you love and a touch of sweetness, plus a full glass of milk for the calcium, calories, and fat that you need. Commandeer an ice cube tray from your freezer or test out one of those handy baby food freezer trays you scored at your shower (the baby will appreciate your commitment to quality control). Divide a 6-ounce/177 ml cup of coffee among the compartments. (A 6-ounce cup makes twelve ½-ounce/15 ml cubes.) When the cubes are frozen, if you're not going to use them immediately, dump them into a resealable plastic freezer bag and stash them in the freezer. If you freeze multiple trays at once, bag them in single servings so you can just grab and blend.

Makes 1 serving

6 ounces/177 ml brewed coffee
(regular or decaffeinated), frozen in cubes
1 cup/237 ml low-fat or whole milk
2 teaspoons blackstrap molasses or pure maple syrup

Add the frozen coffee cubes to a blender with the milk and molasses. Blend for nearly a full minute until a thick, slushy shake comes together in the carafe.

Pour into a glass and enjoy immediately.

Variations: For a mocha thickshake, blend in a tablespoon of the Chocolate Milk Syrup (page 258). For an iced latte, stir a few coffee cubes into the glass of milk. Once the milk is a creamy beige color, add a drizzle of maple syrup or Chocolate Milk Syrup (page 258) and enjoy.

> BELLY BONUS: Drinking milk is one of the easiest ways to get calcium and protein. An 8-ounce glass of low-fat milk has about 110 calories, 300 mg of calcium, and 8 g of protein, not to mention vitamin D to help absorb calcium.

NUTRITION PER SERVING (ABOUT 16 OUNCES/473 ML)

Calories 130 | Total fat 2 g (Saturated 1 g, Poly 0 g, Omega-3 0.01 g, DHA 0.00 g, EPA 0.00 g, Mono 1 g) | Cholesterol 11 mg | Protein 8 g | Sodium 110 mg | Carbohydrates 21 g | Fiber 0 g | Sugars 21 g | Vitamin A 132 mcg | Vitamin B6 0 mg | Vitamin B12 1 mcg | Vitamin C 0 mg | Vitamin D 109 IU | Choline 45 mg | Folate 15 mcg | Calcium 354 mg | Iron 2 mg

Frittata Florentine

Frittatas are fast, excellent vehicles for using up leftovers, and they fill you up with good, balanced nutrition without making you feel uncomfortably full. For all of these reasons, frittatas are perfect for breakfast. Or lunch. And dinner, too. Beaten eggs cooked in a pan without any of the flipping requirements of their omelet siblings, frittatas are supremely customizable. Once you get down the base and technique of frittatas, substitute whatever fillings you prefer instead, including leftovers like roasted vegetables or the herbs hanging out in your fridge or garden. Take a little break from all that painting and arranging in the nursery and express your creativity with eggs and fillings that you fancy instead.

Makes 4 servings

1 tablespoon extra-virgin olive oil	6 large eggs
2 garlic cloves, thinly sliced	¼ teaspoon fine sea salt
2 ounces/57 g baby spinach (or about 1 to 2 cups filling of your choice)	¼ teaspoon freshly ground black pepper (about 20 grinds)

Preheat the oven to 400°F/200°C/Gas 6.

Paint a 10-inch/25 cm or 12-inch/30 cm oven-safe skillet with the oil, taking care to coat halfway up the sides as well as across the bottom of the pan. Set the pan over medium heat. Add the garlic and sauté it for 30 seconds, just until fragrant. Drop the spinach into the pan and stir it several times. Cook it for about 3 minutes, or until the leaves wilt, shrinking the bulk of their volume.

In a large mixing bowl, beat the eggs thoroughly with the salt and pepper. Pour them into the pan over the wilted spinach and garlic and stir to sweep up the greens and disperse them throughout the eggs.

Let the eggs sit there undisturbed for about 30 seconds. They'll start to set up. Give the pan a little shake with the handle and run a large rubber spatula along the edges where the eggs have already started to cook into a pale yellow ring. Loosen the edge just slightly. After about 1 minute, turn off the heat and put the pan in the hot oven.

Bake the frittata for 10 minutes, or until it is almost entirely set and there are no visible pools of egg. When you touch the surface, it should spring back a little like a dampened sponge would. If you shake the pan by the handle (don't forget to use a dry kitchen towel or pot holder to grab it!), the middle might jiggle ever so slightly. Since it's advised that pregnant women consume fully cooked eggs, just be sure there aren't any liquidy spots yet to be baked.

Take the frittata out of the oven and let it rest for about 5 minutes. It might deflate a little bit as it does, which is fine. Cut it into four to six wedges. Serve it with (or on or in between) multigrain toast.

BELLY BONUS: Eggs are brimming with pregnancy-critical nutrients like vitamin A, choline, and good fats. If you're having a tough time stomaching meat (an aversion oft-cited by pregnant women), eggs are another great source of protein. Pregnant women should have about 70 g of protein every day.

Calories 147 | Total fat 11 g (Saturated 3 g, Poly 2 g, Omega-3 0.11 g, DHA 0.04 g, EPA 0.00 g, Mono 5 g) | Cholesterol 279 mg | Protein 10 g | Sodium 264 mg | Carbohydrates 3 g | Fiber 1 g | Sugars 0 g | Vitamin A 145 mcg | Vitamin B6 0 mg | Vitamin B12 1 mcg | Vitamin C 2 mg | Vitamin D 62 IU | Choline 221 mg | Folate 35 mcg | Calcium 55 mg | Iron 2 mg

The Best Part of Waking Up?

FOR LOTS OF MOMS-TO-BE, ONE OF THE MOST JARRING PARTS OF ADAPTING TO PREGNANCY IS GIV-ing up the caffeine they depend on to kick-start the day. Like alcohol, caffeine crosses the placenta and accesses the fetus, whose tiny, rapidly developing system can't metabolize it like our adult bodies do. The cumulative effect of sharing your daily cup(s) can be troublesome for your baby, which is why you are encouraged to avoid it or to limit your intake to 200 to 300 mg of caffeine (about one 12-ounce/355 ml cup of brewed coffee) per day.

Black, green, and oolong teas are safe, non-herbal teas made from tea plant leaves. Though caffeine levels in tea are typically lower than in coffee, they vary by brand and type of tea, so check into your preferences to be sure. Opt for decaffeinated teas whenever possible, espe-cially if you drink a lot of tea throughout the day. Be aware that some decaf teas still have small amounts of caffeine.

Herbal teas are not made from tea plants, but from berries, flowers, roots, and seeds of other types of plants. While some herbs have been proven safe for pregnancy, many have not been tested or have been deemed unsafe. Talk to your healthcare provider for guidance if you are an herbal tea enthusiast.

Honey Peanut Banana Muffins

During my twin pregnancy, after the bout of intense morning sickness during which I could eat practically nothing, I developed a crush on the muffins in my neighborhood coffee shop. The first couple of times, I delighted in the ability to look upon anything edible with even an inkling of desire, and I treated myself for breakfast . . . or second breakfast. I loved every morsel of the buttery sweet crumbs, but I usually felt crummy soon after when my blood sugar plummeted. And despite my legitimate need to add extra calories, I admitted that I didn't need the source to be a jumbo mini cake. Still, mamas deserve good-tasting food that's good for them, too. That's why there are these muffins instead. Naturally sweet bananas, whole grains, and a sprinkle of crushed-up crunch bake into a dozen morning treats and fill in nutritional blanks that a portly cake-muffin won't.

Makes 12 muffins

½ cup/13 g banana chips, crushed (see tip)

⅓ cup/43 g roasted, salted peanuts, crushed or roughly chopped (see tip)

3 medium overripe bananas

1 large egg, beaten

½ cup/118 ml honey

3 tablespoons extra-virgin olive oil, plus more if needed for the pan

1 teaspoon vanilla extract

1¼ cups/162 g whole wheat pastry flour

1 cup/128 g unbleached all-purpose flour

3 tablespoons wheat germ

1 teaspoon baking soda

1 teaspoon baking powder

½ teaspoon fine sea salt

Preheat the oven to 350°F/175°C/Gas 4. Drop paper muffin liners into a standard 12-cup baking tin or rub a drop of olive oil into each cup of the tin.

Mix the crushed banana chips and peanuts together in a small bowl and set aside.

In a large mixing bowl, mash the bananas very well with a fork, potato masher, or pastry cutter until the bananas are mostly a thick paste with some lumps. Stir in the egg, honey, oil, and vanilla until the wet ingredients are completely incorporated.

In a medium mixing bowl, whisk together the whole wheat pastry flour, all-purpose flour, wheat germ, baking soda, baking powder, and salt.

Sprinkle a third of the dry flour ingredients across the surface of the wet ingredients and then use a large rubber spatula to fold everything together several times. Repeat twice more with the remaining dry ingredients. Continue folding into a thick batter void of any hidden pockets of dry ingredients, including any gathered at the bottom of the bowl.

Divide the batter evenly among the muffin cups, filling each about two thirds of the way. Sprinkle 2 teaspoons of the crushed peanuts and banana chips over the surface of each muffin, pressing the bits just slightly into the batter with the back of a spoon (this will help them bake into the muffins rather than tumble off as they bake).

{Recipe continues on next page}

Bake for 25 to 30 minutes, or until the muffins are set and a toothpick inserted in the center of several comes out clean. Let them cool for 5 minutes in the tin and then remove to a rack to cool completely.

Store in an airtight container for up to 1 week. Refrigerate during warmer weather to prevent mold growth. Wrap tightly with plastic and freeze in a resealable bag or airtight container for up to 3 months. Thaw in the refrigerator or at room temperature, or unwrap from the plastic and set in a 350°F/175°C/Gas 4 oven until warmed through, about 10 minutes.

• • •

Tip: To crush the banana chips and peanuts, put both in a resealable plastic bag, press the air out of the bag, and seal it shut. Set the bag down on the countertop and use a rolling pin to roll across it five or six times until the chips and nuts are in bits and pieces small enough for sprinkling on top of the muffins, but not pulverized into a sandy dust.

BELLY BONUS: Wheat germ is a nutrient-rich part of the wheat kernel. It is a source of vitamin E, magnesium, thiamin, phosphorus, zinc, fiber, and folate, the B vitamin especially important for pregnant women. Two tablespoons of wheat germ offers 50 calories, 1.5 g fat, and 4 g protein. Potassium-rich bananas can be used to replace some sugar in recipes because of their natural sweetness. And as a bonus, you'll get fiber, folate, magnesium, vitamin A, and vitamin C.

NUTRITION PER SERVING (1 MUFFIN)

Calories 236 | Total fat 8 g (Saturated 2 g, Poly 1 g, Omega-3 0.04 g, DHA 0.00 g, EPA 0.00 g, Mono 4 g) | Cholesterol 16 mg | Protein 5 g | Sodium 267 mg | Carbohydrates 39 g | Fiber 3 g | Sugars 14 g | Vitamin A 8 mcg | Vitamin B6 0 mg | Vitamin B12 0 mcg | Vitamin C 4 mg | Vitamin D 3 IU | Choline 19 mg | Folate 49 mcg | Calcium 42 mg | Iron 1 mg

Lemon-Berry Barley Scones

Tender barley flour lends its sweet, nutty personality to a mix of grains that make up these scones. They bake into sturdy wedges with a craggy crust and a slightly soft crumb, perfect for pairing with a pot of tea or nibbling on the go, if you must. Lemon and cranberry form a smart, tart duo that adds trademark flavor as well as a good dose of vitamin C. Plenty of scone recipes make sugary, butter-drenched cakes in disguise, but this combination promises nutritive saving graces and a baked good you'll love at the same time.

Makes 8 scones

¾ cup/191 g plain yogurt (regular or Greek-style, low-fat or whole milk, but not nonfat)

¼ cup/55 g granulated sugar

Zest of 1 lemon

1 tablespoon freshly squeezed lemon juice

1 cup/118 g barley flour

½ cup/65 g all-purpose flour

½ cup/59 g white whole wheat flour

2 tablespoons baking powder

½ teaspoon baking soda

½ teaspoon fine sea salt

2 tablespoons cold unsalted butter, cut into tiny cubes

¼ cup/28 g dried cranberries

Preheat the oven to 375°F/190°C/Gas 5. Line a baking sheet with parchment paper.

In a large, spouted measuring cup or a small mixing bowl, thoroughly combine the yogurt, sugar, lemon zest, and lemon juice.

In a large mixing bowl, whisk together the barley flour, all-purpose flour, white whole wheat flour, baking powder, baking soda, and salt. Flick the cold butter bits into the flours and then work them into the mixture using either a pastry cutter or your fingers, quickly squeezing the cubes to coat them with flour and crumble them down into smaller shreds. Scatter the cranberries into the mixture and use your hands to toss them with the flours so they're distributed.

Pour half of the yogurt mixture over the surface of the dry ingredients. Use a large rubber spatula to fold everything together, moistening the dry mix slowly. Add the rest of the yogurt mixture and continue to fold, dampening all the pockets of flour until a very crumbly dough comes together. Gently squeeze the dough into a scraggly pile.

Dump the dough pile and all of the dusty crumbs out onto a kneading board or other clean surface. Knead it crudely, without a ton of effort, tucking in excess crumbs as they stubbornly separate from the mass. Pat the pile into a circle 7½ inches/19 cm in diameter and ¾ inch/2 cm thick. Cut the round in half and then cut each half into four wedges.

Line up the scones an inch/2.5 cm or so apart in rows on the prepared baking sheet. Bake for 15 to 20 minutes, or until they are lightly tanned on the tops, edges, and bottoms. Transfer them to a rack to cool completely (and help yourself to one while it's still warm).

{Recipe continues on next page}

Store the scones in an airtight container at room temperature for about 5 days, or in the fridge for about 1 week. To warm them through again, set them in a warm oven or toaster oven for about 10 minutes, or split in half, toast, and spread with a little jam.

> **BELLY BONUS:** Compared to scones available at coffee shops and bakeries, these pastries are reasonably portioned and therefore pack less calories and fat. This recipe also uses much less butter than a typical scone recipe would. These homemade scones provide the benefits of whole grain flour and calcium from dairy, and they don't require a list of preservatives and additives to extend their shelf life.

NUTRITION PER SERVING (1 SCONE)

Calories 191 | Total fat 4 g (Saturated 2 g, Poly 0 g, Omega-3 0.03 g, DHA 0.00 g, EPA 0.00 g, Mono 1 g) | Cholesterol 9 mg | Protein 5 g | Sodium 597 mg | Carbohydrates 36 g | Fiber 3 g | Sugars 11 g | Vitamin A 28 mcg | Vitamin B6 0 mg | Vitamin B12 0 mcg | Vitamin C 1 mg | Vitamin D 2 IU | Choline 10 mg | Folate 19 mcg | Calcium 254 mg | Iron 1 mg

Belly-to-Belly

On food cravings . . .

Alison G: "Avocado and guacamole because it tasted rich but I could still justify it as healthy. Also, fresh donuts."

Carrie S: "We live near a diner that has an amazing cake display. I'd be stuck between whether I should have cheesecake or carrot cake, and my husband would generally get both to be on the safe side."

Cathy B: "I ate a ton of cooked salmon sushi when I was pregnant. Something about the sweet rice and salmon really got me."

Christine R: "Wasabi, peanut butter and bacon, cinnamon rolls. Once, my husband dared to come home with moo shu pork but *no* hoisin sauce. Of course he went back out. . . ."

Dina V: "I loved making mozzarella and tomato salad so much that my husband asked me to change it up a little at one point."

Laurie F: "Beer. All I wanted was beer. Of course, I didn't drink any, but I tried to satisfy that craving by drinking lots of seltzer water. I'd garnish my glasses with limes or lemons and throw some pomegranate juice in there to make myself feel like I was having a cocktail. For some reason if what I was drinking had bubbles in it or a garnish of some sort, I wasn't so annoyed."

Jessica P: "If I could have moved to a clementine orchard while I was pregnant, I am pretty sure I would have. When clementine season was over, I was in agony."

Jess T: "I had a thing for Cheerios. I'm not a big cereal person, so the unavoidable urge to pour something in a bowl and eat it, over and over, was unusual for me."

Jennifer M: "All I wanted was frozen waffles and root beer. Once I woke my husband in the middle of the night and told him that I needed a waffle 'right now.' Funny because they are both things I don't normally eat or drink."

Amy R: "I had very strong citrus cravings. About a month or so before I was due, I made lemon and lime sorbet and it was so sour that I was the only one who found it not only edible but delicious!"

Carita G: "Never in the middle of the night, but I often requested a slice of buffalo chicken pizza and extra spicy pad thai."

Erika C: "I was at a salad bar and had to physically restrain myself from eating a whole bin of black olives. Couldn't get enough of that briny goodness."

Christine N: "I craved soy sauce, which must've been the salt. My husband always wished I would crave a Big Mac."

Carla L: "I craved water. Strange, I know, but I never drank water like I did when I was pregnant!"

Kris N: "I craved vinegar. I love pickles, olives, and mustard. I also always wanted comfort food, stick-to-your-ribs stuff, like chicken pot pie."

Carrie R: "Early on I ate dried mangoes like they were going out of style."

Lis D: "I ate a lot of Swiss cheese, rye bread, and tomatoes . . . and anything that didn't make me sick."

Caoimhe B: "I couldn't get enough curry coleslaw fries (my favorite Irish junk food) and spicy/sweet/salty/tart things."

Kara C: "In the beginning I wanted macaroni and cheese and lettuce, then lots of fruit."

Molasses Waffles with
Cinnamon Pears

Add a little extra iron to your waffle iron with a good pour of blackstrap molasses. A tablespoon of the deep, dark, sweet syrup provides more than 10% of your daily iron needs. It's also a non-dairy calcium source and abundantly flowing with minerals, including copper, which helps our bodies process iron. Make a batch, cool, wrap, and refrigerate whatever you don't eat, and reheat in a warm oven or in a toaster on subsequent mornings. For an even more intense molasses flavor, use 2 cups/473 ml of milk in lieu of the yogurt, which tempers the blackstrap's bittersweetness.

Makes 5 Belgian-style waffles

1½ cups/179 g white whole wheat flour

1 cup/102 g oat flour

2 tablespoons wheat germ

2 teaspoons baking powder

½ teaspoon baking soda

¼ teaspoon fine sea salt

2 large eggs

1¼ cups/296 ml low-fat milk

¾ cup/191 g plain yogurt
(low-fat or whole milk)

1 tablespoon dark or light brown sugar

¼ cup/59 ml blackstrap molasses

2 tablespoons vegetable oil

4 medium pears (Bosc, Anjou, Comice, Bartlett, or your favorite variety), unpeeled, cored, and cut into ½-inch/1.3 cm cubes

½ teaspoon ground cinnamon

Butter, for serving (optional)

Pure maple syrup, for serving (optional)

Preheat a waffle iron according to the manufacturer's instructions.

In a large mixing bowl, whisk together the white whole wheat flour, oat flour, wheat germ, baking powder, baking soda, and salt.

In a separate mixing bowl or a large, spouted measuring cup, beat the eggs thoroughly and then whisk in the milk, yogurt, brown sugar, molasses, and oil.

Drizzle the wet ingredients over the dry and whisk everything together into a thick batter, making sure there are no hidden pockets of the flour mixture.

Pour about ¾ cup/177 ml of batter onto the hot waffle iron and follow the manufacturer's instructions for baking. (Adjust the batter amount according to the design of your iron, if necessary.) Collect the finished waffles on a plate in a warm oven (300°F/150°C/Gas 2) while the others bake.

Meanwhile, set a large skillet or high-sided sauté pan over medium heat. Put in the pears and sprinkle the cinnamon across the surface of the cubes. Gently stir the pears to distribute the cinnamon. Cover the pan and cook for 10 minutes, or until the pears are soft but still intact and a syrupy puddle has gathered at the bottom of the pan.

Divvy up the cinnamon pears among the waffles. Don't hesitate to spread some butter and a drizzle of maple syrup on your waffle, if desired.

NUTRITION PER SERVING (1 WAFFLE)

Calories 481 | Total fat 11 g (Saturated 2 g, Poly 4 g, Omega-3 0.43 g, DHA 0.01 g, EPA 0.00 g, Mono 2 g) | Cholesterol 80 mg | Protein 16 g | Sodium 519 mg | Carbohydrates 85 g | Fiber 12 g | Sugars 30 g | Vitamin A 68 mcg | Vitamin B6 0 mg | Vitamin B12 0 mcg | Vitamin C 5 mg | Vitamin D 46 IU | Choline 71 mg | Folate 35 mcg | Calcium 329 mg | Iron 5 mg

Gestational Diabetes

GESTATIONAL DIABETES IS A COMPLICATION OF PREGNANCY THAT USUALLY DEVELOPS AFTER THE twentieth week. It happens when the body can't make enough insulin, a hormone secreted by the pancreas, which helps regulate the uptake of glucose from the blood. During pregnancy, weight gain can cause the body to use insulin less effectively, thereby increasing the demand for the hormone. When the body can't produce sufficient amounts, glucose stays in the blood and levels are elevated.

Gestational diabetes is screened around the twenty-fourth to twenty-eighth week of pregnancy. If left untreated, it can cause problems for you and your baby. While midnight runs for Ben & Jerry's may be out of the question, this condition can be managed under the guidance of your healthcare provider through diet, exercise, and medication, if necessary. In general, carbohydrates are an important nutrient for a healthy pregnancy, and most American women don't struggle to get enough. No-carb and low-carb diets are considered dangerously restrictive for pregnancy, but a more measured intake of carbohydrates is required for women with gestational diabetes. Work with your healthcare provider to determine a plan of action.

Nectarine Pecan Baked Oatmeal

When there's a little time for it, maybe on a weekend or one of those mornings you're up extra early with pregnancy insomnia, make this. It's as if a bowl of oatmeal and a pecan bun meet in the oven. Leftovers make for quick, healthy, hearty breakfasts for several days to follow. Wedges with their sugar-crusted tops are portable and sure beat a packaged cereal bar and office decaf. Outside of nectarine and peach season, substitute pears or apples.

Makes 8 servings

2 cups/232 g old-fashioned rolled oats

¼ cup/57 g dark brown sugar

1 teaspoon baking powder

¾ teaspoon fine sea salt

½ teaspoon ground cinnamon

1½ cups/355 ml whole or low-fat milk

½ cup/120 g plain yogurt (whole milk or low-fat)

1 large egg

2 tablespoons coconut oil (melted if solid and cooled slightly) or canola oil, plus more for the pie plate

2 tablespoons pure maple syrup

1½ teaspoons vanilla extract

2 medium ripe nectarines or peaches, cut into ½-inch/1.3 cm pieces

½ cup/51 g pecans, chopped

1 tablespoon turbinado sugar

Preheat the oven to 375°F/190°C/Gas 5. Coat a 9-inch/23 cm pie plate with 2-inch-/5 cm-high sides with about a teaspoon of coconut oil.

In a large mixing bowl, stir to combine the oats, brown sugar, baking powder, salt, and cinnamon. In a separate medium bowl or a large, spouted measuring cup, whisk together the milk, yogurt, egg, coconut oil, maple syrup, and vanilla. Pour the liquid ingredients over the oat mixture and fold everything together with a large rubber spatula. Now stir in the nectarines.

Pour the oat batter into the pie plate. Scatter the pecans and sprinkle the turbinado sugar across the surface. Set the pie plate on a baking sheet and bake the oatmeal for about 50 minutes, or until the whole of it is set so there's no more wobble at the center and the top is crisp with a sugary toasted pecan crust.

Let the oatmeal sit for about 5 minutes before cutting into wedges and serving. Drizzle a little extra maple syrup on top, if you like.

Refrigerate leftovers up to 5 days and reheat servings in the microwave or in a warm oven (325°F/165°C/Gas 3) for 10 to 15 minutes.

BELLY BONUS: Oats are whole grains and can help with maintaining blood sugar levels and getting the digestive system on track. They are also a source of soluble fiber, which can lower LDL or "bad" cholesterol.

NUTRITION PER SERVING (1 WEDGE)

Calories 261 | Total fat 12 g (Saturated 5 g, Poly 2 g, Omega-3 0.11 g, DHA 0.00 g, EPA 0.00 g, Mono 4 g) | Cholesterol 29 mg | Protein 7 g | Sodium 305 mg | Carbohydrates 34 g | Fiber 3 g | Sugars 19 g | Vitamin A 40 mcg | Vitamin B6 0 mg | Vitamin B12 0 mcg | Vitamin C 2 mg | Vitamin D 29 IU | Choline 33 mg | Folate 10 mcg | Calcium 137 mg | Iron 1 mg

Seven-Grain Pancakes Make-Ahead Mix

There are a lot of multigrain pancake recipes, and plenty of boxed mix varieties. With that in mind, you might balk at this particular formula and all the grains it requires. You already feel like you're toting around a 10-pound bag of flour at all times, so do you really need to lug home what seems like another 10 pounds of grains? Yes. Here's why. I should have named this recipe Gateway Pancakes because I'm certain that if you invest in all of these grains now to make these pancakes (which, I promise, are better than any boxed mix you can buy), you will come to love them and feel compelled to use them again and again. In doing so, you will embrace whole grains (see "Whole Lotta Whole Grains," page 260), which are a nutritional boon to your diet. And that baby of yours will grow up loving them, too, because his mom always had a big batch of Seven-Grain Pancake mix for Saturday mornings, and because her cookies (Cocoa Chewy Gem Drops, page 247), cobblers (Apple Cranberry Cobbler, page 236), crisps (Berry Crumbles, page 242), biscuits (Cheddar Rye Drop Biscuits, page 39), scones (Lemon-Berry Barley Scones, page 51), and waffles (Molasses Waffles with Cinnamon Pears, page 54) weren't made with just one-dimensional white flour, but with lots of multidimensional grains (and plenty of love).

Makes enough for 4 batches of mix (yielding 12 pancakes each)

3 cups/362 g white whole wheat flour	1 cup/116 g wheat germ
1 cup/150 g brown rice flour	1 cup/104 g old-fashioned rolled oats
1 cup/115 g rye flour	½ cup/718 g dark brown sugar
1 cup/116 g barley flour	2 tablespoons plus 2 teaspoons baking powder
1 cup/156 g corn flour, also referred to as finely ground cornmeal (coarser stone-ground cornmeal, like the type used for grits and polenta, makes for much grittier cakes)	2 teaspoons fine sea salt
	1¼ teaspoons ground cinnamon

In a large mixing bowl, combine the white whole wheat flour, brown rice flour, rye flour, barley flour, corn flour, wheat germ, oats, brown sugar, baking powder, salt, and cinnamon. Whisk very thoroughly to be sure everything is evenly distributed. The brown sugar tends to clump a bit from its inherent moisture, so just squeeze any little masses to break them apart and continue whisking into the other dry ingredients.

Scoop the mix into an airtight container and store it in a cool, dry place for up to 3 months.

FOR ONE BATCH OF 12 PANCAKES (4 SERVINGS)

2 heaping cups/293 g Seven-Grain Pancakes Make-Ahead Mix (see tip)	1 large egg
	1⅔ cups/394 ml low-fat or whole milk
3 tablespoons vegetable, canola, safflower, or nut oil, plus more for the skillet or griddle	

{Recipe continues on next page}

Be sure to whisk the big batch of pancake mix before measuring some of it out for a single batch, since the ingredients will settle and redistribute in storage.

Dump the pancake mix into a large mixing bowl.

Paint a skillet or griddle with 2 teaspoons of oil and set it over medium heat.

Beat the egg in a medium bowl or a spouted measuring cup and then whisk in the milk and oil. Pour this mixture all over the surface of the dry ingredients in the bowl. Whisk everything together just until incorporated, making sure no dry ingredients are hiding at the bottom of the bowl.

Ladle ¼ cup/59 ml of the batter into a puddle on the hot skillet or griddle for each pancake. Leave about ½ inch/1.3 cm between each pancake as you distribute the batter. Cook for 1 to 2 minutes, or until bubbles form on top of the wet batter and the bottoms are nicely browned. Gently flip the pancakes to the other side with a spatula. Cook for another minute, or until the underside of the pancake is as tanned as you prefer. If necessary, brush the skillet or griddle with a little extra oil between batches of pancakes to prevent sticking.

Serve the hot pancakes right off the skillet or griddle or set them on a platter in a warm oven (300°F/150°C/Gas 2) until ready to serve.

• • •

Tip: As a rule, digging a measuring cup into a bag or bin of flour is ill-advised. Doing so actually ends up mining more than a recipe requires, sometimes considerably more if you're putting any muscle behind it, altering the results. The prescribed method is to spoon the flour into the measuring cup without packing, tamping, or tapping it down, and then level off any excess with the edge of a knife or a pastry bench scraper. In the case of this recipe, I recommend 2 heaping cupfuls of the pancake mix, which you should measure by spooning it into the cup a little above the rim and then not leveling it off. Doing it this way ensures just the right amount for twelve pancakes according to the single batch recipe. Scooping up the mix with your measuring cup will get you upward of ¼ cup more than you need, and unpleasantly dense pancakes.

> **BELLY BONUS:** Your pregnant body requires more protein and fiber than usual, and these stacks have high tallies of each. Both nutrients take more time for the body to digest, giving them the incredible power to satiate. These pancakes are satisfying and filling because of it. Try them when you've got a long day ahead or need a stick-to-your-ribs meal.

NUTRITION PER SERVING (3 PANCAKES)

Calories 452 | Total fat 17 g (Saturated 3 g, Poly 8 g, Omega-3 0.87 g, DHA 0.01 g, EPA 0.00 g, Mono 4 g) | Cholesterol 57 mg | Protein 14 g | Sodium 580 mg | Carbohydrates 62 g | Fiber 7 g | Sugars 10 g | Vitamin A 68 mcg | Vitamin B6 0 mg | Vitamin B12 1 mcg | Vitamin C 0 mg | Vitamin D 62 IU | Choline 57 mg | Folate 69 mcg | Calcium 268 mg | Iron 3 mg

Steel-Cut Oats Breakfast Buffet

Steel-cut oats are the kind of hearty breakfast that will carry you straight through the morning without stopping for a break. Also called whole grain groats, steel-cut oats are cut instead of rolled into tiny pinhead pieces that require way more time to cook than that bag of pre-sugared instant oatmeal (which is cut, rolled, and par-cooked). But if you invest the time in a multiserving pot once during the week, you'll have at least four far more nutritious and satisfying breakfasts ready in the same quick "instant" that single-serving packet requires. This recipe makes at least four servings of plain oatmeal sweetened slightly with maple syrup. You can use water instead of milk, but I love the rich creaminess that comes from cooking steel-cut oats in milk. From this basic recipe, your options are endless for customizing your bowl how you like it. Browse the buffet of suggestions below or fiddle with your own flavor combinations.

Makes 4 to 6 servings

1 cup/170 g steel-cut oats	1 tablespoon unsalted butter
4 cups/946 ml low-fat or whole milk	1 tablespoon pure maple syrup

Set a medium saucepot over medium heat and add the oats. Toast them in the dry pot for about 5 minutes, or until they start to smell a little like baking bread. Carefully add the milk, which will sputter quite a bit when it hits the hot pot. Give the milk about 5 minutes to boil. As soon as it does, reduce the heat to medium low and simmer for 30 minutes, uncovered, stirring often to jostle the grains as they plump and soften, and to prevent the milk from scorching on the bottom. A skin will gather on the top of the oats as they cook. Just stir it back into the oats.

Test the grains for doneness. They should be tender but a little bit chewy. If the consistency of the oatmeal is too stiff or thick, add a little bit more milk or water to loosen it. If you prefer yours thicker than it appears after 30 minutes, continue simmering to the desired consistency.

Add the butter and maple syrup and stir to melt the butter completely. Scoop out about 1 cup of cooked oats per serving and flavor your bowl with one of the following combinations or any that you dream up on your own.

Stir-Ins and Add-Ons, Per Bowl:

Peanut Butter and Jam: 1 tablespoon peanut butter + 2 teaspoons Strawberry Sauce (page 71) or your favorite jam

Apple Cider Walnut: 2 to 4 tablespoons apple cider + 2 tablespoons chopped toasted walnuts + 1 small apple, cubed or grated

Almond Coconut: 1 tablespoon almond butter + 1 tablespoon toasted almond slivers + 1 tablespoon toasted unsweetened shredded coconut

Cinnamon Raisin: A pinch of ground cinnamon + 2 tablespoons raisins

Granola: 3 tablespoons Sweet and Toasty Granola (page 63)

{Recipe continues on next page}

Cherry Maple Pecan: 3 tablespoons dried cherries (or ¼ cup/28 g pitted, chopped fresh cherries) + 2 teaspoons pure maple syrup plus 2 tablespoons chopped toasted pecans

Brown Sugar Banana Cinnamon: 1 tablespoon brown sugar + 1 small banana, cubed + a pinch of cinnamon

Peaches and Vanilla Cream: 1 ripe peach, thinly sliced + ¼ teaspoon vanilla extract stirred into 3 tablespoons whole milk plain yogurt

Molasses Applesauce: 1 tablespoon blackstrap molasses + ¼ cup/61 g unsweetened applesauce

Blueberries and Sunflower Seeds: ¼ cup/43 g fresh blueberries or 2 tablespoons dried blueberries + 2 tablespoons toasted unsalted sunflower seeds

Pomegranate Pistachio: ¼ cup/35 g pomegranate seeds + 2 tablespoons Greek-style yogurt + tablespoon chopped shelled pistachios

Chocolate Raspberry: 1 tablespoon bittersweet chocolate chips (above 60% cacao) + ¼ cup/ 28 g raspberries

Honey Buttermilk: 2 teaspoons honey + ¼ cup/59 ml buttermilk

BELLY BONUS: Whole grain oats pack in 6 g of protein and 4 g of fiber for a mere 150 calories in this recipe. Cooking the oats in milk kick-starts your daily calcium tally.

NUTRITION PER SERVING (1 CUP/255 G PLAIN MAPLE OATMEAL)

Calories 290 | Total fat 8 g (Saturated 4 g, Poly 0 g, Omega-3 0.02 g, DHA 0.00 g, EPA 0.00 g, Mono 1 g) | Cholesterol 20 mg | Protein 15 g | Sodium 108 mg | Carbohydrates 44 g | Fiber 4 g | Sugars 16 g | Vitamin A 166 mcg | Vitamin B6 0 mg | Vitamin B12 1 mcg | Vitamin C 0 mg | Vitamin D 119 IU | Choline 44 mg | Folate 12 mcg | Calcium 332 mg | Iron 2 mg

Sweet and Toasty Granola

Your kitchen will smell like coconut and maple while oats bake to a sweet crunch that you'll want to eat all day long. And you should—with fruit and yogurt, from a snack cup with nuts and dried fruit, or spooned over a scoop of ice cream. At its simplest, a bowlful with milk, you'll add fiber from the whole grain oats and folate from the wheat germ. Unsweetened coconut flakes are just that: desiccated coconut, without the extra sugar and calories that sweetened flakes include. For more flavor, texture, and nutrition, add your favorite ingredients after the granola cools. See the list below for some ideas.

Makes 8 servings

½ cup/118 ml pure maple syrup

3 tablespoons coconut oil, melted if solid and cooled slightly

½ teaspoon vanilla extract

3 cups/348 g old-fashioned rolled oats (not quick-cooking or instant)

¼ cup/28 g unsweetened dried shredded coconut

¼ cup/28 g wheat germ

½ teaspoon fine sea salt

Position the oven racks on the middle and lower settings and set out two rimmed baking sheets. Preheat the oven to 350°F/175°C/Gas 4.

In a small mixing bowl or spouted measuring cup, whisk together the maple syrup, coconut oil, and vanilla.

In a large mixing bowl, combine the oats, coconut, wheat germ, and salt. Pour the maple mixture over the oats and stir to coat. Dump the oats out onto the baking sheets and spread into an even layer on each pan.

Bake the oats for 20 to 25 minutes, rotating the baking sheets and gently turning the oats with a long-handled wooden spoon halfway through, until the oats and coconut are toasty and golden. Remove the trays from the oven and let the granola cool completely. It will get crunchier as it cools.

Store in an airtight container for up to 5 days.

• • •

Variations: If you like, stir in extras like these once the granola has cooled:

1 cup dried fruit, such as raisins, cherries, apricots, blueberries, or a combination of your favorites

1 cup/about 128 g chopped toasted nuts, such as almonds, walnuts, or pecans

½ cup/71 g sunflower seeds

½ cup/85 g dark chocolate chips

1 cup/120 g baked banana chips

1 cup/180 g chocolate-covered raisins

{Recipe continues on next page}

BELLY BONUS: Wheat germ is a valuable source of vitamins and minerals that are important during pregnancy. Besides folate, it contains vitamin E (an antioxidant), magnesium, thiamin, phosphorus, and zinc. It's also a source of fiber and protein. Add it to smoothies, oatmeal, yogurt, baked goods, and even savory things like meatballs and stews. Oats are a great source of fiber, which helps move things along the digestive tract. They also help regulate blood sugar levels, lower cholesterol, and fill you up.

NUTRITION PER SERVING (^{2}/3 CUP/64 G)

Calories 246 | Total fat 10 g (Saturated 7 g, Poly 1 g, Omega-3 0.00 g, DHA 0.00 g, EPA 0.00 g, Mono 1 g) | Cholesterol 0 mg | Protein 5 g | Sodium 71 mg | Carbohydrates 36 g | Fiber 4 g | Sugars 14 g | Vitamin A 0 mcg | Vitamin B6 0 mg | Vitamin B12 0 mcg | Vitamin C 0 mg | Vitamin D 0 IU | Choline 0 mg | Folate 28 mcg | Calcium 23 mg | Iron 2 mg

Sweet Potato Bran Muffins

Enjoy this muffin with a hot tea in a comfy, oversized chair, or at your desk, which seems to be getting farther and farther away from you as your midsection grows. A lot of muffins are really just cupcakes without the icing, courtesy of loads of sugar and butter, and have little by way of nutritional saving graces. These muffins are not that. Still, their sweetness from moist, sugary sweet potatoes suggests they're a treat despite their whole grain fortitude and minimal fats. They take to toasting very well and are a perfect match for a spread of soft cream cheese.

Makes 12 muffins

1 cup/258 g cooked, puréed sweet potato (canned or from 1 roasted medium sweet potato; see tip)

1 large egg, beaten

½ cup/134 g low-fat vanilla yogurt

⅓ cup/79 ml molasses

3 tablespoons coconut oil, melted if solid and cooled to room temperature, plus more for coating the muffin tin

1 teaspoon vanilla extract

1 cup/122 g white whole wheat flour

1 cup/125 g whole wheat pastry flour

½ cup/28 g wheat bran

1 teaspoon pumpkin pie spice

1 teaspoon baking powder

½ teaspoon baking soda

½ teaspoon fine sea salt

Preheat the oven to 375°F/190°C/Gas 5. Coat the bottoms and sides of a 12-cup muffin tin with coconut oil or put paper liners in each cup.

In a large mixing bowl, combine the sweet potato purée, egg, yogurt, molasses, coconut oil, and vanilla, mixing well until blended and smooth.

In a medium mixing bowl, whisk together the flours, wheat bran, pumpkin pie spice, baking powder, baking soda, and salt.

Sprinkle the dry ingredients over the wet ingredients in thirds, using a large rubber spatula to combine. Continue to fold the ingredients together until there are no traces of powdery dry pockets in the thick batter or at the bottom of the bowl.

Scoop the batter evenly among the 12 muffin tins, each cup about half full, and bake for 20 minutes, or until the tops and edges are browned, the muffins are set and don't yield to the gentle nudge of a fingertip, and a fork or toothpick comes out clean when inserted into the middle. Let the muffins sit for 10 minutes before removing them to a rack to cool slightly if not completely.

Store the muffins in an airtight container or resealable bag for up to 5 days. Consider refrigerating during warmer months to prevent mold growth.

• • •

Tip: If you use a roasted sweet potato for these muffins, be sure to purée it. Bake the potato until very soft, scoop out the insides (discarding the skins or snacking on them with a little melted butter and a drizzle of honey), and purée until completely smooth. Hand-mashed sweet potatoes

{Recipe continues on next page}

make the batter too dense and run the risk of contributing lumps that won't disappear when the muffin bakes. Puréeing the potato thoroughly creates the smooth, slightly thin texture of canned sweet potato purée.

BELLY BONUS: Sweet potatoes are packed with carotenoids (precursors to vitamin A), vitamin C, fiber, and blood-pressure-lowering potassium. Molasses, especially blackstrap, is a source of prized pregnancy minerals such as iron, magnesium, calcium, and potassium.

NUTRITION PER SERVING (1 MUFFIN)

Calories 167 | Total fat 4 g (Saturated 3 g, Poly 0 g, Omega-3 0.01 g, DHA 0.00 g, EPA 0.00 g, Mono 0 g) | Cholesterol 16 mg | Protein 4 g | Sodium 206 mg | Carbohydrates 29 g | Fiber 4 g | Sugars 9 g | Vitamin A 174 mcg | Vitamin B6 0 mg | Vitamin B12 0 mcg | Vitamin C 3 mg | Vitamin D 3 IU | Choline 17 mg | Folate 5 mcg | Calcium 78 mg | Iron 2 mg

Toasted Millet and Coconut Porridge

Hot breakfast cereal settles into that category of hearty, stick-to-your-ribs food that fills a belly for the long haul. There's more than just oatmeal in this category, too, and whole grain millet is a great option for mixing in some variety. If you've reached that stage in your forty weeks where you feel ravenous most of the time and your blood sugar plummets without consistent boosts, add this porridge to your morning routine. Natural sugars and sustaining protein from tiny pearls of millet will help keep you feeling balanced.

Makes 6 servings

1¼ cups/240 g millet	1⅔ cups/394 ml light coconut milk
2 tablespoons unsweetened dried shredded coconut	¼ teaspoon fine sea salt
	2 tablespoons pure maple syrup

Set a medium saucepot over medium heat for 2 minutes, or until the bottom gets hot. Sprinkle the millet and coconut into the pot and toast them for 5 minutes, stirring often. After several minutes, the millet will start to sound like itsy bitsy popcorn kernels popping rapidly, and the millet seeds will start to glisten slightly as their oil warms at the surface. Keep a close eye on the seeds and coconut because both will burn in a blink if you're not careful.

Mix the coconut milk with 2 cups/473 ml water. Slowly drizzle the liquid into the pot. It will sputter and spray dramatically when it hits the hot pot. Stir to prevent the millet from clumping and then bring the liquid to a gentle boil, which will take about 2 to 3 minutes.

Cover the pot, reduce the heat to medium low, and simmer the cereal for 25 minutes. Then turn off the heat and let it sit for 5 minutes. Uncover the pot and add the salt and maple syrup. Serve as is or, if you prefer your hot cereal soft and closer to fluid than fluffy, stir in between ¼ cup/59 ml and ½ cup/118 ml water to loosen it.

Scrape leftovers into an airtight container and refrigerate for up to 1 week. To reheat, add about 2 tablespoons water or milk per serving and warm through in a small pot over medium heat or in the microwave. Stir in additional liquid to achieve the consistency you prefer.

BELLY BONUS: A warm bowl of this hot cereal packs a supply of protein, complex carbohydrates, fiber, and fat, making it rich and satisfying, and enough to sustain you throughout long mornings. Millet also contributes B vitamins, antioxidants, and minerals such as iron, magnesium, phosphorus, calcium, and zinc.

NUTRITION PER SERVING (APPROXIMATELY ¾ CUP/251 G)

Calories 226 | Total fat 6 g (Saturated 4 g, Poly 1 g, Omega-3 0.05 g, DHA 0.00 g, EPA 0.00 g, Mono 0 g) | Cholesterol 0 mg | Protein 5 g | Sodium 117 mg | Carbohydrates 38 g | Fiber 4 g | Sugars 6 g | Vitamin A 0 mcg | Vitamin B6 0 mg | Vitamin B12 0 mcg | Vitamin C 0 mg | Vitamin D 0 IU | Choline 0 mg | Folate 34 mcg | Calcium 12 mg | Iron 1 mg

Tomato and Swiss Baked Egg Muffins

Eggs are an ideal food in so many ways. They are a source of non-meat complete protein as well as vitamins A, D, and B6, all of which are critical during pregnancy for you and your growing baby. Recent research has begun to chip away at the bad rap eggs have been given because of high cholesterol content, and some studies suggest that a diet rich in eggs may actually help to maintain better heart health. Aside from the nutritional goldmine tucked inside every shell, eggs are cheap, fast, and versatile. Make a batch of these egg muffins ahead and reheat them for a morning meal on the fly. Sandwich one of them between two sides of a toasted multigrain English muffin, or serve alongside mixed greens and roasted potatoes for supper. Since the tastes of pregnant ladies can swing like a pendulum, substitute fillings to cater to your preferences if tomatoes and Swiss are on the blacklist for now.

Makes 6 muffins

1 tablespoon olive oil

5 large eggs

2 tablespoons low-fat or whole milk

½ teaspoon fine sea salt

¼ teaspoon freshly ground black pepper (about 20 grinds)

1 medium tomato, cored and diced small

½ cup/57 g grated Swiss cheese

2 tablespoons chopped fresh chives

Preheat the oven to 375°F/190°C/Gas 5. Brush a 6-cup muffin pan or 6 cups of a standard 12-cup muffin pan with the olive oil.

Whisk the eggs, milk, salt, and pepper together in a large bowl.

In a small bowl, mix the tomatoes with the cheese and chives. Divide the mixture among the coated muffin cups and pour equal amounts of the whisked eggs on top. Put the muffin pan on top of a baking sheet and transfer to the oven. Bake for 20 to 25 minutes, or until the eggs are cooked through and spring back to the touch.

Run a butter knife between each muffin cup and its muffin to free any stuck edges. Place a rectangular plate or a baking sheet over the muffin pan and then invert it to tip out the muffins.

Cool leftovers, wrap tightly, and refrigerate up to 4 days. To reheat later, place in a 325°F/165°C/Gas 3 oven for 10 to 15 minutes, or until warm. Alternatively, heat in the microwave for 1 minute, or until hot.

Your Way, Right Away

If tomatoes, cheese, and chives don't appeal to your persnickety pregnancy preferences, swap them out for something more appealing. Here are a few suggestions:

• 4 strips cooked bacon, crumbled

• ½ cup/78 g black beans, 3 scallions, sliced, ½ cup/78 g shredded Cheddar cheese

{Recipe continues on next page}

- ¼ cup/11 g pitted, chopped Kalamata olives, ¼ cup/11 g crumbled feta cheese (see page 30 for information on choosing safe cheeses)
- ½ cup/28 g chopped cooked spinach, 1 chopped roasted red pepper
- ½ cup/78 g grated mozzarella cheese, 2 tablespoons thinly sliced basil, 1 small tomato, diced
- ¼ cup/28 g grated Parmesan cheese, 2 tablespoons each minced fresh parsley, thyme, and chives

BELLY BONUS: Protein is a crucial nutrient during pregnancy because it sustains the creation of new cells, which is the name of the game in baby building. While most Americans don't have trouble meeting the daily recommendations for grams of protein, some expectant moms who are suffering meat aversions might need a boost with alternatives. Not only are eggs a complete protein, they are considerably easier and faster to prepare than any meat, making them a must-have fridge staple for quick bites any time of day!

NUTRITION PER SERVING (1 MUFFIN)

Calories 122 | Total fat 9 g (Saturated 3 g, Poly 1 g, Omega-3 0.10 g, DHA 0.02 g, EPA 0.00 g, Mono 4 g) | Cholesterol 164 mg | Protein 8 g | Sodium 263 mg | Carbohydrates 2 g | Fiber 0 g | Sugars 1 g | Vitamin A 101 mcg | Vitamin B6 0 mg | Vitamin B12 1 mcg | Vitamin C 5 mg | Vitamin D 39 IU | Choline 125 mg | Folate 21 mcg | Calcium 109 mg | Iron 1 mg

Yogurt Muesli Parfait
with Strawberry Sauce

Yogurt is a staple convenience food for pregnant women because it offers nutrient-rich quick calories, it's portable, and it's completely customizable. Though there are a gazillion varieties on dairy section shelves, opting for good old plain yogurt and flavoring it yourself with a drizzle of pure maple syrup, honey, or a teaspoon of jam spares you added sugars and additives in general. And because kids usually love yogurt, too, mastering yogurt skills will save you money and spare you the worry that your child is shoveling in too much sugar to make any inherent cultured goodness count. Muesli is a combination of uncooked grains, fruit, and nuts that is usually served with cold milk or yogurt.

Makes 6 servings

2 cups/226 g frozen strawberries

1 tablespoon freshly squeezed lemon juice

2 tablespoons pure maple syrup

1 cup/121 g slivered almonds

½ cup/58 g old-fashioned rolled oats

¼ cup/58 g raisins

4 cups/907 g plain yogurt (low-fat or whole milk) (⅔ cup/171 g per serving)

Put the strawberries in a medium saucepot over medium heat and add the lemon juice. Stir the berries often and continue cooking for about 5 minutes, or until their own juices start to boil up around them slightly. Drop the heat a bit but continue cooking for about 20 minutes, keeping things at a steady simmer, not a rapid boil. Squish the strawberries continuously to encourage them to break down into the pulpy sauce enveloping them.

Pour the thick strawberry sauce into a glass bowl, stir in the maple syrup, cover, and refrigerate for at least 1 hour.

Toast the almonds and oats either in the oven or in a skillet. To use the oven, spill them out across a baking sheet and put them in a preheated 350°F/175°C/Gas 4 oven for 10 minutes, keeping a close eye on them to prevent burning. Pull them out when they are just tanned and smell a little like popcorn or toasted bread. Alternatively, heat a large skillet over medium heat. Add the almonds and oats and toast them in the dry pan for about 7 minutes, stirring occasionally so they tan all over. Let the toasted goodies cool completely before adding the raisins to complete the muesli. Pour the muesli into an airtight container and store up to 2 weeks.

To build a parfait, scoop out ⅔ cup/171 g of the yogurt, ¼ cup/42 g of the muesli, and 2 tablespoons of the strawberry sauce and divide them into layers: place a third of the yogurt into the bottom of a small glass and top with 1 tablespoon of the strawberry sauce and a third of the muesli (a heaping tablespoon or so). Add another third of the yogurt, the second tablespoon of sauce, and another third of muesli. Then top with the remaining yogurt and muesli. Repeat with the remaining parfaits.

{Recipe continues on next page}

This combination is no less delicious dumped into a bowl with no arrangement whatsoever. Stir it altogether and let it sit for 10 minutes so the oats soften like they do in traditional European muesli.

The strawberry sauce is excellent stirred into yogurt, oatmeal, or Toasted Millet and Coconut Porridge (page 67), or spread over Seven-Grain Pancakes (page 59) or on Lemon-Berry Barley Scones (page 51). It keeps well in the refrigerator for up to 2 weeks or frozen for a few months.

BELLY BONUS: If you pick a low-fat or whole milk plain yogurt made from nothing more than milk and natural bacteria, then the ingredient list of this pretty little parfait is made up of nothing more than seven whole foods. That's a refreshing change in our world of breakfast bars.

NUTRITION PER SERVING (1 PARFAIT)

Calories 304 | Total fat 16 g (Saturated 4 g, Poly 3 g, Omega-3 0.05 g, DHA 0.00 g, EPA 0.00 g, Mono 8 g) | Cholesterol 20 mg | Protein 11 g | Sodium 72 mg | Carbohydrates 33 g | Fiber 5 g | Sugars 20 g | Vitamin A 42 mcg | Vitamin B6 0 mg | Vitamin B12 1 mcg | Vitamin C 18 mg | Vitamin D 3 IU | Choline 37 mg | Folate 28 mcg | Calcium 254 mg | Iron 2 mg

CHAPTER 2

Snacks and Sips

When you're pregnant and hungry, you are usually on a mission to find food fast. It's wise to get something good in your system before your blood sugar plummets, leaving you feeling sluggish and sometimes sick to your stomach. Plan ahead to have some nutritious snack options on hand so you don't fall prey to the lure of convenience food and packaged products void of anything worthwhile. The snacks and sips in this chapter range from sweet goodies to savory munchies, and all of them contribute a bit of wholesome balance to your day. Most make several days' worth of servings, so you'll have good options at the ready.

When you buy packaged food, look for those whose labels indicate the fewest ingredients and ones that you recognize and can pronounce! For example, seek out jarred salsas made simply with tomatoes, peppers, vinegar, spices, and other vegetables. Or yogurt made only from milk and cultures rather than varieties loaded with sweeteners and flavorings. Opt for plain instead and sweeten a serving yourself with fruit or a drizzle of honey or maple syrup. Frozen fruits and vegetables are handy, nutritious, and quick to prepare for smoothies or as a pick-me-up on their own, like steamed and lightly salted edamame.

If your glucose screening leads to a conversation with your healthcare provider about gestational diabetes and its requirements of a more calculated diet, peruse this chapter with her or his guidance and pick a few satisfying snacks that will help keep you and your baby healthy.

RECIPE	VITAMIN A	VITAMIN C	VITAMIN D	B6	B12	FOLATE	CHOLINE	CALCIUM	IRON	DHA	FIBER	PROTEIN
Almond Banana Buzz				*	**			**			*	*
Chipotle Black Bean Dip				*							**	
Cherry Lime Fizzer		*										
Citrus Ginger Pops		**										
Crunchies with Buttermilk Dip	**	*						*				
Eggplant and Red Pepper Dip		**									*	
Chickpea Guacamole											**	
Honeydew Kiwi Smoothie		**									*	
Hummus as You Like It (Basic)												
Lemon Hummus												
Olive and Feta Hummus												
Sweet Pepper and Toasted Walnut Hummus											*	
Lime Salsa with Giant Chips		**		*					*		**	
Maple Pecan Popcorn											*	
Olive Oil Parmesan Popcorn												
Mama Nature's Candy Bars											*	
Peaches and Creamsicle Smoothie		**										
Pickled Cukes and Zukes												
Spinach Cheese Dip												
Strawberry Mango Smoothie		**									*	
Trail Mix												
Trail Mix Bars												

KEY:
* = Good Source (10 to 19%)   ** = Excellent Source (>20%)
Note: DHA is based on 200 mg recommendation

Almond Banana Buzz

Sometimes the sugar and acidity of juice-infused smoothies doesn't sit so well in the prone-to-heartburn digestive systems of pregnant women. This blended drink is smooth, creamy, and sweet enough but void of juice. Almond butter gives it a protein boost, and deep, dark blackstrap molasses adds iron. You can substitute cow's milk or any other non-dairy milk, including almond for the soy milk.

Makes 4 servings

2 ripe bananas	1 tablespoon blackstrap molasses
3 tablespoons almond butter	1 cup/124 g ice
2½ cups/591 ml plain, unsweetened soy milk, divided	

Add the bananas, almond butter, and 2 tablespoons of the soy milk to the blender and purée until smooth, about 30 seconds. Pour in the remaining soy milk, molasses, and ice and blend until smooth and thick.

Refrigerate leftovers and either reblend each serving or shake well in a lidded container.

BELLY BONUS: Soy is a great source of plant-based protein. Soy milk can provide up to 12 g of protein per cup. Bananas are a good source of potassium, fiber, B6, and vitamin C, so save a few that are over-ripe in the freezer for the next smoothie. Almond butter is packed with good fats, fiber, calcium, magnesium, and protein.

NUTRITION PER SERVING (10 OUNCES/296 ML)

Calories 184 | Total fat 9 g (Saturated 1 g, Poly 2 g, Omega-3 0.02 g, DHA 0.00 g, EPA 0.00 g, Mono 4 g) | Cholesterol 0 mg | Protein 7 g | Sodium 112 mg | Carbohydrates 21 g | Fiber 3 g | Sugars 11 g | Vitamin A 2 mcg | Vitamin B6 0 mg | Vitamin B12 1 mcg | Vitamin C 5 mg | Vitamin D 47 IU | Choline 13 mg | Folate 32 mcg | Calcium 229 mg | Iron 1 mg

Chipotle Black Bean Dip

Lots of pregnant women I know could single-handedly bolster the annual profit margins of chip and cracker companies. More than Super Bowl party throwers or mothers of finicky three-year-olds, pregnant gals almost always have a stash of some kind of snack chip or crunchy cracker to curb either hunger or nausea. Lots of friends asked for topping and dip alternatives to old standbys like cheese and peanut butter. This dip is full of fiber, rich in protein, low in fat, and loaded with flavor. The recipe makes a big batch that keeps for about a week. Roll it in warm flour tortillas, use it as a sandwich spread with grilled chicken, scoop it up with carrot sticks, or dip your chips and crackers in it. It's fairly mild, but if you are especially averse to spice heat, cut back on the chipotle or skip it altogether.

Makes 5 servings

1 (15-ounce/425 g) can black beans, drained and rinsed, or 1½ cups/258 g cooked beans

1 (15-ounce/425 g) can chickpeas, drained and rinsed, or 1½ cups/256 g cooked beans

1 large roasted red pepper, seeded and chopped (about ½ cup/170 g)

1 small chipotle pepper in adobo sauce, or dried and rehydrated in hot water, seeded and minced (about 1 tablespoon)

2 tablespoons extra-virgin olive oil

2 tablespoons freshly squeezed lemon juice (from about ½ lemon)

1 small garlic clove, minced and smooshed to a paste with the flat side of a knife

½ teaspoon cumin

½ teaspoon coarse sea salt

¼ teaspoon freshly ground black pepper

Combine the black beans, chickpeas, red pepper, and chipotle pepper in the bowl of a food processor. Pulse several times until a chunky paste forms. Add the olive oil, lemon juice, garlic, cumin, salt, and pepper and process for about 10 seconds. Add 2 tablespoons water and blend until very smooth. Transfer to a bowl to serve, or store in ½-cup/226 g servings. Refrigerate in an airtight container up to 1 week.

> **BELLY BONUS:** Legumes are prized as a valuable source of plant protein, folate, and fiber, so black beans and chickpeas make this dip a nutritious choice for snacking. Both beans deliver iron, which many women need, especially during the later trimesters. High vitamin C content in the red pepper helps promote absorption of iron from non-meat sources.

NUTRITION PER SERVING (½ CUP/226 G)

Calories 167 | Total fat 7 g (Saturated 1 g, Poly 1 g, Omega-3 0.06 g, DHA 0.00 g, EPA 0.00 g, Mono 5 g) | Cholesterol 0 mg | Protein 7 g | Sodium 648 mg | Carbohydrates 22 g | Fiber 7 g | Sugars 2 g | Vitamin A 1 mcg | Vitamin B6 0 mg | Vitamin B12 0 mcg | Vitamin C 4 mg | Vitamin D 0 IU | Choline 24 mg | Folate 19 mcg | Calcium 55 mg | Iron 2 mg

Cherry Lime Fizzer

Get a glass good and frosty and fill it with some Fizzer, a mocktail that's just what the doctor ordered. Vibrant flavors of tart cherries and limes will soothe queasiness, satisfy the urge for candy-sweet treats, and quench thirst in the form of a fruit juice without added sugar. If it's cherry season and pitting is a cathartic task for you, substitute fresh for frozen. But blended ice-cold (already pitted for you!) cherries thicken the drink into a slushy texture without watering it down. A glassful with a bendy straw is an easy way to get in extra servings of fruit. And you'll hardly notice if your company is drinking frozen margaritas around you.

Makes 4 servings

2½ cups/591 ml seltzer water

1½ cups/260 g frozen, pitted unsweetened sour cherries

1½ cups/226 g ice

Zest and juice of 2 limes (about ⅓ cup/79 ml juice)

1 teaspoon honey (optional)

Combine the seltzer, cherries, ice, lime zest, lime juice, and honey (if using) in a blender and blend until smooth. Pour into glasses and serve.

Refrigerate any leftovers in a tightly closed container for up to 5 days.

BELLY BONUS: Several studies have shown that drinking tart cherry juice can promote sleep because it contains melatonin, a neurotransmitter that helps moderate the body's sleep-wake cycles. Though a glass of Fizzer won't work on your newborn in the wee hours of the morning, it might help with pregnancy-related insomnia.

NUTRITION PER SERVING (10 OUNCES/296 ML)

Calories 51 | Total fat 0 g (Saturated 0 g, Poly 0 g, Omega-3 0.06 g, DHA 0.00 g, EPA 0.00 g, Mono 0 g) | Cholesterol 0 mg | Protein 1 g | Sodium 3 mg | Carbohydrates 13 g | Fiber 2 g | Sugars 8 g | Vitamin A 39 mcg | Vitamin B6 0 mg | Vitamin B12 0 mcg | Vitamin C 12 mg | Vitamin D 0 IU | Choline 5 mg | Folate 4 mcg | Calcium 13 mg | Iron 0 mg

Citrus Ginger Pops

Citrus and ginger are widely prescribed for pregnant women because of their soothing and refreshing effects on queasy stomachs or wary palates. These pops are aimed at curing what ails you in the form of an icy cold treat that you can take your time with. They'll also answer the call of the sweet tooth and the siren song of candy. If you catch yourself chomping on ice to avert nausea, freeze the juice in very small molds to make lozenges you can suck on safely and comfortably. While lots of people swear by ginger for nausea, if its powerful punch makes yours worse, you can leave it out entirely. And if lollipops or ice pops make you gag (a common problem among pregnant women!), freeze the juice into ice cubes and drop them in a glass of water or seltzer instead.

Makes 5 ice pops

1⅔ cups/394 ml orange juice (not from concentrate)

3 tablespoons freshly squeezed lemon juice

1 teaspoon finely grated fresh ginger

Stir the orange juice, lemon juice, and ginger together in a spouted measuring cup. Pour the juice into 3-ounce/89 ml popsicle molds or small (1 teaspoon) ice cube molds. Stir between pours to redistribute the ginger, which will settle to the bottom of the liquid. Freeze overnight.

> **BELLY BONUS:** These pops don't contain much calcium, but if you want a boost of the bone-building mineral, opt for orange juice that's fortified with it. Some brands offer as much as 330 mg per cup.

NUTRITION PER SERVING (1 ICE POP)

Calories 36 | Total fat 0 g (Saturated 0 g, Poly 0 g, Omega-3 0.00 g, DHA 0.00 g, EPA 0.00 g, Mono 0 g) | Cholesterol 0 mg | Protein 0 g | Sodium 7 mg | Carbohydrates 8 g | Fiber 0 g | Sugars 6 g | Vitamin A 0 mcg | Vitamin B6 0 mg | Vitamin B12 0 mcg | Vitamin C 23 mg | Vitamin D 0 IU | Choline 1 mg | Folate 18 mcg | Calcium 6 mg | Iron 0 mg

Quickie Food and Snacks

HERE'S A LIST OF QUICK GRAB-AND-GO SNACKS AND THEIR NUTRITIONAL BONUSES AS A SUPPLE-ment to the snack recipes throughout the chapter.

- Quick-cooking oats with peanut butter (fiber, protein, B6)
- Almond butter and whole grain crackers (fiber, protein, calcium, folic acid, vitamin E, magnesium)
- Brown rice sushi with avocado (monounsaturated fat, fiber, vitamin C, folate, B6, potassium)
- Greek-style yogurt with honey and almonds (protein, calcium, fiber, vitamin E, calcium, magnesium)
- Whole wheat English muffin with ricotta and strawberries (fiber, folic acid, vitamin C, calcium, protein)
- Whole wheat toast with avocado (fiber, folic acid, vitamin C, B6, potassium)
- Hardboiled eggs and calcium-fortified orange juice (protein, choline, folate, calcium, vitamin C)
- Red bell pepper strips and carrots with hummus (fiber, vitamin A, vitamin C, protein)
- Cheddar cheese and apple (fiber, calcium, protein, vitamin C)
- Kale chips and walnuts (fiber, vitamin C, vitamin A, omega-3s, potassium, magnesium, B6)
- Blueberries and plain yogurt (protein, calcium, fiber, vitamin C, potassium, antioxidants)
- Cottage cheese with fresh or dried fruit (calcium, protein, vitamin C, fiber)
- Edamame (protein, calcium, vitamin A, iron)
- Clementines (vitamin C, fiber)

Crunchies with Buttermilk Dip

Nutritionally, raw veggies are an ideal snack because they are portable, inexpensive, and packed with vitamins and fiber. If you need convincing to choose crunchy vegetables over nutritionally void snacks like chips, this creamy dip, vibrant with chives and garlic, will win you over. Made with thick protein-packed Greek-style yogurt, low-fat buttermilk, and just a scoop of mayo, it tastes like indulgent buttermilk ranch dressing but wrangles in the fat content so you don't have to feel bad about double dipping.

Makes 5 servings

¾ cup/177 ml low-fat buttermilk	¼ teaspoon fine sea salt
½ cup/127 g plain, low-fat Greek-style yogurt	¼ teaspoon freshly ground black pepper (about 20 grinds)
2 tablespoons mayonnaise	3 medium carrots, cut into sticks
1 teaspoon garlic powder	1 large cucumber, sliced into discs
2 tablespoons chopped fresh chives	1 cup sugar snap peas

Whisk together the buttermilk, yogurt, and mayonnaise until the mixture is smooth. Add the garlic powder, chives, salt, and pepper and whisk to combine. Refrigerate the dip for at least 30 minutes to let the flavors meld.

Pack the dip in ¼ cup/64 g portions for snacking. Serve with the carrot sticks, cucumber slices, and sugar snap peas.

BELLY BONUS: Raw cucumbers, carrots, and snap peas (and any edible raw veggie, for that matter) are more than just a vehicle for indulging in dip. They are packed with vitamins, low in or void of calories, fat, and sodium, and a good source of fiber, which comes in handy when you run into roadblocks like constipation (see the "Belly Woes" sidebar on page 38). What's more, they answer the call for something crunchy, a common craving of women busy growing babies.

NUTRITION PER SERVING (¼ CUP/64 G)

Calories 94 | Total fat 3 g (Saturated 1 g, Poly 1 g, Omega-3 0.12 g, DHA 0.00 g, EPA 0.00 g, Mono 1 g) | Cholesterol 5 mg | Protein 6 g | Sodium 227 mg | Carbohydrates 11 g | Fiber 2 g | Sugars 7 g | Vitamin A 318 mcg | Vitamin B6 0 mg | Vitamin B12 0 mcg | Vitamin C 10 mg | Vitamin D 1 IU | Choline 14 mg | Folate 19 mcg | Calcium 111 mg | Iron 1 mg

Eggplant and Red Pepper Dip

I love when a snack is a tool for shoveling in extra nutrients, but you don't even think about that bonus because you're paying way more attention to the tastiness. Get out your shovel of choice: whole grain crackers, pretzels, toasted pita triangles, grilled bread, tortilla chips, or whatever else you like, and scoop away. Filling fiber, vitamins and minerals, and a ton of flavor are packed into each mound of dip. As a sandwich spread, paired with roasted turkey (page 216) or sliced tomatoes and a pile of baby arugula, it contributes all of its merits, which typical condiments can't boast.

Makes 6 servings

1 medium or 3 small eggplants (about 1 pound/454 g), unpeeled, cut into 1-inch/2.5 cm cubes

1 medium red bell pepper, cut into 1/2-inch/1.3 cm cubes

2 garlic cloves, halved

3 tablespoons extra-virgin olive oil, divided

1/2 cup/78 g cooked white beans

2 teaspoons balsamic vinegar

6 large fresh basil leaves

1/4 teaspoon dried oregano

1/4 teaspoon fine sea salt

1/8 teaspoon freshly ground black pepper (about 10 grinds)

Preheat the oven to 375°F/190°C/Gas 5.

Scatter the eggplant, pepper, and garlic across a baking sheet. Drizzle 2 tablespoons of the olive oil over everything and then use a large rubber spatula or your hands and toss to coat everything with the oil. Roast the vegetables for 35 minutes, lifting and flipping with a spatula once or twice to help prevent sticking, until the eggplant is very tender and creamy and the peppers are soft and sweet.

Scrape the roasted veggies into a food processor. Add the remaining tablespoon of olive oil, the beans, vinegar, basil, oregano, salt, and pepper. Process for a full minute, or until almost completely smooth. Stop to scrape down the sides or loosen any ingredient buildup around the blade if necessary.

Adjust the seasoning to taste. Enjoy immediately or refrigerate to allow the flavors to come together. The dip keeps nicely refrigerated in an airtight container for up to 1 week.

BELLY BONUS: Red bell peppers are one of the best sources of vitamin C, the nutrient you and your baby need for healthy bones, teeth, and gums. It also helps the body absorb iron. The fat in the dip is mostly from olive oil, a monounsaturated fat that is heart healthy. Having adequate amounts of "good" fat in the diet during pregnancy is also important because it helps the body absorb fat-soluble vitamins like A, D, E, and K.

NUTRITION PER SERVING (1/3 CUP/71 G)

Calories 112 | Total fat 7 g (Saturated 1 g, Poly 1 g, Omega-3 0.08 g, DHA 0.00 g, EPA 0.00 g, Mono 5 g) | Cholesterol 0 mg | Protein 2 g | Sodium 94 mg | Carbohydrates 10 g | Fiber 3 g | Sugars 4 g | Vitamin A 33 mcg | Vitamin B6 0 mg | Vitamin B12 0 mcg | Vitamin C 27 mg | Vitamin D 0 IU | Choline 12 mg | Folate 38 mcg | Calcium 26 mg | Iron 1 mg

Drink to That: Getting Enough Water

WATER DOESN'T JUST QUENCH YOUR THIRST. IT KEEPS YOU HYDRATED AND PLAYS AN IMPORTANT role in electrolyte balance; helps combat constipation; prevents and helps manage hormone-induced headaches; and participates in the production and maintenance of all that extra blood volume that's put to use during pregnancy. Proper hydration prevents against uterine (and other muscle) cramping and preterm labor and keeps amniotic fluid at healthy levels. Though water content in other fluids and food like coffee, tea, juice, soup, fruits, and vegetables count toward meeting your goal of 3 liters, cool, clear water is your best bet for refreshment and the work that needs to be done for a healthy pregnancy. (Read more about water in "General Pregnancy Guidelines" on page 15 and "Major Nutrients for Pregnancy" on page 20.)

Some women struggle to drink the recommended daily minimum of a little less than a gallon of water (3 liters/101 ounces, or about twelve 8-ounce glasses). If you're having a hard time, try a few tricks to up your totals.

FIND THE RIGHT TEMP: I like my water ice cold, but drink it room temperature, lukewarm, or hot if that feels better going down.

CONTAIN IT: Pick a favorite vessel or several to drink from. I like my 32-ounce (1 liter) bottle because it helps me keep track of how much I've had and how much more I need. Plus, I can dump ice into it without fuss and fill it up easily. If you like to drink water from a coffee mug, the pilsner or wine glass you're not otherwise using at the moment, or a cup with a crazy straw, have at it!

JAZZ IT UP: Add slices or squeezes of lemon or lime juice, or flavored ice cubes (try the cubed variation of Citrus Ginger Pops, page 81) to your water glass if the pure stuff is just too plain. The fizziness of sparkling or seltzer water can be a nice change of pace, too.

WATER IT DOWN: Fruit juice has a lot of extra sugar and calories, so depending on it for hydration is not ideal. Instead, combine 4 ounces of fruit juice with 12 ounces of water to get the best of both worlds. Diluting the juice also adds flavor to your water. This trick will come in handy later if you are trying to rein in consumption by a juice-loving kiddo.

LEAVE IT AROUND: When I was pregnant with the twins, I was simultaneously distracted by lots of other life and work and I often forgot to drink the water I really needed. Someone suggested that I fill up water bottles and leave them around the house so that I would walk into a room, find water, and be reminded to drink up. Ask your partner to help you out that way, or by filling up bottles every morning and leaving them in the fridge so your 3-liter quota is ready to go.

Chickpea Guacamole

Scoop it up with chips, spread it on a toasted tortilla, stuff it into a pita with grilled chicken, or spoon it up on its own. However you like it, enjoy this ramped-up guac knowing it's boosted further by the filling fiber stores of chickpeas, which will help you feel fuller longer. Avocados are an important source of monounsaturated fats ("good" fats) and omega-3 fatty acids, which can benefit the heart. They also offer a roster of pregnancy-fueling nutrients such as fiber, vitamins E and K, folate, and minerals (potassium, iron, and magnesium).

Makes 4 servings

1 (15-ounce/425 g) can chickpeas, drained and rinsed, or 1½ cups/256 g cooked beans

1 small garlic clove

1 large ripe avocado, pitted and peeled

¼ cup/7.5 g loosely packed fresh cilantro leaves

2 teaspoons freshly squeezed lime juice (from about ½ small lime)

¼ teaspoon fine sea salt

Put the chickpeas and garlic in a food processor and pulse about fifteen times, or until both are well pulverized. Add the avocado, cilantro, lime juice, salt, and 2 tablespoons water and pulse again fifteen to twenty times, or until the guacamole is as textured or smooth as you like it.

Serve immediately or cover tightly with plastic wrap or store in an airtight container and refrigerate for up to 3 days.

BELLY BONUS: Chickpeas, also called garbanzo beans, are one of the most widely consumed legumes in the world and a great source of protein, folate, and fiber. A half-cup contains 6 g of fiber, about a quarter of what you need every day.

NUTRITION PER SERVING (½ CUP/113 G)

Calories 165 | Total fat 6 g (Saturated 1 g, Poly 1 g, Omega-3 0.04 g, DHA 0.00 g, EPA 0.00 g, Mono 3 g) | Cholesterol 0 mg | Protein 6 g | Sodium 163 mg | Carbohydrates 22 g | Fiber 6 g | Sugars 1 g | Vitamin A 6 mcg | Vitamin B6 0 mg | Vitamin B12 0 mcg | Vitamin C 4 mg | Vitamin D 0 IU | Choline 5 mg | Folate 31 mcg | Calcium 48 mg | Iron 1 mg

Honeydew Kiwi Smoothie

Add this to your partner's Honey-Do list. Melon is a superb ingredient for smoothies because its juicy bulkiness blends silky-smooth, and its mellow sweetness is an agreeable backdrop to almost anything. Baby spinach lends its vibrant color and a load of nutrients including vitamin C and calcium, yet practically none of its grassy flavor, to a pretty green dairy-free smoothie that should be on juice bar menus everywhere.

Makes 4 servings

2 ripe kiwis, peeled and quartered

4 cups peeled, cubed honeydew melon
(about 24 ounces/680 g)

2 cups/57 g baby spinach

¾ cup/177 ml pineapple juice

Combine the kiwi, melon, spinach, and pineapple juice in a blender and blend for a full minute, or until completely smooth. Serve immediately and refrigerate any leftovers in the refrigerator for up to 5 days. As the smoothie sits, the fruit pulp will rise up above the juice. Before serving again, stir or shake vigorously to recombine.

BELLY BONUS: This smoothie is a great source of vitamin C, which boosts the immune system and helps your body absorb iron from plant foods, called non-heme iron. Kiwis are packed with nutrients such as fiber, vitamins C and E, folate, magnesium, and potassium.

NUTRITION PER SERVING (10 OUNCES/296 ML)

Calories 111 | Total fat 0 g (Saturated 0 g, Poly 0 g, Omega-3 0.07 g, DHA 0.00 g, EPA 0.00 g, Mono 0 g) | Cholesterol 0 mg | Protein 2 g | Sodium 56 mg | Carbohydrates 27 g | Fiber 3 g | Sugars 21 g | Vitamin A 35 mcg | Vitamin B6 0 mg | Vitamin B12 0 mcg | Vitamin C 75 mg | Vitamin D 0 IU | Choline 16 mg | Folate 41 mcg | Calcium 32 mg | Iron 1 mg

Hummus as You Like It

Whether you use it for a dip, a spread, or as part of the main event in a sandwich, hummus has you covered on nutrients from fiber to vitamins and minerals. Sure, you can buy tubs of it at any store, but it's a snap to make and you can customize it with any flavor combos you dream up. Here's a basic base recipe and a few variations to get you started. If you're a hummus addict, double the recipe for three times the amount you'd get at the store. This is news you can use for future reference, because kids tend to like hummus, too.

Basic Hummus

Makes 6 servings

1 (15-ounce/425 g) can chickpeas, drained and rinsed, or 1½ cups/256 g cooked beans

1 garlic clove

½ teaspoon granulated sugar

½ teaspoon fine sea salt

¼ cup/65 g tahini

2 tablespoons freshly squeezed lemon juice

2 tablespoons extra-virgin olive oil

Put the chickpeas, garlic, sugar, and salt in a food processor and process for 30 seconds, or until the mixture starts to stick to the walls of the bowl. Stop the machine and scrape down the sides. Add the tahini and process again for 20 seconds. When the mixture starts to make its way up the sides again, stop and scrape. Whisk the lemon juice and olive oil together with ¼ cup/59 ml water in a spouted measuring cup. With the motor running, pour the olive oil mixture in a slow stream through the food chute. Let the machine run for a full minute. Stop, scrape down the sides again, and then continue processing for another minute, or until the hummus is smooth, soft, and whipped.

NUTRITION PER SERVING (⅓ CUP/71 G)

Calories 144 | Total fat 11 g (Saturated 1 g, Poly 3 g, Omega-3 0.08 g, DHA 0.00 g, EPA 0.00 g, Mono 6 g) | Cholesterol 0 mg | Protein 4 g | Sodium 282 mg | Carbohydrates 9 g | Fiber 2 g | Sugars 1 g | Vitamin A 0 mcg | Vitamin B6 0 mg | Vitamin B12 0 mcg | Vitamin C 3 mg | Vitamin D 0 IU | Choline 0 mg | Folate 12 mcg | Calcium 24 mg | Iron 1 mg

Variations
Lemon Hummus

To the Basic Hummus recipe above, add 1 packed teaspoon lemon zest (from 1 large lemon) to the mixture after you process the tahini and just before adding the oil and water. To the oil and water, add ¼ cup/59 ml freshly squeezed lemon juice (from 1 large lemon), and then proceed with the recipe instructions. Makes 6 servings.

NUTRITION PER SERVING (⅓ CUP/71 G)

Calories 146 | Total fat 11 g (Saturated 1 g, Poly 3 g, Omega-3 0.08 g, DHA 0.00 g, EPA 0.00 g, Mono 6 g) | Cholesterol 0 mg | Protein 4 g | Sodium 282 mg | Carbohydrates 10 g | Fiber 2 g | Sugars 1 g | Vitamin A 0 mcg | Vitamin B6 0 mg | Vitamin B12 0 mcg | Vitamin C 5 mg | Vitamin D 0 IU | Choline 1 mg | Folate 13 mcg | Calcium 25 mg | Iron 1 mg

{Recipe continues on next page}

Olive and Feta Hummus

To the Basic Hummus recipe above, add 1¼ cups/42 g crumbled feta cheese and 1¼ cups/42 g pitted olives (Kalamata or your favorite variety) after you add the lemon juice, olive oil, and water and process until smooth. Pulse the olive and feta into the hummus about ten times, or until the hummus is the texture you prefer (pulse less for bigger bits of the olives and cheese or more to make it very smooth).

NUTRITION PER SERVING (¼ CUP/60 G)

Calories 180 | Total fat 14 g (Saturated 3 g, Poly 3 g, Omega-3 0.10 g, DHA 0.00 g, EPA 0.00 g, Mono 6 g) | Cholesterol 6 mg | Protein 5 g | Sodium 508 mg | Carbohydrates 10 g | Fiber 2 g | Sugars 1 g | Vitamin A 9 mcg | Vitamin B6 0 mg | Vitamin B12 0 mcg | Vitamin C 3 mg | Vitamin D 1 IU | Choline 1 mg | Folate 14 mcg | Calcium 59 mg | Iron 1 mg

Sweet Pepper and Toasted Walnut Hummus

To the Basic Hummus recipe above, add ½ cup/57 g toasted walnuts, 1 medium roasted red pepper, jarred or homemade (note that some jarred roasted peppers are marinated and will add extra saltiness to the final hummus), and ¼ cup/42 g black raisins along with the tahini and proceed with the recipe.

> **BELLY BONUS:** Chickpeas are a valued source of fiber and folate, along with protein, potassium, and zinc, all of which are important nutrients for keeping you and your baby healthy. Tahini is a paste made from sesame seeds and is a source of fiber, iron, calcium, and potassium.

NUTRITION PER SERVING (⅓ CUP/71 G)

Calories 251 | Total fat 17 g (Saturated 2 g, Poly 7 g, Omega-3 0.94 g, DHA 0.00 g, EPA 0.00 g, Mono 7 g) | Cholesterol 0 mg | Protein 6 g | Sodium 470 mg | Carbohydrates 19 g | Fiber 3 g | Sugars 6 g | Vitamin A 17 mcg | Vitamin B6 0 mg | Vitamin B12 0 mcg | Vitamin C 4 mg | Vitamin D 0 IU | Choline 5 mg | Folate 21 mcg | Calcium 43 mg | Iron 1 mg

Lime Salsa with Giant Chips

Some days the urge to dip some chips is insatiable, so you might as well make the most of it by choosing a more nutritious, but no less delicious, option. If you like salsa mild, follow the recipe as is. If you prefer a kick, add a minced chipotle in adobo sauce, some diced jalapeño, or a sprinkle of chipotle powder. Giant tortilla chips are easy to make and store, plus they cut back on the fat and sodium fried into most varieties. For smoother, saucier salsa, choose crushed tomatoes, but if you like chunks, pick diced or "chef's cut" crushed.

Makes 4 servings

½ teaspoon coarse sea salt

2 garlic cloves, minced

1 (28-ounce/794 g) can or 1 (26.46-ounce/750 g) aseptic box crushed tomatoes

¼ cup/7.5 g fresh cilantro leaves, chopped (roughly or finely chopped, depending on preference)

Zest of 1 medium lime

1 tablespoon freshly squeezed lime juice

¼ teaspoon granulated sugar

1 tablespoon extra-virgin olive oil

¼ teaspoon ground cumin

8 (6-inch) corn tortillas (yellow, white, or blue)

Preheat the oven to 350°F/175°C/Gas 4.

Sprinkle the sea salt over the minced garlic on a cutting board. Use the flat side of a chef's knife to crush the garlic into a paste, pulling the blade across the surface of the garlic toward you. Repeat this motion ten to twenty times, or until the garlic is mostly smooth. Scrape the paste off the board with the blade of the knife and drop into a medium mixing bowl.

Add the tomatoes, cilantro, lime zest, lime juice, sugar, olive oil, and cumin. Stir and refrigerate for at least 30 minutes to let the flavors come together.

Carefully lay the corn tortillas directly onto the oven rack. Toast for about 10 minutes, or until the tortillas are crisp and only starting to brown. Remove from the oven and let cool on a rack for about 5 minutes.

Serve the giant chips whole, breaking them apart as you dip them into the salsa.

Refrigerate leftover salsa for up to 1 week. Store extra toasted chips in a resealable bag or an airtight container at room temperature for up to 1 week.

BELLY BONUS: Corn tortillas contain less calories, fat, and sodium than a similar-sized flour tortilla, and if they are processed the traditional way with slaked lime (calcium hydroxide), they can provide a significant amount of calcium. Blue corn tortillas contain anthocyanins, plant-based pigments, which function like antioxidants. With each scoop, a serving of this snack tackles the munchies with a bonus dose of vitamin C plus a bit of folate and iron, too.

NUTRITION PER SERVING (¾ CUP/186 G SALSA AND 2 GIANT CHIPS)

Calories 173 | Total fat 5 g (Saturated 1 g, Poly 1 g, Omega-3 0.04 g, DHA 0.00 g, EPA 0.00 g, Mono 3 g) | Cholesterol 0 mg | Protein 5 g | Sodium 521 mg | Carbohydrates 30 g | Fiber 6 g | Sugars 10 g | Vitamin A 23 mcg | Vitamin B6 0 mg | Vitamin B12 0 mcg | Vitamin C 19 mg | Vitamin D 0 IU | Choline 24 mg | Folate 25 mcg | Calcium 87 mg | Iron 3 mg

Maple Pecan Popcorn

When I was pregnant with our twin sons, we drove up to Vermont to visit friends who are maple syrup producers just as I was emerging from months of perpetual morning sickness. The fresh air and tromping through snow provided a welcome recharge after so much time spent curled up on the couch feeling unable to move much. Equally rejuvenating was reacquainting with the long-lost desire for food that happened to return in the presence of maple kettle corn, one of my favorite snacks. This make-at-home version is just the thing for a sweet treat. A bowlful is light and satisfying, and you can munch on the pieces one by one for a while the way I did with my stash of kettle corn on our long trip home to Philadelphia. If you don't care for pecans, simply omit them.

Makes 6 servings

½ cup/50 g pecan halves, roughly chopped

1 tablespoon canola oil

½ cup/113 g popcorn kernels

½ teaspoon fine sea salt, divided

1 tablespoon unsalted butter

⅓ cup/79 ml grade A medium-amber pure maple syrup

Preheat the oven to 350°F/175°C/Gas 4 to toast the pecans first. Line a rimmed baking sheet with parchment paper and spill the nuts across it. Set the pan in the oven and toast the nuts just until you start to smell them, about 5 to 7 minutes. Pay close attention since nuts go from toasted to burned quickly! Carefully lift the parchment with the nuts off the baking sheet and set it on a rack to cool. Let the pecans cool completely. Pour the cooled pecans into a bowl and set aside. Return the parchment paper to the baking sheet.

Reduce the oven temperature to 200°F/95°C/Gas ¼.

Heat the oil and a single popcorn kernel in an uncovered medium saucepan over medium-high heat. Wait for the kernel to pop. When it does, add the rest of the kernels, shake the pan gently two or three times, and then cover the pan with a lid. Shake the pot frequently, using a kitchen towel to hold the lid down and to grasp the side handles. The kernels will begin to pop rapidly. After about 2 minutes, the popping will begin to slow. When it does, lower the heat to low and wait for the popping to stop almost completely. Dump half the popcorn into a large, wide bowl and sprinkle it with half the salt. Dump the remaining popcorn into another bowl and sprinkle it with the remaining salt. Remove unpopped kernels as it cools.

In a small saucepan, heat the butter and the maple syrup to a boil over medium heat, whisking once or twice to blend as the butter melts. Boil undisturbed until it thickens slightly, about 3 minutes. Turn off the heat and add the toasted nuts to the syrup mixture, coating quickly.

Drizzle half of the syrup mixture over one of the bowls of popcorn, folding it in with a large rubber spatula to coat the popcorn as you do. Gradually add the other bowl of popcorn to this mix, drizzling the rest of the syrup while folding. This process can take a few minutes of patience to disperse the cooling syrup over each piece of fluffed corn. Pour the coated corn in a single layer onto

{Recipe continues on next page}

the prepared baking sheet and spread it out to the edges of the pan with the rubber spatula. Put the popcorn in the oven to dry for 1 hour.

Remove the pan from the oven and let the popcorn cool for at least 5 minutes before scooping it into a serving bowl or storage container. You can break up the sticky popcorn into individual pieces or leave the bigger clusters intact. Store cooled popcorn in an airtight container or resealable plastic freezer bag. It will keep for several days at room temperature or in the freezer for up to 3 months. Bring it to room temperature before devouring.

BELLY BONUS: It's tough to come across a sweet-enough snack that adds fiber to your diet, but this popcorn does it. Pecans add good fats, fiber, and iron to this whole grain snack.

NUTRITION PER SERVING (1$\frac{2}{3}$ CUPS/13 G)

Calories 204 | Total fat 11 g (Saturated 2 g, Poly 3 g, Omega-3 0.31 g, DHA 0.00 g, EPA 0.00 g, Mono 6 g) | Cholesterol 5 mg | Protein 3 g | Sodium 183 mg | Carbohydrates 24 g | Fiber 3 g | Sugars 12 g | Vitamin A 16 mcg | Vitamin B6 0 mg | Vitamin B12 0 mcg | Vitamin C 0 mg | Vitamin D 1 IU | Choline 4 mg | Folate 12 mcg | Calcium 26 mg | Iron 1 mg

Olive Oil Parmesan Popcorn

Stovetop popped kernels become billowing bowls that satisfy hunger and the urge to munch with a dose of fiber, which may also help keep your digestive system in check when it tends toward sluggishness under the lull of pregnancy progesterone. Treat yourself to a bottle of good-quality, buttery smooth extra-virgin olive oil, which is high in heart-healthy monounsaturated fats, for drizzling, and you may never go back to buttered popcorn again.

Makes 6 servings

3 tablespoons extra-virgin olive oil, divided

½ cup/113 g popcorn kernels

1 teaspoon fine sea salt

2 tablespoons freshly grated Parmigiano-Reggiano cheese

Heat 1 tablespoon of the oil and a single popcorn kernel in a medium saucepot over medium-high heat. Wait for the kernel to pop. When it does, add the rest of the kernels, shake the pan gently two or three times, and then cover the pan with a lid. Shake the pot frequently, using a kitchen towel to hold the lid down and to grasp the side handles. The kernels will pop rapidly for about 2 minutes before the popping begins to slow. When it does, reduce the heat to low and wait for the popping to stop almost completely.

Dump the popcorn into a large, wide bowl and sprinkle with the salt while still hot. Drizzle 1 teaspoon of oil and sprinkle about 1 teaspoon of cheese over each serving of popcorn (about 1⅔ cups/13 g) just before eating.

Store leftover popcorn (without oil or cheese) in an airtight container or a tightly folded paper bag for up to 3 days.

BELLY BONUS: Popcorn is a whole grain snack and contains more antioxidants and fiber than any potato chip. Whole grains can help maintain blood sugar levels and help you feel fuller longer. While cheese is a good source of calcium, it's also packed with fat and calories. Make a big impact with smaller amounts by using flavorful cheeses like Parmesan or sharp Cheddar.

NUTRITION PER SERVING (1⅔ CUPS/13 G)

Calories 130 | Total fat 8 g (Saturated 1.5 g, Poly 1 g, Omega-3 0.06 g, DHA 0.00 g, EPA 0.00 g, Mono 6 g) | Cholesterol 2 mg | Protein 3 g | Sodium 397 mg | Carbohydrates 11 g | Fiber 2 g | Sugars 0 g | Vitamin A 5 mcg | Vitamin B6 0 mg | Vitamin B12 0 mcg | Vitamin C 0 mg | Vitamin D 1 IU | Choline 0 mg | Folate 10 mcg | Calcium 27 mg | Iron 0 mg

Mama Nature's Candy Bars

Chewy and rich, sweet and a little salty, here's a bar that tastes like candy but is not. Cut them into bars as suggested, or into whatever size and shape you wish for a portable, poppable protein boost and dose of natural sugars that will help keep your energy balanced between meals. These are excellent any time of day, straight up to a bedtime snack with a cup of tea.

Makes 12 bars

1 cup/135 g roasted unsalted cashews

1 cup/143 g roasted unsalted almonds

¼ teaspoon fine sea salt

2 tablespoons unsweetened cocoa powder

½ cup/100 g combination of raisins and dried cherries

½ cup/100 g dates (about 6 dates), pitted and stem ends removed

Dump the cashews, almonds, and salt into a food processor and pulse about fifteen times to pulverize to a bitty meal. Sprinkle the cocoa across the mixture and then pulse another fifteen times to work it into the meal.

Add the cherries, raisins, and dates and process in intervals of 20 to 30 seconds four times, stopping to scrape down the sides. Blending the ingredients will be noisy at first, but the sound will dull to a hum as the ingredients are ground together into a finer meal. When the mixture is ready, it will still appear crumbly, but it should stick together if you squeeze a bit of it in your fist. The nut oils and natural stickiness of the fruit will bind everything as it is rolled and chilled.

Scrape the mixture out onto a large piece (about 24 inches/61 cm) of waxed or parchment paper and squeeze it together into a pile situated on one half of the paper. Fold the other half of the paper over the pile and push it down with the palm of your hand into a relatively even thickness in a shape that resembles a rectangle. Then use a rolling pin to roll the paste into an 8 x 6-inch/20 x 15 cm rectangle about ½ inch/1.3 cm thick. Don't worry too much about the exactness of the rectangle and the precision of the edges, just work it into a shape from which you can easily cut relatively evenly sized bars. Transfer to the freezer for 15 to 30 minutes, or until cold and firm but not frozen. Peel off the paper and cut into twelve equal-size bars about 4 inches/10 cm long and 1 inch/2.5 cm wide.

Refrigerate in an airtight container with waxed paper or parchment paper between each layer of bars for up to 5 days.

BELLY BONUS: Almonds have more bone-building calcium, fiber, protein, and vitamin E than any other tree nut. One serving (23 almonds) provides 75 mg of calcium. Cocoa powder contains flavanols, plant-based compounds that are known to reduce blood pressure and improve blood flow to the brain and heart.

NUTRITION PER SERVING (1 BAR)

Calories 177 | Total fat 11 g (Saturated 1 g, Poly 2 g, Omega-3 0.02 g, DHA 0.00 g, EPA 0.00 g, Mono 6 g) | Cholesterol 0 mg | Protein 5 g | Sodium 48 mg | Carbohydrates 19 g | Fiber 4 g | Sugars 11 g | Vitamin A 1 mcg | Vitamin B6 0 mg | Vitamin B12 0 mcg | Vitamin C 0 mg | Vitamin D 0 IU | Choline 13 mg | Folate 15 mcg | Calcium 47 mg | Iron 1 mg

Peaches and
Creamsicle Smoothie

Even without the cream, peaches, orange juice, and (give it a chance) silken tofu make for a drink-able creamsicle that's as much of a delight as the one on a stick. Frozen peaches lend a cold thick-ness to the blend, which isn't quite as sweet as the ice cream treat, but still enough so to satisfy a craving. When peaches are at their peak, substitute fresh ones for frozen if you like, and throw in a fistful of ice cubes to keep the chill.

Makes 4 servings

1 cup/241 g silken tofu

1½ cups/ 213 g sliced frozen peaches,
or 2 medium fresh peaches, peeled, pitted, and sliced

1½ cups/355 ml orange juice

Combine the tofu, peaches, orange juice, and ½ cup/118 ml water in a blender and blend for a full minute, or until completely smooth. If the frozen peaches halt the blade, stop the blender and use a wooden spoon to nudge them around a little before proceeding.

Serve immediately and store any leftovers in the refrigerator for up to 3 days. Stir or shake the smoothie if it separates while stored.

BELLY BONUS: If you're not a dairy lover, you can still get bone-building calcium through the tofu and orange juice in this drink. Some brands of silken tofu offer up to 300 mg of calcium per serving. Besides calcium, OJ can also provide folate, B vitamins, and potassium, and peaches are a good source of vitamin C.

NUTRITION PER SERVING (10 OUNCES/296 ML)

Calories 93 | Total fat 2 g (Saturated 0 g, Poly 1 g, Omega-3 0.01 g, DHA 0.00 g, EPA 0.00 g, Mono 0 g) | Cholesterol 0 mg | Protein 3 g | Sodium 3 mg | Carbohydrates 16 g | Fiber 1 g | Sugars 12 g | Vitamin A 9 mcg | Vitamin B6 0 mg | Vitamin B12 0 mcg | Vitamin C 72 mg | Vitamin D 0 IU | Choline 5 mg | Folate 26 mcg | Calcium 55 mg | Iron 1 mg

Pickled Cukes and Zukes

That whole pregnancy pickle popularity rumor isn't a fable. Like most cravings, the ones for the sour-salty-crunchy combo are real and very common. These pickles respect the urge and offer a fix. Snappy cucumbers and tender zucchini take a bath in a sweet, salty, and sour vinegar mixture and emerge soaked with flavor. Homemade fridge pickles like these are virtually void of additives found in lots of manufactured jarred pickles (yellow #5, I'm looking at you) and cut way back on sodium, too. Best of all, the spears keep well up to a week in the fridge (if they last), so you won't have to send anyone out hunting for pickles at midnight. (Please note that this recipe is not intended for shelf-stability, so do not store these outside the refrigerator.)

Makes 2 quarts

1 cup/237 ml distilled vinegar	¼ teaspoon celery seeds
1 cup/237 ml cider vinegar	¼ teaspoon cumin seeds
2 tablespoons granulated sugar	1 pound/454 g cucumbers (about 2 medium)
2 tablespoons kosher salt	1 pound/454 g zucchini, green or yellow (about 2 medium)
½ teaspoon whole black peppercorns	

In a medium saucepot over medium-high heat, combine 2 cups/473 ml of water with the vinegars, sugar, salt, peppercorns, celery seeds, and cumin seeds. Bring the liquid to a boil for about 5 minutes to dissolve the sugar and kosher salt.

While the liquid boils, cut the cucumbers and zucchini in half horizontally and then cut each half into eight spears. Put the spears into two 1-quart glass jars or a 2-quart glass storage container with a lid. (Try to avoid stuffing the spears too tightly into one container, which will limit the amount of pickling liquid you can add.)

Pour or ladle half of the hot liquid (about 2 cups/473 ml) into each jar to fill it (or pour all of the liquid over all of the vegetables if using a single container). Fit the jar with a lid, or cover the container tightly and refrigerate until cold, at least 2 hours. The pickles keep well refrigerated up to 1 week.

BELLY BONUS: Cucumbers are great for hydration during pregnancy and lactation; they are 96% water and low in calories, too! Zucchinis are fat-free, cholesterol-free, sodium-free, low in calories, and high in vitamin C.

NUTRITION PER SERVING (1 SPEAR)

Calories 5 | Total fat 0 g (Saturated 0 g, Poly 0 g, Omega-3 0.00 g, DHA 0.00 g, EPA 0.00 g, Mono 0 g) | Cholesterol 0 mg | Protein 0 g | Sodium 180 mg | Carbohydrates 1 g | Fiber 0 g | Sugars 1 g | Vitamin A 1 mcg | Vitamin B6 0 mg | Vitamin B12 0 mcg | Vitamin C 2 mg | Vitamin D 0 IU | Choline 0 mg | Folate 2 mcg | Calcium 3 mg | Iron 0 mg

Belly-to-Belly

On favorite pregnancy clothes . . .

Amy M: "I had a shirt that said, 'With bump, not plump.' I loved that!"

Adelaide L: "Leggings, duh."

Christine R: "I was pregnant before they made cute pregnancy clothes. You wore tents and leggings in my pregnancy age."

Christine V: "Tight maternity tops to show my belly. I was proud and consider pregnancy to be beautiful!"

Laurie F: "I splurged on a pair of designer maternity jeans, and it was the best $100 I spent. They made me feel normal and like less a gigantic whale."

Jessica P: "When I was pregnant with my twins, I had a sweater that I loved. I have since held it up to my body . . . and I can now use it as a blanket on a cold winter night."

Julie S: "Black soft, stretch pants that felt more like pajamas. I almost felt guilty wearing them to work."

Kat B: "I loved me some full-panel pregnancy lounge pants or comfy jeans, along with a soft maternity tee and a cozy sweater or sweatshirt."

Lari R: "Overalls—the farmer kind."

Lauren B: "I wore flip-flops until I tripped and fell in them when I was seven months pregnant. Then it was laceless Keds. The sneakers were for safety, and they were laceless so I wouldn't have to bend over to tie them!"

Nicole R: "Nothing with elastic that sat on my bladder."

Tara H: "I am eternally grateful that leggings came back into fashion shortly before I started gestating."

Carita P: "Any pants that tucked up over my belly and didn't make me feel dumpy."

Erika C: "I discovered the wonder of dresses while pregnant. I didn't wear them too often before then, and realized how easy they were to throw on and be comfy."

Spinach Cheese Dip

I do love a creamy dip for dunking things to munch, but we can all do better than a supermarket tub of onion dip or one of those packets of powdered stuff destined for a cup each of mayonnaise and sour cream. Softened shallots and sautéed garlicky spinach flavor a thick, creamy base of cottage cheese and beans in a dip that fills empty snack calories with fiber and protein. Dunk carrots, celery, pretzels, tortilla chips, or toasted pita, or spread some on a sandwich as a condiment. The soft-cheese warning for pregnant women doesn't apply here, as cottage cheese is made from pasteurized milk. What about the leftover beans from this recipe, you ask? Toss them with some of the leftover spinach you'll likely have, along with tomatoes and cucumbers, for a quick salad with a boost of fiber and protein.

Makes 4 servings

2 tablespoons extra-virgin olive oil

1 small shallot, minced

2 garlic cloves, sliced

3 cups/85 g baby spinach

½ cup/114 g low-fat cottage cheese

1 (15-ounce/425 g) can cannellini beans, drained and rinsed, or 1¼ cups/284 g cooked beans

¼ teaspoon fine sea salt

Heat the olive oil in a large sauté pan over medium heat. Add the shallots and sweat them in the hot oil for about 3 minutes, or until their purple hue begins to fade just a little. Add the garlic and sauté for 30 seconds, or until fragrant. Drop the spinach into the pan and sauté for 2 to 3 minutes, or until it is completely wilted and dark green and all of the water it releases has evaporated from the pan.

Scrape the cooked spinach, shallots, and garlic into a food processor. Add the cottage cheese, beans, and salt and process until smooth, about 30 seconds.

Transfer the dip to an airtight container and refrigerate for at least 30 minutes to let the flavors meld together before enjoying. Keep refrigerated up to 1 week.

> **BELLY BONUS:** Spinach is an excellent source of vitamins A, C, and K, as well as folate, a nutrient that can help guard against neural tube defects. The leafy greens are also a good source of magnesium, potassium, and iron. Cottage cheese is a valuable source of protein and calcium, supplying 14 g of protein per ½ cup/114 g serving.

NUTRITION PER SERVING (¼ CUP/71 G)

Calories 126 | Total fat 8 g (Saturated 1 g, Poly 1 g, Omega-3 0.00 g, DHA 0.00 g, EPA 0.00 g, Mono 5 g) | Cholesterol 1 mg | Protein 6 g | Sodium 296 mg | Carbohydrates 10 g | Fiber 3 g | Sugars 2 g | Vitamin A 41 mcg | Vitamin B6 0 mg | Vitamin B12 0 mcg | Vitamin C 4 mg | Vitamin D 0 IU | Choline 6 mg | Folate 7 mcg | Calcium 49 mg | Iron 1 mg

Strawberry Mango Smoothie

My husband and I became big smoothie drinkers once we started training for endurance races like marathons, which require long runs early on weekend mornings. Smoothies were the go-to fuel post-run because they are quick, portable, and packed with energizing nutrients. I put pregnancy in the "endurance sport" category and think that blended fruit drinks can come in just as handy for moms-to-be on the go. But during my pregnancies I found our usual smoothies too sweet and acidic for my prone-to-heartburn digestive system. So I created this one, which is mellow, creamy (though dairy-free), and just sweet enough. You can swap whatever liquid you prefer if you don't care for coconut milk, but know that substituting juices will up the acidity and sweetness I aimed to tame. Try regular milk or plain non-dairy milks such as soy or almond.

Makes 4 servings

2 cups/228 g fresh strawberries, hulled

2 large ripe mangoes, peeled and cubed

1 (13.5-ounce/400 ml) can light coconut milk

1 cup/130 g ice cubes

Add the strawberries, mango, coconut milk, and ice to a blender and blend for a full 30 seconds. Stop the blender and let everything settle. Blend an additional 30 seconds, or until the shake is thick and smooth.

Enjoy immediately and refrigerate leftovers for up to 3 days. Stir, shake, or blend again before pouring additional servings.

• • •

Tip: In the off-season, if you can't come by good strawberries or mangoes, you can substitute frozen, but it's best to thaw them both at least partially first. The shake is still delicious with fruit that is frozen solid, but it becomes more spoonable than sipable. Mangoes naturally contribute significant thickness to the body of this shake, even more so when frozen.

BELLY BONUS: Mangoes are considered one of the most nutritious fruits. Not only are they a source of fiber and potassium, they are an excellent source of vitamins A and C. Strawberries also provide a significant amount of vitamin C (eight strawberries provide more vitamin C than an orange) and are high in antioxidants.

NUTRITION PER SERVING (10 OUNCES/296 ML)

Calories 131 | Total fat 6 g (Saturated 4 g, Poly 0 g, Omega-3 0.08 g, DHA 0.00 g, EPA 0.00 g, Mono 0 g) | Cholesterol 0 mg | Protein 1 g | Sodium 34 mg | Carbohydrates 22 g | Fiber 3 g | Sugars 16 g | Vitamin A 45 mcg | Vitamin B6 0 mg | Vitamin B12 0 mcg | Vitamin C 63 mg | Vitamin D 0 IU | Choline 10 mg | Folate 49 mcg | Calcium 19 mg | Iron 0 mg

Trail Mix (Bars)

Trail mix, the snack of sustenance for long hikes in the woods, served me well during both pregnancies. I like its salty sweetness and how it occupies my hands and mouth for a while as I work my way through it. An espresso cup is the perfect container for a single serving (¼ cup/28 g). Alternatively, you can turn the mix into sticky, salty, sweet bars bound together by peanut butter and honey. You can swap any other nut butter, including sunflower seed butter, in equal measure for the PB. Either version of this concoction is a sensible source of protein and natural sugars that will help keep your blood sugar balanced as you hike ahead through your day.

Makes 9 servings of trail mix or 12 bars

⅓ cup/28 g banana chips

⅓ cup/57 g roasted, salted peanuts

⅓ cup/62 g raisins

¼ cup/42 g bittersweet chocolate chunks (60 to 70% cacao)

1 cup/0.18 g unsweetened puffed whole grain cereal (try puffed kamut or wheat)

¼ cup/70 g natural creamy peanut butter (if making bars)

3 tablespoons honey (if making bars)

To make the trail mix, snap or crush the banana chips into big pieces and toss them in a medium mixing bowl. Add the peanuts, raisins, chocolate, and cereal. Mix everything together to distribute evenly. Store the mix in a glass jar or other airtight container for up to 2 weeks. Scoop out ¼ cup/28 g servings.

To make the trail mix bars, start by lining an 8-inch/20 cm square baking dish with parchment paper so that the paper covers the bottom and at least halfway up the sides.

Dump the banana chips, peanuts, raisins, chocolate chunks, and cereal in a food processor and pulse the blade twenty to thirty times to pulverize everything into a coarse mixture. Spill it out into a medium mixing bowl.

Put the peanut butter and honey in a small saucepot over medium heat and melt them together, stirring constantly, into a warm, viscous, spoonable paste. Scrape the peanut butter and honey into the pulverized trail mix and use a large wooden spatula to fold and stir it all together, coating the mix with the paste thoroughly.

Scrape the mixture into the parchment-lined dish and press it out as evenly as you can. Refrigerate for at least 1 hour so that the peanut butter binding sets everything together.

When the mixture is cold and set, cut it into twelve bars (three rows of four). Cover and keep refrigerated for up to 1 week.

{Recipe continues on next page}

BELLY BONUS: Peanuts are nutrient dense, meaning they pack a lot of nutrients in a small amount of space. A small (1-ounce/28 g) handful of peanuts provides 170 calories, 7 g of protein, 14 g of mostly healthy fats, and 2 g of fiber. If you're worried that your nut consumption may set your child up for nut allergies, you can breathe a sigh of relief. A new study published in *JAMA Pediatrics* finds that eating nuts during pregnancy dramatically decreases the odds of having a child with nut allergies.

NUTRITION PER SERVING OF TRAIL MIX (¼ CUP/28 G)

Calories 108 | Total fat 6 g (Saturated 3 g, Poly 1 g, Omega-3 0.00 g, DHA 0.00 g, EPA 0.00 g, Mono 2 g) | Cholesterol 0 mg | Protein 3 g | Sodium 45 mg | Carbohydrates 12 g | Fiber 2 g | Sugars 7 g | Vitamin A 0 mcg | Vitamin B6 0 mg | Vitamin B12 0 mcg | Vitamin C 0 mg | Vitamin D 0 IU | Choline 5 mg | Folate 10 mcg | Calcium 11 mg | Iron 1 mg

NUTRITION PER SERVING (1 BAR)

Calories 128 | Total fat 8 g (Saturated 2 g, Poly 1 g, Omega-3 0.00 g, DHA 0.00 g, EPA 0.00 g, Mono 2 g) | Cholesterol 0 mg | Protein 3 g | Sodium 55 mg | Carbohydrates 13 g | Fiber 2 g | Sugars 8 g | Vitamin A 0 mcg | Vitamin B6 0 mg | Vitamin B12 0 mcg | Vitamin C 0 mg | Vitamin D 0 IU | Choline 4 mg | Folate 8 mcg | Calcium 8 mg | Iron 1 mg

CHAPTER 3

Easy Meals for Noon and Night

I always encourage people to spend quality time in their kitchens tinkering with tools, learning about new ingredients, and taking a few extra steps to cook from scratch. I am a preacher of the merits of homemade food. I truly believe the kitchen is the heart of a house.

But during my pregnancy, I learned to appreciate other rooms in my house, too, like the ones with reclining furniture. On the nights when my body begged for bedtime a little earlier, or the days when my back, feet, and waning energy nudged me out of the kitchen, I embraced the merits of fast and easy cooking and the extra throw pillows on the couch in front of the television. I became adept at creating quick and simple recipes that promised the nutrients I needed and whatever else I craved. If something was ever going to drive me to climb aboard the popular 30-minute-meal bandwagon, pregnancy was it. And it did.

I knew that if I lacked the stamina most days for any kind of extensive meal making, most moms-to-be did, too. Yet nutritious food is more important than ever for women when they are pregnant and responsible for the well-being of *two* (or more) vulnerable people. So I was motivated to stay away from processed fast food and to design good-for-me fast food instead.

Most of these recipes take less than one hour to make, start to finish, with minimal active time. Necessity is the mother of invention, and this chapter is the result of my pregnant self's need for delicious, satisfying meals that came together fast and gave me the fuel and nutrients I needed. Most of them became regulars in the repertoire long after pregnancy because they grew into family favorites. Food that's good for you during pregnancy, after all, is good for anyone all the time!

RECIPE	VITAMIN A	VITAMIN C	VITAMIN D	B6	B12	FOLATE	CHOLINE	CALCIUM	IRON	DHA	FIBER	PROTEIN
Baked Potatoes with Broccoli and Bacon Vinaigrette	*	**		**		*			*		**	**
Gotta Have 'Em Burgers and Oven Square Fries				**	**		**		*		*	**
Whole Wheat Couscous with Cherries, Almonds, and Arugula											**	*
Ginger Bok Choy Stir-Fry	**	**		**		*		**			*	
Grilled Skirt Steak Fajitas	**	**		**	**	*	*		*		**	**
Grilled Tomato, Red Onion, and Mozzarella Cheese Sandwiches								**			**	**
One-Pot Pearl Couscous with Shrimp and Tomatoes	*	*		**			*			*		**
Kickin' Chicken with Pineapple Salsa		**		**			**					**
Linguine with Chard and White Beans	*	*				**			*		**	**
Pork and Peanut Noodles	*	**		**	*	**	*		**		**	**
Salmon and Quinoa Two Ways		*	**	**	**		*			**		**
Bulgur with Sausage, Kale, and Mushrooms	**	**		**				*	*		**	**
Smoky Penne Pomodoro		*										**
Sushi-Fix Veggie Hand Roll with Scallion Mayo	*										*	
Sweet Potato Black Bean Hash	**	**		*	*			**	*		**	**
Smoky Turkey Tacos with Celery Avocado Relish		**		**	**	*			*		**	**

Key:
* = Good Source (10 to 19%) ** = Excellent Source (>20%)
Note: DHA is based on 200 mg recommendation

Baked Potatoes with Broccoli and Bacon Vinaigrette

During my first pregnancy, plain baked potatoes with a pat of butter and a pinch of salt fueled me through some queasy early days. Their simplicity, far from bland but nowhere near an assault on my heightened senses of smell and taste, was all I wanted some nights when I sat beside my husband, whose dinner plate popped with color and flavor and texture. Pregnant or not, baked potatoes make an excellent meal, and this treatment rounds out their nutritional merit with plenty of extras, including a healthy helping of calcium and vitamin C–rich broccoli. The vinaigrette is a lighter change of pace from typical baked potato toppings like sour cream and cheese.

Makes 4 servings

4 medium russet potatoes

3 strips thick-cut bacon, cut into 1/4-inch/0.6 cm pieces

1 small broccoli crown, cut into medium florets and 1/4-inch/0.6 cm stem pieces

1/4 cup/28 g minced shallot

2 tablespoons cider vinegar

1 tablespoon balsamic vinegar

3 tablespoons extra-virgin olive oil

2 teaspoons dark brown sugar

1/4 teaspoon fine sea salt

1/8 teaspoon freshly ground black pepper (about 10 grinds)

Preheat the oven to 375°F/190°C/Gas 5. Position a rack in the middle of the oven.

Scrub the skins of the potatoes under cold water, pat them dry, and then poke them all over with the tines of a fork. Set the potatoes directly on the middle rack and bake for 1 hour. When they are done, the skins should feel crisp and slightly stiff. The insides should give way easily to a fork or a knife and yield to a gentle squeeze around the middle.

While the potatoes bake, make the broccoli filling. Start by heating a large skillet or high-sided sauté pan over medium-high heat. Put in the bacon and cook it until it's crisp, about 5 to 7 minutes, stirring occasionally. Lift the crunchy bits out of the pan with a slotted spoon, leaving the fat in the pan, and set them on a paper towel.

Add the broccoli and shallots to the pan and sauté over medium-high heat for 5 minutes, or until the broccoli becomes a deep, bright green and starts to soften toward tender. Drizzle 2 tablespoons of water into the pan and scrape any browned bits off the bottom as it sizzles. Reduce the heat to low and cover the pan for about 5 minutes, just enough to steam the broccoli slightly.

Meanwhile, in a small mixing bowl or spouted measuring cup, whisk together the cider vinegar, balsamic vinegar, oil, brown sugar, salt, and pepper. Turn off the heat, uncover the broccoli, scatter the bacon into the pan, and drizzle the vinaigrette over everything. Toss the broccoli several times to dress it with the vinaigrette.

{Recipe continues on next page}

Split the potatoes in half, break up the insides, and fluff with a fork. Season the potato with a pinch of salt and a grind of pepper if you like, and then top each with about ½ cup/78 g of the bacon broccoli.

• • •

Tip: To make a single serving of this same recipe, either quarter all of the ingredients or make the entire recipe and refrigerate and reheat the leftovers. Cool the baked potatoes to room temperature and refrigerate in an airtight container or wrapped in foil. Reheat the potatoes in a warm oven (about 350°F/175°C/Gas 4) for 10 to 15 minutes, or slice in half and microwave for 30 seconds to 1 minute, or until heated through. Refrigerate the broccoli mixture and reheat in a skillet over medium heat or in the microwave.

> **BELLY BONUS:** Broccoli is considered a nutrition powerhouse because it's rich in vitamin C, fiber, vitamin A, iron, calcium, magnesium, and a host of phytonutrients. Vitamin C may be known for cold prevention, but it's also important for iron absorption and the prevention of anemia in pregnant women. One serving of this dish packs in 93 mg of vitamin C, over 100% of what you need in a day. And there's nothing wrong with plain white potatoes: they're a source of vitamin C, potassium, and fiber (with skins).

NUTRITION PER SERVING (1 POTATO WITH ½ CUP/78 G BROCCOLI)

Calories 402 | Total fat 18 g (Saturated 5 g, Poly 1 g, Omega-3 0.21 g, DHA 0.00 g, EPA 0.00 g, Mono 8 g) | Cholesterol 21 mg | Protein 18 g | Sodium 738 mg | Carbohydrates 50 g | Fiber 6 g | Sugars 5 g | Vitamin A 128 mcg | Vitamin B6 1 mg | Vitamin B12 0 mcg | Vitamin C 93 mg | Vitamin D 0 IU | Choline 29 mg | Folate 95 mcg | Calcium 74 mg | Iron 3 mg

Gotta Have 'Em Burgers and Oven Square Fries

Countless moms-to-be, most notably the ones who don't go jonesin' for fast food normally, get an urge for it during the forty weeks of the mystery that is pregnancy. These burgers and fries have redeemable nutritional qualities and are built to satisfy. A flat fry-pan burger is the antithesis of big, thick gourmets, tumbling with fancy toppings. This one is the kind that screams for crunchy pickles and a "special sauce," which is usually no more than a whirl of condiments under a soft, squishy bun. Complete with hot, salty oven fries, this happy little meal saves face with a healthier preparation of better ingredients than any you'll get through your car window.

Makes 4 servings

4 small russet potatoes, skin on and scrubbed	½ teaspoon coarse sea salt, plus more for seasoning
3 tablespoons vegetable or olive oil	¼ teaspoon freshly ground black pepper (about 20 grinds), plus more for seasoning
1 pound/454 g 90% lean ground beef, preferably grass-fed	4 whole wheat burger buns

OPTIONAL TOPPINGS

4 ounces thinly sliced Cheddar cheese	Chopped Pickled Cukes and Zukes (page 99) or your favorite jarred variety
3 large romaine leaves, sliced into ¼-inch/0.6 cm strips	Ketchup
1 small tomato, sliced	Mustard

Preheat the oven to 400°F/200°C/Gas 6. Position a rack in the middle of the oven. Put a baking sheet in the oven while it preheats.

Cut the potatoes lengthwise into quarters and then crosswise into ½-inch-/1.3 cm-thick chunks. In a medium mixing bowl, toss the potatoes with the oil to coat. Remove the hot baking sheet from the oven and pour the potatoes onto it, scraping any excess oil from the bowl onto the potatoes. The potatoes will sizzle as you spread them out across the pan in an even single layer. Transfer to the middle rack and roast, turning with a spatula halfway through, until brown and crisp, about 45 minutes.

When the potatoes are nearly ready, make the burgers. Divide the meat into four equal portions (4 ounces) and roll each into a ball. Season the top of each ball with a bit of the salt and pepper.

Heat a large cast-iron skillet or a sauté pan over high heat. When the pan is very hot and just starting to smoke, add the meatballs, seasoned-side down. Cook for 1 minute and then flip each ball over. Using a spatula, flatten the meat to less than ½ inch/1.3 cm thick and about 4 inches/ 10 cm in diameter, and cook for 2 minutes. Flip the burgers over, press them down with the spatula, season the surface with more of the salt and pepper, and cook for 2 to 3 minutes more, or until the bottoms have browned and the meat is cooked all the way through. If the pan cannot accommodate all four burgers at once, do this in batches to prevent crowding and steaming the meat. (To make a

cheeseburger, after the second flip, top the cooked sides of the burgers with slices of cheese and let it melt while the burger cooks through.)

Slide the cooked burgers onto the buns and add your favorite toppings and condiments.

When the potatoes are done, remove them from the oven and sprinkle with salt and freshly ground black pepper to taste. Serve immediately with the burgers.

BELLY BONUS: Despite being typically lumped into the junk food category for fat content and over-sized portions, more carefully prepared burgers like these can be an excellent addition to the diet of moms-to-be. Lean beef is a prized source of iron, a critical pregnancy nutrient, especially in the second and third trimesters when lack of it often leads to anemia. And while a bag of fries won't win a spot on the best-foods-for-the-bump list, these oven fries, baked with skin on in a bit of oil, instead of peeled and dunked in a vat of hot fat, deliver leg-cramp-fighting potassium and nausea-swatting vitamin B6. A 4-ounce patty and small potato is an actual super-sized meal that satisfies cravings and delivers nutrients.

NUTRITION PER SERVING (1 BURGER AND 1/2 CUP/70 G FRIES)

Calories 494 | Total fat 24 g (Saturated 6 g, Poly 8 g, Omega-3 0.88 g, DHA 0.00 g, EPA 0.00 g, Mono 8 g) | Cholesterol 74 mg | Protein 29 g | Sodium 575 mg | Carbohydrates 43 g | Fiber 5 g | Sugars 4 g | Vitamin A 0 mcg | Vitamin B6 1 mg | Vitamin B12 3 mcg | Vitamin C 6 mg | Vitamin D 5 IU | Choline 101 mg | Folate 36 mcg | Calcium 75 mg | Iron 5 mg

Whole Wheat Couscous with Cherries, Almonds, and Arugula

A beautiful bowlful, flecked with vivid green arugula and deep red cherries, is ready to eat in 15 minutes flat. The toasted almond slivers stay crunchy for a few days, so make a batch big enough for leftovers. I loved this salad throughout my pregnancy because it required so little time on my feet and was satisfying enough to call a meal, but not so filling that it left me uncomfortable when baby started encroaching on my digestive real estate. Try couscous with other dried fruit, such as apricots or raisins, or use plain warm couscous as a bed for roasted or grilled meat and fish. You're likely to go into labor before you run out of options.

Makes 4 servings

1 cup/173 g dry whole wheat couscous

4 teaspoons extra-virgin olive oil, divided

½ cup/71 g dried cherries

½ cup/57 g slivered almonds, toasted

2 cups/60 g baby arugula, roughly chopped

1 tablespoon white balsamic or white wine vinegar

½ teaspoon coarse sea salt

¼ teaspoon freshly ground black pepper (about 20 grinds)

Bring 1¼ cups/296 ml water to a boil in a medium pot over high heat. Add the couscous and 2 teaspoons of the olive oil and stir to combine. Sprinkle the cherries on top, remove from the heat, and cover the pot tightly. Let the couscous sit for 10 minutes.

While the couscous cooks, combine the toasted almonds and the chopped arugula in a large mixing bowl. Whisk together the remaining 2 teaspoons of olive oil and the vinegar.

Uncover the pot of couscous, fluff with a fork, and then scrape it into the mixing bowl with the arugula and almonds. Season with the salt and pepper and toss everything together. Drizzle the oil and vinegar on top and toss again to coat. Serve immediately, warm or at room temperature, or cool. Cover and refrigerate leftovers for up to 3 days.

BELLY BONUS: A scoop of this couscous offers manganese and magnesium, both of which are put to good use growing babies by supporting bone growth and reproduction. Manganese helps to maintain blood sugar, which comes in handy when hormone fluctuations wreak havoc out of the blue. It has also been tied to mood, teaming up with B vitamins to keep things balanced in the face of anxiety, stress, or frustration . . . in the event that you might experience them from time to time over this forty-week journey.

NUTRITION PER SERVING (2 CUPS/300 G)

Calories 347 | Total fat 12 g (Saturated 1 g, Poly 2 g, Omega-3 0.05 g, DHA 0.00 g, EPA 0.00 g, Mono 8 g) | Cholesterol 0 mg | Protein 11 g | Sodium 277 mg | Carbohydrates 54 g | Fiber 12 g | Sugars 9 g | Vitamin A 12 mcg | Vitamin B6 0 mg | Vitamin B12 0 mcg | Vitamin C 2 mg | Vitamin D 0 IU | Choline 9 mg | Folate 16 mcg | Calcium 82 mg | Iron 3 mg

Ginger Bok Choy Stir-Fry

Bok choy, or Chinese white cabbage, is crisp, tender, mild, and excellent in stir-fry because it retains all of those qualities under high heat. Outside of its appetizing adaptability, bok choy is part of the revered collection of dark leafy greens that are prized as a source of folate, the nutrient that is essential for the neural tube development of growing babies. Add to that the abundance of vitamins and minerals from carrots, celery, and edamame, and this quick meal gets multiple gold stars. Enjoy the veggies on their own, pile them on top of hot cooked rice (choose whole grain brown rice for added fiber), or toss with your favorite kind of Asian noodles.

Makes 4 servings

1 tablespoon vegetable oil

1 tablespoon minced fresh ginger (about one 2½-inch/6 cm piece of ginger, peeled)

3 garlic cloves, minced

2 medium carrots, halved lengthwise and sliced into very thin half-moons

2 medium celery stalks, halved lengthwise and sliced very thin

½ cup/75 g shelled edamame (frozen or fresh)

1 medium bok choy, halved lengthwise and sliced thin across the leaves and stem into ½-inch-/1.3 cm-thick pieces

2 tablespoons soy sauce

1½ tablespoons rice vinegar

¼ teaspoon Sriracha

½ teaspoon dark brown sugar

Pour the oil into a wok and swirl it around to coat the bottom and a little bit of the sides. (Alternatively, use a large, wide skillet.) Set the wok over medium-high heat. When the oil is hot, add the ginger and garlic and sauté for 1 minute, stirring constantly to prevent the aromatics from burning. Add the carrots and celery and stir-fry for 2 minutes, or until the veggies start to sweat and suggest that they might soften slightly. Scatter in the edamame and cook for 30 seconds before piling on the bok choy.

Fold the bok choy continuously as it starts to loosen and then wilt, and continue to stir-fry for 5 to 7 minutes. The leafy tops of the bok choy will shrivel into soft dark green threads, and the wide white stems will retain just a little bit of crunch, as will the carrots and celery.

Whisk together the soy sauce, vinegar, Sriracha, and brown sugar in a small bowl. Pour the mixture over the vegetables and toss everything together. Serve immediately on its own or over cooked rice; soba, udon, or ramen noodles; or rice vermicelli.

BELLY BONUS: Bok choy is an excellent source of vitamin A, which helps with vision and bone growth and is essential for healthy skin. Ginger lends an aromatic and pungent flavor to the dish and can provide some relief from first-trimester nausea.

NUTRITION PER SERVING (1½ CUPS/273 G)

Calories 107 | Total fat 5 g (Saturated 0 g, Poly 2 g, Omega-3 0.34 g, DHA 0.00 g, EPA 0.00 g, Mono 1 g) | Cholesterol 0 mg | Protein 6 g | Sodium 613 mg | Carbohydrates 12 g | Fiber 4 g | Sugars 6 g | Vitamin A 682 mcg | Vitamin B6 0 mg | Vitamin B12 0 mcg | Vitamin C 76 mg | Vitamin D 0 IU | Choline 16 mg | Folate 112 mcg | Calcium 206 mg | Iron 2 mg

Grilled Skirt Steak Fajitas

Quick and uncomplicated, a fajita fiesta gets dinner and extra iron on the table and into your system fast. Iron is essential during pregnancy because it transports oxygen around the body and helps with cell growth. Plus, one serving of these fajitas supplies more than half of the daily protein recommendations for pregnant women. Just a few ingredients make for a colorful, well-rounded meal that requires minimal prep and cleanup.

Makes 4 servings

½ teaspoon ground cumin

½ teaspoon ancho chili powder

¼ teaspoon fine sea salt

¼ teaspoon freshly ground black pepper (about 20 grinds)

1 pound/454 g skirt steak

1 teaspoon vegetable oil

3 large bell peppers (any color or combination)

1 large Vidalia onion or very large yellow onion

8 (6-inch) flour tortillas

½ cup/127 g sour cream (optional)

1 cup/113 g grated mild Cheddar cheese (optional)

Heat the grill to medium high (about 400°F/204°C).

In a small bowl, stir together the cumin, chili powder, salt, and pepper. Set the steak on a plate or platter and sprinkle the seasoning over both sides, using your fingers to rub it all over the surface of the steak. Drizzle ½ teaspoon of the oil on each side of the steak and set it aside.

Stand the peppers upright on a cutting board and cut them into wide planks, which will lie flat on the grill. You'll have three or four pieces per pepper. Discard the cores and scrape off the seeds and membranes that remain. Peel the onion and cut it into ¼-inch-/0.6 cm-thick round slices.

Stack the flour tortillas and wrap them in foil.

Grill the pepper planks and onion rings 5 minutes per side, or until blackened just slightly and starting to soften. Don't fret if you lose an onion ring or two between the grates. It happens. Set the pile of wrapped tortillas on the grill toward the back to warm through.

Stack the hot cooked veggies on a plate or in a bowl and cover them with foil or a lid, letting the steam soften them further while keeping them warm.

Set the steak on the hottest part of the grill and cook 2 to 3 minutes per side with the grill covered. Flip over the pile of tortillas to continue warming through.

Let the meat rest uncovered for 5 minutes before slicing it very thin against the grain. While the steak rests, cut the peppers into strips and separate the onions into individual rings.

Assemble the fajitas with a few slices of steak, peppers, and onions per warmed tortilla. Add 1 tablespoon of sour cream and 2 tablespoons of cheese per fajita, if you like.

BELLY BONUS: Heme iron, which is found in the skirt steak and other animal protein sources, is more efficiently absorbed by the body than non-heme iron. Thanks to the bell peppers, you'll also get loads of vitamins A and C, key vitamins for helping the little one grow in utero. Vitamin C also helps along the absorption of iron by the body.

NUTRITION PER SERVING (2 FAJITAS)

Calories 450 | Total fat 15 g (Saturated 5 g, Poly 1 g, Omega-3 0.14 g, DHA 0.00 g, EPA 0.00 g, Mono 4 g) | Cholesterol 71 mg | Protein 33 g | Sodium 803 mg | Carbohydrates 46 g | Fiber 6 g | Sugars 10 g | Vitamin A 170 mcg | Vitamin B6 1 mg | Vitamin B12 2 mcg | Vitamin C 139 mg | Vitamin D 3 IU | Choline 61 mg | Folate 67 mcg | Calcium 36 mg | Iron 3 mg

Grilled Tomato, Red Onion, and Mozzarella Cheese Sandwiches

On the nights during my pregnancies when I was too tired to cook, my husband's grilled cheese sandwiches often saved dinner. They are as fast as convenience food gets, but his in particular don't taste like some kind of quickie afterthought. His perfectly toasted bread doesn't yield to a bite without sounding a crackly crunch, and it encloses melted cheese that oozes out of the edges. His are plain and simple—bread, butter, and usually Cheddar—and I'll take one whenever he offers. This version is a riff that makes room for seasoned tomatoes and red onion and depends on hearty multigrain bread to hold it all together. Use a rustic artisan boule or loaf rather than packaged sandwich bread if you can.

Makes 4 sandwiches

1 large tomato, thinly sliced

¼ teaspoon garlic powder

¼ teaspoon dried oregano

Pinch of fine sea salt

Pinch of freshly ground black pepper

¼ cup/28 g very thinly sliced red onion

1⅓ cups/170 g grated part-skim mozzarella cheese

8 slices multigrain bread (the good stuff from the bakery case)

1 tablespoon plus 1 teaspoon extra-virgin olive oil

Set the tomato slices in a single layer on a plate or small platter. Mix together the garlic powder, oregano, salt, and pepper and then sprinkle pinches of the seasoning across the tomatoes. Scatter the onions across the surface of the tomatoes and set aside for at least 15 minutes, or up to several hours refrigerated.

Heat a large skillet (cast iron works beautifully here) over medium heat. Assemble a sandwich: Sprinkle about 3 tablespoons of cheese across the surface of a piece of bread. Pile two or three slices of tomato and several onions on top. Scatter another 3 tablespoons of cheese and then top with a second slice of bread. Brush the surface of the top piece with olive oil (about ½ teaspoon). Set the sandwich oiled-side down on the hot skillet and press down firmly with the back of a spatula. Grill for 2½ to 3 minutes, or until the bottom of the sandwich is toasty brown. Brush the top-facing slice of bread with olive oil (another ½ teaspoon). Carefully flip the sandwich over and grill that side an additional 2½ to 3 minutes, or until the sandwich is crisp and browned and the cheese is completely melted.

Repeat to make three additional sandwiches. Serve them immediately.

• • •

Tip: Artisan bread boules are often about 8 inches/20 cm in diameter, but the sizes of these bakery-fresh loaves vary vastly. If your bread slices are on the smaller side and don't quite accommodate the cheese and tomatoes as prescribed in the recipe, just use your judgment to resituate as needed on the slighter slices. It might mean you get to indulge in one and a half or two sandwiches instead!

BELLY BONUS: Consider cheese for your calcium tallies that you need to build the little one's bones and to strengthen your own. The mineral also helps the nervous, muscular, and circulatory systems stay in tip-top shape. If you don't eat enough, your body will draw from your bones and give it to your baby, so aim for at least 1,000 mg a day from sources such as green leafy vegetables, milk, fortified drinks (OJ, soy milk, almond milk), and yogurt. Not only do multigrain or whole grain breads provide necessary energy to keep us going, they have extra fiber, iron, and B vitamins. If the bread is made from fortified flour, it'll also supply folic acid, also known as vitamin B9, which can help prevent birth defects.

NUTRITION PER SERVING (1 SANDWICH)

Calories 371 | Total fat 18 g (Saturated 6 g, Poly 0 g, Omega-3 0.03 g, DHA 0.00 g, EPA 0.00 g, Mono 4 g) | Cholesterol 23 mg | Protein 19 g | Sodium 689 mg | Carbohydrates 34 g | Fiber 7 g | Sugars 6 g | Vitamin A 19 mcg | Vitamin B6 0 mg | Vitamin B12 0 mcg | Vitamin C 7 mg | Vitamin D 0 IU | Choline 4 mg | Folate 40 mcg | Calcium 351 mg | Iron 2 mg

One-Pot Pearl Couscous with Shrimp and Tomatoes

Here's a change of pace from weeknight pasta, with the same quick-fix ease. Pearl couscous, which looks similar to acini di pepe pasta, those itsy pasta balls, softens into chewy little bits spiked with the intense flavors of olives and lemon. Its texture is markedly different from the tiny grains of durum wheat couscous that turn into soft, dry granules. The shrimp, which cooks in an instant, adds a little extra protein to your day and is a smart choice of low-mercury seafood. Seek out the freshest wild shrimp you can find. Frozen shrimp is often your best bet, since much of the shrimp available in grocers' fish cases has been frozen and thawed, which sometimes threatens the quality of texture and flavor.

Makes 4 servings

1 tablespoon extra-virgin olive oil

1¼ cups/214 g pearl (Israeli) couscous

1 small shallot, finely chopped

2 large garlic cloves, minced

½ teaspoon dried oregano

8 ounces/227 g shelled, deveined shrimp (about 10 ounces/284 g unpeeled shrimp), cut into ½-inch/1.3 cm pieces

2 cups/56 g baby spinach

1½ cups/227 g grape tomatoes, halved

¼ cup/56 g pitted Kalamata olives, chopped

Zest of 1 lemon

1 tablespoon freshly squeezed lemon juice (from about ¼ of 1 large lemon)

¼ teaspoon freshly ground black pepper (about 20 grinds)

Pinch of fine sea salt (optional)

Heat the olive oil in a large, high-sided sauté pan over medium heat. Add the couscous, shallot, and garlic and cook for 2 minutes, stirring several times to toast the couscous and soften the shallot. Pour in 2¼ cups/532 ml water and the oregano. Stir and then bring the liquid to a boil. Partially cover the pan and reduce the heat to medium low. Simmer for 10 minutes, or until almost all of the liquid has been absorbed and the couscous is tender.

Fold the shrimp into the hot couscous and cover the pan again for 2 minutes to allow the shrimp to cook through. Add the spinach, tomatoes, olives, lemon zest, lemon juice, and pepper, plus any salt to taste. Fold everything together a number of times, until the spinach is wilted and the tomatoes are just warmed through. Serve immediately.

Refrigerate leftovers for up to 3 days. Enjoy as a cold pasta salad, or gently reheat with a splash of water, either in a small saucepot over medium heat, or in the microwave until heated through. (Stovetop reheating is gentler on already cooked shrimp, which tend to toughen up under the harsh zap of a microwave.)

BELLY BONUS: Protein requirements almost double during pregnancy to help facilitate growth in mom and fetus; pregnant women should have about 70 g per day. A serving of this dish provides about a quarter of the protein you need every day.

NUTRITION PER SERVING (1$\frac{1}{2}$ CUPS/216 G)

Calories 343 | Total fat 8 g (Saturated 1 g, Poly 0 g, Omega-3 0.07 g, DHA 0.02 g, EPA 0.02 g, Mono 3 g) | Cholesterol 71 mg | Protein 16 g | Sodium 640 mg | Carbohydrates 53 g | Fiber 2 g | Sugars 2 g | Vitamin A 79 mcg | Vitamin B6 0 mg | Vitamin B12 1 mcg | Vitamin C 14 mg | Vitamin D 1 IU | Choline 51 mg | Folate 23 mcg | Calcium 56 mg | Iron 1 mg

Kickin' Chicken with Pineapple Salsa

A little bit of heat from ancho chili powder and jalapeño lights up the freshness of this concoction. Grilled chicken and fresh salsa is filling without being heavy and is well rounded enough to qualify as a meal. Warm flour tortillas, toasted corn tortillas, or rice bulk things up if you need something extra. And leftovers make a speedy lunch with no need to reheat.

Makes 4 servings

1 packed teaspoon lime zest (from 1 large lime), divided

2 tablespoons freshly squeezed lime juice (from 1 large lime), divided

1 tablespoon extra-virgin olive oil

½ teaspoon ancho chili powder

¼ teaspoon ground cumin

¼ teaspoon fine sea salt

¼ teaspoon freshly ground black pepper (about 20 grinds)

4 boneless, skinless chicken breasts (a little over 1 pound/454 g)

2 cups/248 g grape or cherry tomatoes, quartered

1 cup/156 g small diced pineapple

2 tablespoons finely chopped fresh chives

1 small jalapeño, seeded and minced

¼ cup loosely packed fresh cilantro leaves, chopped

In a medium mixing bowl, combine half of the lime zest and half of the lime juice with 2 tablespoons water, the oil, chili powder, cumin, salt, and pepper. Add the chicken to the bowl and turn it around and around in the marinade to coat it well. Cover the bowl and set aside at room temperature for 30 minutes, or in the refrigerator for up to 1 hour.

Meanwhile, make the salsa in another medium bowl. Combine the remaining lime zest and juice with the tomatoes, pineapple, chives, jalapeño, and cilantro and gently fold everything together. (If you're heat averse, or not sure of the potency of your jalapeño, add only what you like.) Set the salsa aside at room temperature while you grill the chicken, or cover and refrigerate it up to 1 day. Bring it to room temperature before serving.

Heat the grill to medium high (about 400°F/204°C). Add the chicken (discarding any remaining marinade), close the cover, and grill for 5 to 7 minutes. Uncover, flip the chicken over, and grill for 5 to 7 more minutes, or until cooked through (registering 165°F/74°C on an instant-read thermometer).

Top the chicken with the salsa and serve. Refrigerate leftovers for up to 3 days.

BELLY BONUS: Thanks to the chicken, a serving of this dish provides a third of your daily pregnancy protein needs of about 70 g. Protein is especially crucial in helping the baby grow during the last two trimesters. Tomatoes, pineapple, and jalapeño are brimming with vitamin C, which promotes iron absorption and healthy bones, teeth, and gums.

NUTRITION PER SERVING (1 CHICKEN BREAST WITH ¾ CUP/135 G SALSA)

Calories 181 | Total fat 5 g (Saturated 1 g, Poly 1 g, Omega-3 0.05 g, DHA 0.00 g, EPA 0.00 g, Mono 2 g) | Cholesterol 73 mg | Protein 25 g | Sodium 207 mg | Carbohydrates 9 g | Fiber 2 g | Sugars 6 g | Vitamin A 50 mcg | Vitamin B6 1 mg | Vitamin B12 0 mcg | Vitamin C 36 mg | Vitamin D 6 IU | Choline 91 mg | Folate 25 mcg | Calcium 22 mg | Iron 1 mg

Linguine with Chard and White Beans

Pasta is a blank canvas for nutritional flourishes like the ones that tangle with the linguine here: beans and greens. If you love hot twirls of pasta dishes, but you've been avoiding most because tomato sauces light up your heartburn, try this tomato-free recipe that works in fiber from creamy cannellini beans and calcium and folate from colorful rainbow chard (though any variety of chard will work). Treat yourself to a little jar of all-natural smoked salt, which lends flavor reminiscent of bacon here and anywhere else you sprinkle it.

Makes 6 servings

1 pound/454 g linguine

¼ cup/59 ml extra-virgin olive oil, divided

1 small bunch of rainbow chard, cut into ¼-inch-/0.6 cm-thick strips across the leaves and stems

½ medium red onion, thinly sliced

3 garlic cloves, sliced

1 (15-ounce/425 g) can cannellini beans, drained and rinsed, or 1¼ cups/284 g cooked beans (navy beans or other white beans work well, too)

2 teaspoons balsamic vinegar

½ teaspoon smoked salt (or coarse sea salt)

¼ teaspoon freshly ground black pepper (about 20 grinds)

Freshly grated Parmigiano-Reggiano, for serving (optional)

Cook the linguine according to package directions. Just before draining, reserve 1 cup/237 ml of the water.

While the water boils and the pasta cooks, heat 1 tablespoon of the olive oil in a large, high-sided sauté pan over medium-high heat. Add the chard to the hot pan and push it around a little for a few minutes to help it wilt down into a more manageable mass. After about 5 minutes, once the chard has shrunken down and released much of its water, add the onions and garlic and continue cooking for another 5 minutes, or until the onions have softened and turned pale purple.

Add the beans, vinegar, salt, and pepper and stir several times to combine and heat the beans through. Drain the pasta and immediately add it to the chard and beans, along with the reserved cup of water and the remaining 3 tablespoons of olive oil. Toss everything together several times. Adjust the seasoning to taste and serve immediately, topping with grated Parmigiano-Reggiano, if you like.

BELLY BONUS: Also called white kidney beans, cannellini beans are an inexpensive source of fiber, iron, protein, and calcium. A serving of this linguine provides about a quarter of your fiber needs, helpful in combating constipation or a slow-down in the digestive system.

NUTRITION PER SERVING (1½ CUPS/227 G)

Calories 424 | Total fat 10 g (Saturated 2 g, Poly 1 g, Omega-3 0.07 g, DHA 0.00 g, EPA 0.00 g, Mono 7 g) | Cholesterol 0 mg | Protein 15 g | Sodium 409 mg | Carbohydrates 69 g | Fiber 6 g | Sugars 5 g | Vitamin A 116 mcg | Vitamin B6 0 mg | Vitamin B12 0 mcg | Vitamin C 12 mg | Vitamin D 0 IU | Choline 8 mg | Folate 169 mcg | Calcium 70 mg | Iron 4 mg

Pork and Peanut Noodles

If you crave Chinese takeout for all of its saucy, salty goodness, better to make some at home, where you can rein in the extra sodium that's not doing anything to help your swelling ankles. In general, homemade dishes are the way to go if you're trying to eat better. Here, just a little bit of ground pork adds flavor, texture, and, yes, vitamins and minerals to an otherwise very vegetable-packed stir-fry. Peanut butter fortifies an already umami-rich sauce, and chopped peanuts deliver extra crunch to top it all off.

Makes 4 servings

6 ounces/170 g medium-width egg noodles

2 tablespoons natural creamy peanut butter

1 tablespoon red chili paste

1 teaspoon dark brown sugar

3 tablespoons reduced-sodium soy sauce

1 tablespoon sesame oil

1 tablespoon vegetable oil

3 garlic cloves, minced

4 ounces/112 g ground pork

1 pound/454 g asparagus, cut into ½-inch/1.3 cm pieces

8 ounces/226 g broccoli, chopped into bite-size pieces of florets and stems

¼ cup/48 g roasted, salted peanuts, chopped

3 scallions, white and green parts thinly sliced

In a medium saucepot, cook the egg noodles according to package directions. Reserve 1 cup/ 237 ml of the water before draining. Set the drained noodles aside.

Return the saucepot to the stove with the heat turned off. Add the peanut butter, chili paste, and brown sugar and stir, working the sugar and thick pastes together. Add the soy sauce and sesame oil, stirring again to loosen the mixture. Slowly drizzle in the reserved hot water from the noodles, stirring constantly until all of it has been incorporated, making a sauce.

Pour the vegetable oil into a wok or a large, high-sided sauté pan over medium-high heat. Scrape in the garlic and stir-fry it for 30 seconds before adding the pork. Stir-fry the pork for 3 minutes, or until most of the pink is cooked away to brown. Scatter in the asparagus and stir-fry for 2 minutes. Then drop in the broccoli and cook for 3 minutes, moving everything constantly with a wok spatula or a wooden spoon, as the vegetables become bright green and consider giving away some of their tough rawness for tenderness.

Pour the sauce over the veggies and pork and continue cooking and pushing everything around until the asparagus and broccoli stems are tender but still holding on to a bit of crunch, about 5 minutes.

Dump the reserved noodles into the wok and stir them in, coating them with the saucy pork and vegetables. Add the peanuts and scallions, or wait to add them per serving to preserve their crunchy contributions if you anticipate leftovers.

{Recipe continues on next page}

Tip: If you are a heat seeker, sprinkle ¼ teaspoon crushed red pepper flakes in with the pork or squirt a few drops of Sriracha onto your serving just before digging in. The red pepper flakes contribute no additional sodium but plenty of kick.

BELLY BONUS: This meal is heavy on nutrient-rich veggies, but it also delivers on the meat, in small amounts. Pork is an excellent source of protein and energy-promoting B vitamins: thiamin, niacin, riboflavin, and B6. It's also a good source of zinc and potassium. Asparagus, a source of fiber, folate, and vitamins A, C, E, and K, is a natural diuretic (because of amino acid asparagine) and can flush out excess fluid in the body. This can be especially beneficial for those swollen ankles and that high blood pressure.

NUTRITION PER SERVING (1½ CUPS/299 G)

Calories 485 | Total fat 25 g (Saturated 5 g, Poly 5 g, Omega-3 0.39 g, DHA 0.00 g, EPA 0.00 g, Mono 5 g) | Cholesterol 56 mg | Protein 22 g | Sodium 715 mg | Carbohydrates 46 g | Fiber 7 g | Sugars 6 g | Vitamin A 141 mcg | Vitamin B6 0 mg | Vitamin B12 0 mcg | Vitamin C 62 mg | Vitamin D 5 IU | Choline 53 mg | Folate 206 mcg | Calcium 94 mg | Iron 6 mg

Safe Fish: What's the Catch?

FIRST THINGS FIRST: IT IS WIDELY HELD AND SUPPORTED THAT THE BENEFITS OF PREGNANT WOMEN eating good quality fish far outweigh the risks, and that avoiding fish altogether is more detrimental than any problems associated with eating the right fish from a reliable supply.

Fish is one of the best sources of the omega-3 polyunsaturated fatty acids needed for various functions in the body. Our bodies can't make them, so we have to get them from food or supplements. During pregnancy, these fats are incredibly important because they help with the baby's brain and eye development. They may also reduce the risk of allergies during infancy, premature birth, and postpartum depression. Omega-3s are composed of three types: eicosapentaenoic acid (EPA), docosahexaenoic acid (DHA), and alpha-linolenic acid (ALA). Research has shown that EPA and DHA have the best benefits during pregnancy; they can be found in fish such as salmon, sardines, and trout. The recommended intake of omega-3s is 200 to 300 mg every day. Pregnant women should aim to include about 12 ounces of fish per week in their diets.

I use salmon, tuna, cod, shrimp, scallops, and sardines in this book because they are generally low in contaminants, and dependable sources are easily accessible in supermarkets, specialty stores, farmers' markets, and even online. These varieties are also very easy to cook with. But there are lots of other fish in the sea that are safe for moms-to-be. If you love fish of all kinds, take some time to explore the websites of the watch groups and consumer resources mentioned below. They will help you reel in the facts about what's safe and beneficial for you and your baby.

The big concern about fish consumption is contamination. Because mercury exists in oceans, lakes, and rivers, most fish have some levels of the metal in their bodies. They may also be contaminated with polychlorinated biphenyls (PCBs) and dioxins, environmental pollutants that pose a danger to human health.* The key is not to avoid fish, but to find seafood that is low in contaminants.

The types of fish most commonly advised against are the large predatory fish—shark, swordfish, king mackerel, and tilefish—which consistently register high levels of methylmer-

---

*A note about radiation contamination in fish: At the time of printing of this book (January 2014), concern about radiation contamination of Pacific Ocean fish from the 2011 catastrophe at Japan's Fukushima nuclear power plant was being allayed by reports from reliable resources in the scientific research community. Statements held that radiation contaminants were being recorded at levels that were not cause for alarm or

cury and mercury in tests. In short, this is because they are higher up on the food chain and have eaten smaller fish contaminated with mercury. That mercury accumulates in anything that consumes it. It is not processed out or excreted, so the impurities stockpile over time, and the totals are amplified. Bigger fish equate to much bigger quantities of contaminants.

Though eating fish known to be highly contaminated is not recommended, it's important to understand that the worrisome aspect is the cumulative effect of consuming the pollutants that are present in fish. You are not going to subject your baby to mercury poisoning with one swordfish dinner. Eat swordfish or any other of the species that are known to contain high levels of mercury every week for the duration of your pregnancy, however, and you're asking for trouble (and so would be your non-pregnant partner for doing the same).

This precaution is entirely different from the counsel against consuming raw fish. The heat of cooking renders powerless the bacteria and parasites that may lurk in raw fish and that could make you seriously ill with one exposure. The threat you are avoiding by passing up raw fish for nine months is not cumulative.

So what about farmed fish versus wild-caught fish? By and large, food from its natural environs is better for you and for the animal. On the whole, most fish farming has a less-than-stellar environmental impact with a track record of introducing disease and parasites into oceans and threatening wild and native populations. In many cases, tests of farmed fish return high levels of contaminants, especially PCBs and dioxins. Some well-managed fish farms are producing fish that is safe and good, but you have to do your research to find trustworthy producers. Supermarkets in the United States are required to label fish in their cases "farmed" or "wild."

Wild Alaskan salmon is an excellent choice because of its nutritional worth and its high rating on the scale of environmental sustainability. Alaska's fishing industry is bound by regulations that exist to safeguard the waters of Alaska and its fish. Wild Alaskan salmon season is from May through October, but frozen-at-sea, or FAS, practices help extend access year round. Canned wild Alaskan salmon is also an excellent option. Salmon is among the most abundant food sources of DHA. Note that Atlantic salmon is usually farm raised and not recommended.

Canned tuna is a terrific convenience and has been deemed safe for pregnant women in certain amounts. If you eat a tuna sandwich every day, maybe give it a rest during pregnancy.

---

avoidance of Pacific Ocean fish. Historically, however, consequences of environmental disasters on this scale continue to surface or remain to be seen for years after the fact. For this reason, it is wise for all consumers of fish, especially pregnant women, to pay close attention to any updates available from trustworthy sources to be sure the consensus continues to be that consumption of Pacific Ocean fish, including Alaskan catch, remains advisable.

But don't cut tuna out all together! Its nutritional virtues outweigh contaminant risks. Try it in Black Rice Salad with Roasted Asparagus and Tuna (page 157), where you'll get the benefits of the fish and everything else that makes the salad. Tuna steaks and canned albacore register higher mercury levels, and guidelines advise to limit consumption of these types to 6 ounces per week. Light tuna, which is also called skipjack, bluefin, yellowtail, or tongol, can be eaten in quantities of about 12 ounces per week.

Fish that is packed in water retains more nutrients than those packed in oil. Ideally, seek out fish that is placed in the can raw and cooked only once by the heat of the canning process. This fish is more flavorful and holds on to more nutrients. Some popular supermarket brands are cooked twice: they're baked and deboned, and then packed in cans with additives or flavoring before being cooked again during canning.

Though the industry is widely moving toward BPA-free canning, some manufacturers have not transitioned completely. Companies such as Wild Planet mention "BPA-free" on their cans, and if you can find those or other brands with the same guarantee, certainly choose those. (See "Can We Use Cans?" on page 208 for more information on BPA in cans.)

Definitely include fish in your list of good eats for a healthy pregnancy! Learn more from these organizations dedicated to the preservation of sustainable seafood and to helping consumers find fish that's safe to eat.

- Marine Stewardship Council (www.msc.org)
- Monterey Bay Aquarium Seafood Watch Program (www.montereybayaquarium.org or www.seafoodwatch.org)
- Safe Harbor (www.safeharborfoods.com)
- American Pregnancy Association (www.americanpregnancy.org)

FISH RECIPES FOUND IN THIS BOOK:
- Salmon and Quinoa Two Ways (page 133)
- One-Pot Pearl Couscous with Shrimp and Tomatoes (page 122)
- Alaskan Niçoise Salad with Lemon Vinaigrette (page 151)
- Black Rice Salad with Roasted Asparagus and Tuna (page 157)
- Simple Fish Stew (page 221)

Salmon and Quinoa Two Ways

Salmon continues to win out as a close ally on your quest to ingest ample DHA during your pregnancy for your baby's developing brain. Wild salmon is the best choice for quality fish and for the environment. Canned salmon is an excellent and convenient choice, and wild Alaskan varieties, some of the best salmon you can get, are readily available in most grocery stores. Use it with quinoa to make cakes, or follow the variation instructions below to make salmon salad sandwiches instead. Either way you'll get a fortified spin on a nutrient-rich food. And for future reference, kids consider these a catch, too!

Makes 4 cakes

¼ cup/43 g quinoa (white, red, black, or multicolored)

½ cup/15 g loosely packed fresh flat-leaf or curly parsley leaves, finely chopped, divided

2 tablespoons minced fresh chives (about 20), divided

3 tablespoons mayonnaise, divided

¼ cup/61 g chopped cornichons or finely chopped dill pickles

½ cup/127 g plain Greek-style yogurt

2 tablespoons freshly squeezed lemon juice (from about 1 small lemon or half of 1 large)

1 cup/227 g flaked cooked or canned salmon, preferably any species of wild Alaskan (see tip)

¼ teaspoon sea salt, plus more as needed

¼ teaspoon freshly ground black pepper (about 20 grinds), plus more as needed

¼ cup/12 g panko breadcrumbs

2 to 4 teaspoons extra-virgin olive oil

Boil ½ cup/118 ml of water in a small saucepot over high heat. Stir in the quinoa, let the water return to a boil, and then reduce the heat to low and cover the pot for 15 minutes to steam the grains. Then turn off the heat and let the pot sit for 5 minutes more.

Meanwhile, make a yogurt sauce for spreading on sandwiches or topping the cakes. Put 2 teaspoons of the chopped parsley and 2 teaspoons of the minced chives in a small mixing bowl (dump the rest into a medium mixing bowl that you'll use to make the salmon mixture later). Stir 1 tablespoon of the mayonnaise into the herbs and then add the cornichons, yogurt, and lemon juice. Mix thoroughly into a smooth sauce and add salt and freshly ground black pepper to taste. Set aside.

Add the salmon and the remaining 2 tablespoons of mayonnaise to the medium mixing bowl with the parsley and chives and then use a fork to mix everything together, poking at the salmon to break it into smaller flakes if necessary.

After the quinoa has steamed and rested, scrape it into the salmon mixture. (Hot or warm quinoa helps bind everything together better than cool or cold grains.) Sprinkle in the ¼ teaspoon salt and ¼ teaspoon pepper, toss, and fold the ingredients to mix thoroughly, packing everything together with every stir. Taste and adjust the seasoning to your preference.

Sprinkle in the panko breadcrumbs and work them into the mix evenly and thoroughly. Divide the salmon mixture into four ½-cup/113 g portions, patting them into cakes about ¾ inch/2 cm thick and about 3 inches/7.5 cm in diameter.

{Recipe continues on next page}

Heat 2 teaspoons of the olive oil in a large sauté pan over medium heat. When the oil starts to shimmer a little, add as many of the cakes as possible without crowding and pan-fry them for 3 minutes, or until a dark brown crust forms on the bottom. (Frying them in batches as needed avoids steaming, which will inhibit the forming of a crunchy crust. Usually no more than two cakes will comfortably fit in a 10-inch/25 cm pan.) Gently turn the cakes over with a spatula and pan-fry the other side for another 3 minutes, or until the same crisp crust forms. Set them on a paper towel–lined plate while you cook the remaining cakes in the same manner, adding more oil as needed.

Serve each hot salmon cake with about 2 tablespoons of the yogurt sauce. To round out the meal, enjoy with a salad, green beans, or a baked potato.

Refrigerate leftovers for up to 2 days. To reheat, either microwave on medium power for 40 seconds to 1 minute, or until heated through, or set in a sauté pan over medium-low heat for about 5 minutes per side until heated through.

• • •

Variation: To make quinoa and salmon salad sandwiches instead of salmon cakes, don't add the breadcrumbs to the salmon and quinoa mixture. Stuff ½ cup/113 g of the mixture per sandwich into a warmed whole wheat pita along with a few leaves of crunchy romaine or several pinches of baby arugula and about 2 tablespoons of the yogurt sauce. Or make both. For fewer than four cakes, add only 1 tablespoon of panko breadcrumbs per cake into the salmon mixture. For instance, if you want one salmon salad sandwich and three cakes, follow the recipe through making the base, which doubles as the salmon salad, remove ½ cup/113 g of the mixture for the sandwich, and then add 3 tablespoons of breadcrumbs to the remaining salmon mixture to carry on with making the cakes.

• • •

Tip: Cans of salmon range in size from about 5 ounces/142 g to upward of 14.5 ounces/411 g. The weight listed on the label is a net total including water or oil for packing, and the amount of fish in the can is actually less. So for this recipe, you'll need two 5-ounce/142 g cans or about three quarters of a 14.5-ounce/411 g can to yield 1 cup, about 8 ounces/227 g (you can use the extra salmon from the bigger can in pasta or salad). If you use fresh salmon that you grill, poach, or roast instead, you'll need a piece that weighs between 10 and 12 ounces when it's raw (283 to 340 g). If you have a heaping cup of fish or an ounce or two more than the recipe prescribes, that's okay. But too much more or less than 8 ounces/227 g will change the structure of the cakes, potentially making them crumble or crack when you cook them.

BELLY BONUS: Besides providing fiber and iron, quinoa is considered a "complete" protein, meaning that it contains all the twenty-two essential amino acids that our bodies must get from food.) Fatty fish like salmon are great sources of DHA (docosahexaenoic acid), an omega-3 fatty acid that's good for the heart and brain. During pregnancy, DHA is especially important for the growth and development of the fetus's eyes and central nervous system.

NUTRITION PER SERVING (1 CAKE WITH 2 TABLESPOONS OF YOGURT SAUCE)

Calories 308 | Total fat 18 g (Saturated 5 g, Poly 4 g, Omega-3 1.43 g, DHA 0.47 g, EPA 0.30 g, Mono 8 g) | Cholesterol 40 mg | Protein 20 g | Sodium 304 mg | Carbohydrates 15 g | Fiber 1 g | Sugars 2 g | Vitamin A 50 mcg | Vitamin B6 0 mg | Vitamin B12 3 mcg | Vitamin C 10 mg | Vitamin D 256 IU | Choline 88 mg | Folate 35 mcg | Calcium 66 mg | Iron 1 mg

Bulgur with Sausage, Kale, and Mushrooms

In a nutritious jumble of vegetables and grains, a few crumbles of sausage plus the crunch of apples and almonds lend texture and taste. Bulgur wheat, a whole grain that cooks without much effort, offers plant-food protein and fiber that should win it a permanent spot in your pantry. A meatless version of this recipe is as simple as skipping the sausage step, but still as satisfying.

Makes 4 servings

1 cup/157 g medium-coarse bulgur wheat

1 tablespoon plus 2 teaspoons extra-virgin olive oil, divided

1 tablespoon balsamic vinegar

¼ teaspoon honey

¼ teaspoon garlic powder

¼ teaspoon fine sea salt

⅛ teaspoon freshly ground black pepper (about 10 grinds)

8 ounces/226 g fresh chicken sausage (try spinach and feta, apple sage, sweet Italian, or whatever blend you prefer)

8 ounces/226 g cremini mushrooms, thinly sliced

3 garlic cloves, roughly chopped

1 medium bunch Lacinato kale, sliced across the leaves into ¼-inch-/0.6 cm-thick strips

1 medium crisp apple (such as Honeycrisp or Gala), unpeeled and diced small

½ cup/58 g thinly sliced red onion (about ¼ of 1 large red onion)

½ cup/57 g slivered almonds, toasted

Bring 1 cup of water to a boil and pour it over the bulgur in a large mixing bowl. Cover the bowl with a tight-fitting lid or plastic wrap for 30 minutes.

In a small mixing bowl, jar, or spouted measuring cup, briskly whisk together 1 tablespoon of the oil with the vinegar, honey, garlic powder, salt, and pepper. Set the vinaigrette aside.

Meanwhile, heat the remaining 2 teaspoons of oil in a large skillet or high-sided sauté pan over medium-high heat. Push the sausage out of the casings (discard casings), drop it into the pan, and use a wooden spoon to break it up into bits and bite-size pieces. Cook for about 3 to 5 minutes, stirring often, or until no longer pink.

Spill the mushrooms in and sauté for about 3 minutes, or until the pan is dry enough to begin to brown them. Add the garlic and sauté for 30 seconds, just until it is fragrant. Drop the kale in by two or three bunches, letting it wilt a bit before you add the next handful. Cook for 5 to 7 minutes, stirring often, or until the kale has wilted and shrunk to about a quarter of its original volume and is tender, no longer stiff, and chewy. Stir in the apple and onion and cook for another minute to heat them through.

Fluff the bulgur and taste a forkful for doneness. It should be soft but with a bite like al dente pasta. Spoon the sausage, mushroom, and kale mixture onto the bulgur, drizzle the vinaigrette over the top (rewhisk it first if it has separated), and gently toss everything together to dress it all. Sprinkle the almonds over it just before serving to let their toasted crunch shine.

Refrigerate leftovers in an airtight container. Reheat in a skillet over medium heat with a tablespoon of water, stirring often, for about 5 minutes, or in the microwave until hot.

BELLY BONUS: Kale is full of fiber, vitamins A, C, and K, calcium, and iron. It can also be eaten raw or cooked. Doesn't hurt to get the little one hooked on it in utero! Bulgur is the result of wheat kernels that have been boiled, dried, and cracked. It adds 5 g of protein and 7 g of fiber per ¼ cup/35 g dry.

NUTRITION PER SERVING (1½ CUPS/291 G)

Calories 451 | Total fat 21 g (Saturated 4 g, Poly 3 g, Omega-3 0.16 g, DHA 0.00 g, EPA 0.00 g, Mono 9 g) | Cholesterol 63 mg | Protein 21 g | Sodium 616 mg | Carbohydrates 51 g | Fiber 12 g | Sugars 9 g | Vitamin A 285 mcg | Vitamin B6 0 mg | Vitamin B12 0 mcg | Vitamin C 72 mg | Vitamin D 2 IU | Choline 34 mg | Folate 53 mcg | Calcium 157 mg | Iron 3 mg

Smoky Penne Pomodoro

If your prenancy stretches over the peak of tomato and basil season, when summer markets are filled to the brim with bright red orbs, then make the kind of pasta sauce you can only daydream about the rest of the year. This quick sauce calls for lots of the ripest tomatoes, just a little bit of bacon, and smoked mozzarella for their trademark flavors, plus plenty of basil to round it all out. This sauce will be a healthful staple long after your baby grows up.

Makes 6 servings

24 ounces/679 g fresh plum or Roma tomatoes, diced small (about 4 cups)

4 garlic cloves, thinly sliced

1/4 cup/59 ml extra-virgin olive oil

1 tablespoon white wine vinegar

1/4 teaspoon freshly ground black pepper (about 20 grinds)

1/2 teaspoon fine sea salt

3 strips bacon, sliced into 1/4-inch/0.6 cm pieces

1 pound/453 g penne

2 ounces/60 g smoked mozzarella, diced small (about 1/3 cup)

10 large basil leaves, torn into small pieces

Pile the diced tomatoes into a large glass mixing bowl. Add the garlic, oil, vinegar, pepper, and salt and mix thoroughly. Set aside for at least 30 minutes, or cover and refrigerate up to 24 hours.

Set a wide, high-sided sauté pan over medium heat. When the pan is hot, scatter the bacon across the surface and cook for about 7 minutes, pushing it around in the pan frequently, until it's crispy. Turn off the heat and lift the bacon out of the pan with a slotted spoon, leaving the rendered fat in the pan, and set it on a paper towel to cool.

Cook the pasta according to the package directions.

About 5 minutes before the pasta is due to be al dente, turn the heat under the sauté pan back to medium. When the pan and the bacon fat in it are hot, add the tomato mélange and simmer to warm it through so that the tomatoes shrivel a little as they release their juices and make a sauce. Scoop out 1/4 cup/59 ml of the hot pasta water before you drain the pasta, and add the water to the tomato sauce.

Drain the pasta and then dump it into the tomatoes. Stir to coat the pasta with the sauce and then sprinkle the cheese and torn basil leaves into the mix. Top each serving with the bits of bacon.

BELLY BONUS: Tomatoes provide vitamins A and C, important nutrients for pregnancy, as well as lycopene, a phytonutrient that may be protective against cancer. When tomatoes are cooked, the cell walls break down, making lycopene more available for our bodies to absorb.

NUTRITION PER SERVING (1 1/2 CUPS/227 G)

Calories 452 | Total fat 16 g (Saturated 4 g, Poly 1 g, Omega-3 0.07 g, DHA 0.00 g, EPA 0.00 g, Mono 7 g) | Cholesterol 16 mg | Protein 17 g | Sodium 502 mg | Carbohydrates 60 g | Fiber 3 g | Sugars 6 g | Vitamin A 49 mcg | Vitamin B6 0 mg | Vitamin B12 0 mcg | Vitamin C 16 mg | Vitamin D 0 IU | Choline 8 mg | Folate 18 mcg | Calcium 67 mg | Iron 1 mg

Sushi-Fix Veggie Hand Roll
with Scallion Mayo

Survey a group of ten pregnant women and put money on at least half of them lamenting the loss of sushi for nine months. Some may quietly admit that they haven't stricken it from their diet (see "But *They're* Doing It!" on page 141), but most just wait it out, longing for the time when they can belly up to the sushi bar and indulge in the omakase again. If you've decided to play it safe and skip the raw stuff until your baby arrives, satisfy your hankering with this vegetable version. The nori and rice will nip that craving. Assembling hand rolls are as easy as rolling up a burrito. Make a recipe's worth and store them for several days for quick snacks or lunch.

Makes 4 servings

½ cup/112 g short-grain brown rice	1 medium carrot, or 1 cup/110 g shredded carrot
¼ cup/52 g mayonnaise	1 ripe avocado
1 teaspoon soy sauce	2 tablespoons rice wine vinegar
1 large scallion, white and green parts minced	1 teaspoon granulated sugar
1 small cucumber	6 nori sheets, cut in half

Combine the brown rice and 1¼ cups/296 ml water in a medium saucepot and bring the water to a boil. Cover the pot and reduce the heat to low. Simmer on low for 40 minutes. Remove from the heat and let the rice sit, covered, for an additional 10 minutes. While the rice cooks, prepare the sauce and the vegetables.

In a small mixing bowl, combine the mayonnaise, soy sauce, and scallions. Mix well and refrigerate until ready to use.

Peel the cucumber, cut it in half lengthwise, and scoop out the seeds with a spoon. Cut the seeded cucumber in half horizontally and then into ¼-inch/0.6 cm slices lengthwise. Peel the carrot and trim the stem end. Cut the carrot in half horizontally; slice it lengthwise into ¼-inch/0.6 cm planks and then ¼-inch/0.6 cm sticks. Halve the avocado and peel away the skin from each half. Discard the pit and slice into ¼-inch/0.6 cm strips.

When the rice is finished, transfer it to a large glass bowl. Sprinkle the hot rice with the vinegar and sugar and toss several times to coat. Allow the rice to cool completely before assembling the hand rolls.

To make each hand roll, hold one half sheet of nori in your palm, supporting the length of the sheet with your fingers. Pile 2 tablespoons of rice on the end of the nori in the palm of your hand. With wet fingers, pat the rice down to spread it out just slightly, leaving about ½-inch/1.3 cm margin at the edge. Top with 1 teaspoon of the scallion mayo and several slices of cucumber, carrot, and avocado.

{Recipe continues on next page}

Starting with the side in your palm, fold the lower corner of the nori sheet diagonally across the ingredients to form a cone, and tuck at the bottom edge of the filling. Continue rolling the nori into a cone shape. Set the completed hand roll on a plate, seam-side down, and continue rolling new ones with the remaining ingredients.

BELLY BONUS: Aside from being exceptionally low in calories and saturated fat, these hand rolls are loaded with vitamins, minerals, and fiber from vegetables, whole grain brown rice, and seaweed. More than just the binder of the stuffing inside the rolls, nori is a source of calcium, iron, folic acid, and omega-3 fatty acids.

NUTRITION PER SERVING (3 ROLLS)

Calories 228 | Total fat 11 g (Saturated 1 g, Poly 3 g, Omega-3 0.34 g, DHA 0.00 g, EPA 0.00 g, Mono 5 g) | Cholesterol 4 mg | Protein 4 g | Sodium 267 mg | Carbohydrates 31 g | Fiber 4 g | Sugars 5 g | Vitamin A 146 mcg | Vitamin B6 0 mg | Vitamin B12 0 mcg | Vitamin C 7 mg | Vitamin D 1 IU | Choline 11 mg | Folate 47 mcg | Calcium 35 mg | Iron 1 mg

But They're Doing It!

IT'S TRUE THAT ON THE OTHER SIDE OF THE WORLD, YOUR PREGNANT JAPANESE DOPPELGANGER IS most likely dunking her hamachi sashimi into soy sauce, sounding a diabolical laugh at the notion of your avoiding sushi for nine-plus months. If you saw her in person, you'd slap her, steal her sashimi, and . . . and . . . eat it? Sigh. Probably not.

Pregnant women are advised against eating raw fish and raw meat because of possible risk of parasites or other sources of food-borne illness. Raw shellfish, such as clams and oysters, are even more likely carriers of harmful bacteria. Incidentally, significantly more food poisoning cases are linked to cooked chicken than raw sushi-grade fish (which may correlate to the fact that people in the United States are eating far more chicken than sushi), but the message stands that cooking to total doneness kills potential critters, and we tend to err on the side of caution when it comes to food safety during pregnancy.

Across the world, pregnant women are eating, drinking, and doing things American women are advised against. In France, raw milk cheeses are as ubiquitous as Velveeta in a Midwestern church cookbook (for the record, I'd feel safer eating the raw milk cheese), and many women there trust their source to process it in the safest way possible, limiting every opportunity for dangerous bacteria like *Listeria monocytogenes* to rear their ugly little heads.

Still, all it takes is just one story too close to home to scare the craving out of you for nine months. Do your research (see page 30 for a list of foods to avoid during pregnancy), and, with your doctor's input, make an educated decision about what you feel is safe or worth the risk for you and your baby.

Sweet Potato Black Bean Hash

On the other end of the spectrum from one-dimensional sits this concoction, brimming with flavor, texture, and, most important, nutrients of the best kind for you and your little growing sweet potato. Another bonus is that the hash reheats perfectly, which makes for a quick lunch or dinner of leftovers later. The sweet and spicy mishmash of roasted potatoes and wilted kale spiked with chorizo and studded with beans begs to be topped off with an egg, one of pregnancy's super foods. But skip it with no love lost if you don't have a taste for them.

Makes 4 servings

2 medium sweet potatoes, unpeeled and diced into ½-inch/1.3 cm cubes

1 tablespoon plus 2 teaspoons vegetable or olive oil, divided

3 ounces/85 g smoked chorizo sausage, cut into ½-inch/1.3 cm cubes

½ medium bunch kale (curly or Lacinato), halved lengthwise and cut across the leaves into ½-inch/1.3 cm strips

1 (15-ounce/425 g) can black beans, drained and rinsed, or 1½ cups/258 g cooked beans

¼ teaspoon ground cumin

¼ teaspoon ancho chili powder

¼ teaspoon fine sea salt

4 (6-inch) corn tortillas

2 teaspoons unsalted butter (if making the eggs)

4 large eggs (optional)

1 cup/113 g grated Cheddar cheese

4 large scallions, white and green parts thinly sliced (about ½ cup/50 g)

¼ cup/60 g sour cream

½ cup/124 g salsa (Lime Salsa, page 91, or your favorite)

Preheat the oven to 400°F/200°C/Gas 6. Set a baking sheet in the oven for 5 minutes to heat up.

Toss the potatoes with 1 tablespoon of the oil in a large mixing bowl. Take the baking sheet out of the oven and dump the oiled potatoes out across it. Shake the pan to spread the cubes out into a single layer and then roast them for about 25 minutes, or until they are soft with browning edges.

Meanwhile, heat the remaining 2 teaspoons of oil in a large sauté pan over medium-high heat. Scrape the chorizo into the pan and cook it for 2 minutes, moving the bits around with a wooden spoon regularly. Drop fistfuls of the kale into the pan in three batches, allowing the greens to wilt and shrink for a minute between each to make room for more. After all the kale has been added, sauté it with the chorizo for another 2 minutes.

Drizzle ¼ cup/59 ml water into the pan, scraping the bottom to lift any bits or brown pieces that may have clung from the chorizo and kale. Add the beans, cumin, chili powder, and salt and stir to combine. Cover the pan and reduce the heat to medium low to cook for another 5 minutes, or until the potatoes are done roasting.

Set the corn tortillas directly on the middle rack in the oven to toast for 5 minutes, or just until crunchy and barely tanned, shortly before assembling the dish.

If you like, crown the hash with a fried egg for extra protein, iron, and vitamin D. Add 1 teaspoon of butter to a large sauté pan over medium-high heat and swirl it around as it melts to coat the bottom of the pan. When the pan is hot, crack one or two eggs, if space permits, into the pan. Cook for 30 seconds, letting the translucent egg white start to set into a firm, stark white. Using a fork or a sharp knife, poke the egg yolk, letting it flatten and run a little bit out over the white. Cook an additional 30 seconds to 1 minute, or until the white is completely set and the yolk is starting to cook through. Use a spatula to flip each egg over and continue to cook an additional 1 to 2 minutes, or until the egg yolk is completely set and light yellow. Repeat with the remaining butter and eggs.

Divide the roasted potatoes for four servings, scooping them onto plates and topping each with a quarter of the kale and beans. Add ¼ cup/28 g cheese, 2 tablespoons scallions, and 1 tablespoon sour cream on top of each serving. Snap the corn tortillas into big pieces and stick them into the hash. Top each serving with a fried egg, if using. Serve the salsa on the side.

> **BELLY BONUS:** A serving packs in over a third of your daily fiber needs thanks to fiber-rich foods like sweet potatoes, kale, and black beans. The jumble also accounts for notable amounts of vitamin A, folate, calcium, and iron.

NUTRITION PER SERVING (1 CUP/144 G OF HASH PLUS TOPPINGS)

Calories 461 | Total fat 21 g (Saturated 9 g, Poly 4 g, Omega-3 0.60 g, DHA 0.00 g, EPA 0.00 g, Mono 5 g) | Cholesterol 56 mg | Protein 22 g | Sodium 967 mg | Carbohydrates 51 g | Fiber 11 g | Sugars 9 g | Vitamin A 1 |095 mcg | Vitamin B6 0 mg | Vitamin B12 0 mcg | Vitamin C 50 mg | Vitamin D 9 IU | Choline 22 mg | Folate 38 mcg | Calcium 358 mg | Iron 3 mg

Smoky Turkey Tacos with
Celery Avocado Relish

While you're at it in the kitchen, double the relish recipe (this one yields 2 cups) and save half of it for snacking on later with chips (like the Giant Chips on page 91). Use the other half to pile on top of veggie-studded ground turkey seasoned with a blend of spices and folded into warm tortillas. Smoked paprika (whose smokiness differentiates it from Hungarian, sweet, or hot varieties) lacks the smoldering heat of chipotle powder, which is smoky in the midst of its spiciness, so use whichever you prefer. To spare you a few extra minutes on your feet, you can use a food processor to chop the celery, pepper, red onion, and cilantro for the relish, but pulse the blade instead of running it continuously to prevent pulverizing to a paste.

Makes 4 servings

FOR THE RELISH

2 teaspoons extra-virgin olive oil	½ of 1 small orange bell pepper, finely diced
2 teaspoons white wine vinegar	2 tablespoons minced red onion
½ teaspoon honey	¼ cup/7.5 g loosely packed fresh cilantro leaves, chopped
¼ teaspoon fine sea salt	1 medium avocado, pitted, peeled, and diced
1 large celery stalk, finely diced	

FOR THE TACOS

1 tablespoon olive oil	½ teaspoon sea salt
1 pound/454 g ground turkey breast	½ teaspoon ancho chili powder (or any variety)
3 garlic cloves, minced	1 small zucchini, diced small
¼ cup/60 g tomato paste	½ cup/84 g corn kernels (fresh or frozen, thawed)
½ teaspoon ground cumin	12 (6-inch) corn tortillas (white, yellow, or blue)
¼ teaspoon smoked paprika or chipotle powder	

For the relish: Whisk together the oil, vinegar, honey, and salt in a small mixing bowl. Add the celery, pepper, onion, cilantro, and avocado and fold the ingredients gently to coat with the vinegar mixture. Refrigerate until ready to serve the tacos.

For the tacos: Heat the oil in a large skillet or high-sided sauté pan over medium-high heat. Add the ground turkey to the pan and use a wooden spoon to break it up and move it around the pan as it cooks, about 2 minutes. Add the garlic and sauté for 30 seconds. Stir in the tomato paste, cumin, smoked paprika, salt, and chili powder and stir to melt the tomato paste and incorporate everything with the turkey.

{Recipe continues on next page}

Add the zucchini, corn, and ¾ cup/177 ml water. Cover the pan, lower the heat to medium low, and simmer the mixture for 5 to 10 minutes, or until the vegetables are tender and the turkey is saucy.

While the turkey cooks, warm the tortillas either in a stack in the microwave for about 1 minute, or wrapped in foil and set in a 350°F/175°C/Gas 4 oven for 10 minutes.

Pile ¼-cup/60 g scoops of the turkey into each warm tortilla and top with 2 tablespoons of the relish.

BELLY BONUS: To help support the growing baby inside you, you'll need to eat extra protein, about 25 g per day more than when you weren't pregnant. Protein is necessary for many of our bodies' normal functions such as growth and repair, as well as the manufacture of muscle, hormones, and antibodies. Complete proteins, which include all nine essential amino acids, are common in animal products such as turkey, but they are rare in plant products. Zinc is important in the growth and maintenance of tissues. Good sources are meat, such as turkey, and whole grain cereals.

NUTRITION PER SERVING (3 TACOS)

Calories 441 | Total fat 17 g (Saturated 2 g, Poly 2 g, Omega-3 0.16 g, DHA 0.01 g, EPA 0.00 g, Mono 10 g) | Cholesterol 70 mg | Protein 34 g | Sodium 489 mg | Carbohydrates 41 g | Fiber 9 g | Sugars 8 g | Vitamin A 36 mcg | Vitamin B6 1 mg | Vitamin B12 1 mcg | Vitamin C 53 mg | Vitamin D 0 IU | Choline 18 mg | Folate 84 mcg | Calcium 77 mg | Iron 3 mg

Belly-to-Belly

On aversions during pregnancy . . .

Karin M: "I remember almost passing out at the grocery store from the smell of the deli counter. It seemed like I smelled it for days afterwards!"

Adelaide L: "My sense of smell was so strong, I was sick riding the trains, especially in the morning with everyone's perfume!"

Cathy B: "There was something about basil, which I normally love, that turned me off. Being around raw meat was particularly stomach turning. I could not stand being by the meat counters at the grocery store."

Christine R: "In my first trimester, I could not bide the smell of the wool oriental rug we inherited from Andy's grandparents. I made him deodorize it two or three times a week."

Christine V: "I had a strong aversion to avocados during my first trimester, which is a food I usually love to eat. Interestingly, avocado is now my baby's favorite food!"

Dina V: "I wanted to run away from anyone who'd even had a sip of red wine. It made me want to smack people. Cigarette smoke from blocks away made me gag (as a former smoker, this shocked me completely)."

Grace R: "I could not stomach coffee, not even the smell, which I grew up loving. In fact, I realized I was pregnant with our third because I couldn't drink my latte."

Jess T: "For the first trimester of my pregnancy, I couldn't eat meat. When I put a bite into my mouth, I felt a body-wide urge to spit it out, like I was eating something poisonous."

Jennifer M: "I would come home from work with the best of intentions to cook dinner, and take one look in the fridge and retreat to another room. Once I stayed outside in the yard until my husband finished cooking because the smell was too much for me to take."

Julie S: "Oh man: major aversions to all protein (except for tofu), including nuts and cheeses. I could not be in the same room if chicken or salmon were being prepared. I also had aversions to granola bars that I was obsessed with pre-pregnancy."

Kat B: "I got it in my head once that I needed fried chicken—something I probably eat less than once a year. I asked my husband to drive out of his way to pick it up. Then, when he got home with it, I couldn't eat it."

Lari R: "Could not go down the soap aisle in the grocery store without gagging."

Tara H: "During the first trimester of both pregnancies, I didn't want any food hot. I had to have everything chilled or at least room temperature. If we got takeout pizza for dinner, I had cereal instead and my slices went in the fridge and I ate them for breakfast the next day."

Nancy M: "I am a huge chocolate lover, but it made me nauseated to even think about it while pregnant with my first. At the time I was a pastry chef, and the restaurant owner pointed out that I hadn't made a chocolate special since I became pregnant."

CHAPTER 4

Salads and Soups

When it comes to eating, I'm no shrinking violet. I can put down a notable amount without a struggle. But during pregnancy, when my stomach starting losing space to a growing baby or babies, my strategy for noshing had to change. I simply couldn't fit in typical portions of food comfortably without suffering heartburn or uncomfortable fullness, even if I sometimes still felt hungry!

Salads and soups became staples because they can pack a punch of nutrients without stuffing a stomach silly. What's more, good ones are usually exceptionally well-rounded meals with all that color and variety in a single bowl or plate.

Salads take a little bit of prep work, but if you keep great ingredients stocked and even wash, chop, and store ahead of time, lunch or dinner can be ready in a jiffy. Some of the salads included in the following pages can be completely assembled and eaten for several days afterward without unpleasant sogginess or dulling of flavors. Try Everlasting Kale and White Bean Salad (page 167), Black Rice Salad with Roasted Asparagus and Tuna (page 157), or Rainbow Farro Salad (page 171).

Soups are a gift that keeps on giving. Since a single recipe almost always yields at least four servings, usually more, if you invest the time once, you save tons of time by only having to reheat lunch or dinner thereafter. This kind of streamlining will save you when you're too tired to cook while pregnant, and later, too harried to wait for simmering with a demanding baby on your hip. Soups are also usually excellent candidates for freezing, which extends their worth even more. The ones in this chapter require relatively little time (and some are downright speedy) for big results. Chapter 5, "For Now and Later," includes more soups and stews that take slightly longer to prepare.

Colorful meals with a variety of ingredients are a great gauge for nutritional worth. Good salads and soups can really maximize potential in smaller portions.

RECIPE	VITAMIN A	VITAMIN C	VITAMIN D	B6	B12	FOLATE	CHOLINE	CALCIUM	IRON	DHA	FIBER	PROTEIN
Alaskan Niçoise Salad with Lemon Vinaigrette	**	**	**	**	**	*	**			**	*	**
Apple Salad with Pepitas and Honey Cider Vinaigrette	**							*			*	*
Bacony Bean Soup	*	*		**		**	**	*	*		**	**
Black Rice Salad with Roasted Asparagus and Tuna	*	**		*	**	*		*	*	**	**	**
Escarole and Brown Rice Minestrone	**	**		*		**		*	*		**	*
Cranberry Pistachio Salad with Chive Vinaigrette	*	*		*				*				*
Curry Noodle Soup	**	**		**	*						**	*
Green Grape and Avocado Salad with Lime Yogurt Dressing	*	*		*		*					*	
Everlasting Kale and White Bean Salad	**	**						**			*	*
Potato, Leek, and Broccoli Soup		**		**		*					*	*
Rainbow Farro Salad	**	**		*							**	*
Red and Orange Sunflower Salad	**	**		*		*					*	
Seriously Speedy Homemade Chicken Soup	**	**		*	**	**	**	*	*		**	**
Spicy Cabbage Crunch		**		*		*					*	
Spring Mix with Strawberries, Pine Nuts, and Goat Cheese	**	**							*			
Steak and Orange Salad with Sesame Dressing	**	**		**	**	**	**	*	*		**	**
Tomato-Basil Bread Soup		**		**		**	*	*	*		**	**
Watermelon Salad with Muddled Mint Vinaigrette		**						·			*	*

Key:
* = Good Source (10 to 19%)   ** = Excellent Source (>20%)
Note: DHA is based on 200 mg recommendation

Alaskan Niçoise Salad
with Lemon Vinaigrette

Salad Niçoise is a classic recipe from the French Riviera city of Nice that composes a meal of tuna, green beans, boiled eggs, tomatoes, and anchovies, sauced with vinaigrette. It's a wholly well-rounded meal and the inspiration for this version, which sources its ingredients from the complete opposite landscape and context. Wild Alaskan salmon is some of the best fish on the planet (see "Safe Fish: What's the Catch?" on page 130) and is an excellent choice for pregnant women because of its abundant supply of DHA, a type of omega-3 fatty acid. It boasts the most of any fish species. I learned this foil-roasting method in the shadows of a glacier in Cordova, Alaska, where Copper River salmon are sustainably plucked from Prince William Sound. It's my favorite way to prepare salmon, it couldn't be easier, and it cleans up in a jiffy. While the oven is on, potatoes and, yes, green beans, share the space and bulk up the finished dish that's brightened by a lemony dressing and the salty bite of olives.

Makes 4 servings

16 ounces/456 g fingerling potatoes or small new potatoes, quartered

8 ounces/226 g green beans, stem ends trimmed

¼ cup/59 ml plus 1 teaspoon extra-virgin olive oil, divided

¼ teaspoon fine sea salt, divided

¼ teaspoon freshly ground black pepper (about 20 grinds), divided

1 pound/456 g wild Alaskan salmon (any species)

1 large lemon

2 large eggs

1½ tablespoons mayonnaise

¼ teaspoon Dijon mustard

2 tablespoons white wine vinegar or white balsamic vinegar

½ medium head romaine lettuce, cut into bite-size pieces

1 small cucumber, peeled, halved lengthwise, and sliced into ¼-inch/0.6 cm pieces

½ cup/72 g pitted olives (Niçoise or your favorite variety), chopped

Situate two racks in the oven at the middle and lower positions and preheat the oven to 400°F/200°C/Gas 6. Set a baking sheet on the lower rack to get hot.

Put the potatoes and green beans in a large mixing bowl, drizzle with 1 tablespoon of the olive oil, and season with half of the salt and pepper. Toss to coat the vegetables with the oil. Take the hot pan out of the oven and spill the potatoes and beans onto it. They'll sizzle noisily when they hit the pan. Roast them on the lower rack for 30 minutes, or until the potatoes are very tender when poked with a fork, and the green beans have shriveled and browned a bit, becoming very sweet in the process.

Meanwhile, set the salmon on a piece of foil long enough to fold over onto itself (about 25 inches/60 cm), encasing the salmon in between. Finely zest the lemon and scrape the zest into a

{Recipe continues on next page}

small mixing bowl. Then cut the lemon in half and squeeze the juice from one of the halves into the lemon zest. (You should get about 1½ tablespoons of juice. If the lemon half isn't all that juicy, just supplement with extra vinegar.) Set aside for the dressing. Now slice both halves of the lemon (there's still plenty of flavor in the juiced half!) into thin ⅛-inch/0.3 cm rounds. Distribute the lemon rounds across the top of the salmon, drizzle 1 teaspoon of the oil, and sprinkle the remaining salt and pepper over the fish. Fold the foil up over the salmon and then turn the edges onto themselves to make a pouch, sealing in the fish. Set the pouch on another baking sheet and roast it on the middle rack for 15 to 20 minutes, or until the fish is firm and cooked through.

While the vegetables and fish cook, set the eggs in a small saucepot filled with cold water. Put the pot over high heat and bring the water to a boil. When it boils, cover the pot and turn off the heat. Let the eggs sit in the hot water for 15 minutes. Pour off the hot water and let cold water run over the eggs until they are cool enough to handle. Tap each lightly on a hard surface to crack the shells and then gently peel the shells from the eggs. Cut each egg into quarters or thirds and set aside.

Let the roasted potatoes and beans cool down to warm and unwrap the fish to do the same.

Stir the mayonnaise and mustard into the lemon zest and juice in the small mixing bowl. Add the remaining 3 tablespoons of oil in a slow drizzle, mixing to incorporate it evenly. Whisk in the vinegar to finish the dressing.

Toss the romaine together with the cucumbers and olives in a wide serving bowl. Add the warm potatoes and beans and fold them into the mix. Drizzle the vinaigrette over the salad and toss to dress it. Divide the roasted fish and eggs among four servings of the salad (the lemon slices are entirely edible, so add to the salad if you like or simply discard).

If you anticipate leftovers, assemble the salad per serving minus the dressing, keeping the roasted vegetables and fish separate from the undressed salad until you're ready to eat. Either reheat the potatoes, beans, and salmon (in a small sauté pan, covered, over medium heat until warmed through, or in the microwave) or simply add them to the salad cold. Drizzle the vinaigrette just before serving.

• • • •

Tip: If four servings of this salad seems like too much for your household, you can cut the ingredient amounts in half, but consider roasting the same amount of fish and repurposing anything you don't eat with the salad. Make Salmon and Quinoa Two Ways (page 133), flake cooked fillets into pasta with peas and lemon sauce, fold up chunks of it into warm corn tortillas with crunchy slaw for fish tacos, or add to soups and stews like the Simple Fish Stew (page 221).

BELLY BONUS: Romaine lettuce is a dark, leafy green, a champion in the nutrition world. It is high in vitamin A and folate and low in calories. Egg yolks are a source of choline, a nutrient important in the functioning of cells in the body, and for memory (feeling forgetful?). It's also important in the development of your baby's brain and may play a role in his or her cognitive function. You'll need 450 mg a day. One egg yolk provides 126 mg, or 28% of your daily needs.

NUTRITION PER SERVING (1 SALAD)

Calories 502 | Total fat 28 g (Saturated 5 g, Poly 5 g, Omega-3 2.14 g, DHA 0.76 g, EPA 0.49 g, Mono 16 g) | Cholesterol 145 mg | Protein 32 g | Sodium 673 mg | Carbohydrates 30 g | Fiber 4 g | Sugars 3 g | Vitamin A 296 mcg | Vitamin B6 1 mg | Vitamin B12 5 mcg | Vitamin C 39 mg | Vitamin D 430 IU | Choline 212 mg | Folate 100 mcg | Calcium 92 mg | Iron 3 mg

Apple Salad with Pepitas and Honey Cider Vinaigrette

Sweet and crunchy, toasty and smoky, the textures and flavors of this simple salad elevate it out of the ordinary. Pepitas, or pumpkin seeds, pack a surprising nutritional punch for being so small. In particular, a fistful of them adds a notable amount of protein and iron, plus zinc for healing and fiber for keeping your system running smoothly.

Makes 4 servings

½ cup/129 g unsalted pepitas

1 medium head red-leaf lettuce, washed, spun dry, and torn into bite-size pieces

1 medium apple (Honeycrisp, Gala, or similar crisp, sweet variety), cored, quartered, and thinly sliced

½ cup/56 g grated smoked Cheddar cheese

½ teaspoon Dijon mustard

2 teaspoons honey

3 tablespoons cider vinegar

¼ cup/59 ml extra-virgin olive oil

Pinch of fine sea salt

Pinch of freshly ground black pepper

Set a small sauté pan over medium heat and add the pepitas. Toast them for about 2½ minutes, or until they start to brown a bit and smell toasty. As they toast, they'll puff up and even pop like popcorn, so beware of jumping pepitas! Once they are toasted, scatter them out on a plate to cool.

In a wide serving bowl, toss the lettuce with the apples, cheese, and cooled pepitas.

In a small mixing bowl, whisk the mustard and honey together into a sticky golden paste. Add the vinegar and whisk again into a uniform liquid. Pour the olive oil into the bowl in a slow, steady stream, whisking constantly until a thickened vinaigrette forms. Add the pinches of salt and pepper and stir again. Drizzle the vinaigrette over the salad and toss to coat the lettuce and apples in the dressing.

If you are making the full recipe to eat over a couple of days, combine the lettuce and apples in an airtight container or bowl covered tightly with plastic wrap and refrigerate along with the grated cheese and the dressing in separate containers. Store the toasted pepitas at room temperature in a little jar or resealable plastic bag. Assemble the salad per serving.

BELLY BONUS: Apples are a great source of two types of fiber: soluble and insoluble. The soluble type helps prevent the buildup of cholesterol in our arteries; the insoluble type provides bulk in our digestive systems and helps to quickly move things through. Most of the fiber is concentrated in the skin, so it's best to eat apples unpeeled. If you're concerned about pesticide use, opt for organic apples. Almost all the vitamin A in the dish comes from red-leaf lettuce.

NUTRITION PER SERVING (1 SALAD)

Calories 355 | Total fat 29 g (Saturated 6 g, Poly 6 g, Omega-3 0.13 g, DHA 0.00 g, EPA 0.00 g, Mono 14 g) | Cholesterol 15 mg | Protein 11 g | Sodium 195 mg | Carbohydrates 16 g | Fiber 3 g | Sugars 8 g | Vitamin A 267 mcg | Vitamin B6 0 mg | Vitamin B12 0 mcg | Vitamin C 5 mg | Vitamin D 0 IU | Choline 23 mg | Folate 39 mcg | Calcium 138 mg | Iron 3 mg

Organic or Panic?

THE LABEL "ORGANIC" HAS BECOME SO UBIQUITOUS THAT YOU ARE EVEN FACED WITH THE CHOICE OF organic cotton onesies and organic crib mattresses as you fill out your registry. But let's stay focused on what to do about filling up your grocery cart. Organic is a label that refers to the way food was grown, handled, and processed. It is used to classify food from apples and milk to flour and grains, and the chocolate in between. It's a voluntary label that companies can use if they follow the USDA's program standards for organic foods.

The benefits of eating organic foods, from lower pesticide exposure to environmental impact, are well known. Choosing organic minimizes your and your baby's exposure to chemicals used in conventional growing practices. Still, there is no consensus on nutrition. Some studies have found organics to be more nutritious than conventional counterparts, but some have found no difference.

Organic foods are usually more expensive than conventional products, with some exceptions. Look for sales and discounted store-brand organic products. It may also make sense to pick and choose which items you will pay more for the organic certification. The Environmental Working Group (www.ewg.org) publishes lists of fruits and vegetables that contain the highest and lowest amount of residues (called "The Dirty Dozen" and "The Clean Fifteen") that can help you decide.

It's important to keep in mind that not all farms, especially small ones, participate in the USDA's organic program because of cost and administrative requirements. Ask farmers at local farmers' markets about their growing methods before passing on their food.

Bacony Bean Soup

First and foremost, this soup is rich and creamy without an ounce of cream. Natural starches make the simple herbaceous broth a velvety, substantial backdrop to beans and vegetables that account for enough fiber, vitamins, and minerals to fuel your day. Folate is a water-soluble nutrient that's extremely important for the prevention of neural tube defects, and for blood production and rapid cell growth. One serving of this soup packs close to half of the 600 mcg of folate recommended per day for pregnant women. Crunchy bacon confetti tops off thick, hot bowlfuls that are already redolent with its smoky trademark charm.

Makes about 6 servings

1 teaspoon extra-virgin olive oil

4 strips thick-cut bacon, sliced into ¼-inch/0.6 cm pieces

1 large yellow onion, diced small (about 1½ cups/173 g)

1 large carrot, diced small (about ½ cup/65 g)

2 medium celery stalks, diced small (about 1 cup/101 g)

1 large russet potato, peeled and diced small (about 3 cups/227 g)

3 garlic cloves, minced

4 (15-ounce/425 g) cans navy beans, drained and rinsed, or 6 cups cooked beans (16 ounces/453 g dried) (great Northern or cannellini beans can be substituted)

1½ teaspoons sea salt

½ teaspoon freshly ground black pepper

6 large sage leaves, very thinly sliced

1 teaspoon fresh thyme leaves (from about 6 sprigs), chopped

6 cups/1.4 L chicken stock (page 214, or low-sodium store-bought)

Heat the oil in a large Dutch oven or saucepot over medium-high heat. Add the bacon and cook until crisp, stirring often with a wooden spoon, 7 to 10 minutes. Lift the bacon out with a slotted spoon, leaving the rendered fat in the pot, and scatter it across a paper towel in one layer. Set aside.

Reduce the heat to medium and add the onion, carrot, and celery to the pot and sweat the vegetables for 5 minutes, to get them on their way to softening and to draw out their natural sugars a bit. Add the potato and garlic and cook for 5 minutes more.

Dump the beans into the pot along with the salt, pepper, sage, thyme, stock, and 1 cup/237 ml water. Stir everything together and bring the liquid to a boil, which will take about 10 minutes. Reduce the heat to medium low and simmer the soup, with the pot partially covered, for 1½ hours, or until the vegetables are completely tender and the stock has thickened from the starches of the beans and potatoes.

Enjoy the soup as is, after a good, long simmer, or you can purée it a little to make it thicker, like a chowder. Scoop about 2 cups/340 g into a blender and purée until smooth. Scrape the mixture back into the pot and stir to incorporate completely. Alternatively, if you have an immersion blender, use it to buzz the veggies and beans into the stock for about 20 seconds, or just enough to bulk up the body of the soup to the thickness you prefer.

{Recipe continues on next page}

Sprinkle some of the crisp bacon over each serving of soup.

Refrigerate leftover soup in an airtight container for up to 5 days, or freeze for up to 6 months. To reheat from frozen, either thaw overnight in the refrigerator or run warm water over the outside of the covered container until the frozen block of soup comes loose. Put the frozen block of soup in a pot with about ¼ cup/59 ml water, cover, and melt it over medium heat, stirring occasionally. Continue to heat until warmed all the way through. Do not refreeze.

BELLY BONUS: Beans are complex carbohydrates and low on the glycemic index, making them ideal for people (and pregnant women!) looking to manage their blood sugar. They're a source of protein, fiber, antioxidants, and vitamins and minerals such as folate, potassium, iron, magnesium, and manganese.

NUTRITION PER SERVING (ABOUT 1^2/3 CUPS/304 G)

Calories 439 | Total fat 10 g (Saturated 4 g, Poly 1 g, Omega-3 0.36 g, DHA 0.00 g, EPA 0.00 g, Mono 1 g) | Cholesterol 19 mg | Protein 30 g | Sodium 1,149 mg | Carbohydrates 65 g | Fiber 21 g | Sugars 3 g | Vitamin A 105 mcg | Vitamin B6 0 mg | Vitamin B12 0 mcg | Vitamin C 10 mg | Vitamin D 0 IU | Choline 98 mg | Folate 266 mcg | Calcium 161 mg | Iron 5 mg

Black Rice Salad with Roasted Asparagus and Tuna

Here, shiny black rice makes a dramatic backdrop for a jumble of color and texture, and a substantial conduit for a healthful helping of tuna. The medium grains of black rice, also called forbidden rice, are chewy and mildly nutty. They absorb the dressing and tomato juices without becoming soggy or bloated like other rice has a tendency to do, so the salad keeps exceptionally well for several days, making an ideally quick and portable meal. If you have the choice, opt for wild-caught skipjack, or light tuna, from the Pacific Northwest or British Columbia. Though limited consumption of albacore tuna (no more than 6 ounces per week) is considered safe, it does contain more mercury than its skipjack cousin. Keep consumption of light tuna to about 12 ounces a week, and use it in recipes like this one that call for smaller quantities with lots of other good-for-you ingredients.

Makes 4 servings

1 cup/218 g black rice

¼ cup/59 ml plus 2 teaspoons extra-virgin olive oil, divided

Juice of 1 medium lemon

1 small garlic clove, minced

¼ teaspoon fine sea salt

¼ teaspoon freshly ground black pepper (about 20 grinds)

2 cups/294 g grape tomatoes, halved

1 pound/454 g asparagus, trimmed of tough ends and cut into 1½-inch/4 cm pieces

1 (15-ounce/425 g) can cannellini beans, drained and rinsed, or 1¼ cups/284 g cooked beans

1 (4.2-ounce/118 g) can light tuna (skipjack, light, or Pacific albacore; see "Safe Fish: What's the Catch?" on page 130)

¼ cup/0.14 g coarsely grated Parmesan cheese

Pour 1⅔ cups/394 ml water into a medium saucepot and stir in the rice. Bring the water to a boil over high heat and then cover the pot, reduce the heat to low, and let the rice simmer for 30 minutes. Turn off the heat and let the rice sit, covered, for another 10 minutes. Drain any remaining water and then spill the rice out into a large, wide serving bowl to cool to room temperature.

Preheat the oven to 425°F/220°C/Gas 7. Set a baking sheet in the oven to get hot.

In a large mixing bowl, whisk together ¼ cup/59 ml of the olive oil and the lemon juice. Add the garlic, salt, and pepper and whisk again to distribute it all throughout the oil and juice. Dump in the tomatoes and stir to coat them well with the dressing. Set the bowl aside at room temperature while you work on the rest.

Take the hot pan out of the oven and drop the asparagus onto it. Drizzle the remaining 2 teaspoons of oil over the asparagus and then use a spatula to roll the pieces around, coating them in the oil. Spread the asparagus out across the surface of the pan, giving the pieces space to roast instead of steam. Return the pan to the oven for 15 minutes, or until the asparagus starts to shrivel and is

{Recipe continues on next page}

tender but not at all soggy when you test it. Let the asparagus cool slightly to warm and then scrape the pieces into the bowl of tomatoes, stirring to combine.

Once the rice is cool, dump the tomato mixture into it, scraping all of the dressing and juices into the rice, too. Add the beans, tuna, and Parmesan and stir to combine everything well. Adjust the seasoning to your taste and enjoy immediately or refrigerate in an airtight container for up to 5 days.

BELLY BONUS: Black rice is a member of the whole grain family and contains a host of vitamins, minerals, and fiber. Its advantage over brown rice comes from anthocyanins, pigments that give foods and plants red-purple colors. Anthocyanins also function as antioxidants and have been linked to decreased risk of heart disease and cancer. Canned tuna is a good source of protein and omega-3s, and it has less mercury than tuna steaks.

NUTRITION PER SERVING (ABOUT 2 CUPS/399 G)

Calories 490 | Total fat 21 g (Saturated 4 g, Poly 2 g, Omega-3 0.21 g, DHA 0.06 g, EPA 0.01 g, Mono 14 g) | Cholesterol 13 mg | Protein 20 g | Sodium 309 mg | Carbohydrates 62 g | Fiber 11 g | Sugars 6 g | Vitamin A 86 mcg | Vitamin B6 0 mg | Vitamin B12 1 mcg | Vitamin C 21 mg | Vitamin D 15 IU | Choline 33 mg | Folate 73 mcg | Calcium 121 mg | Iron 5 mg

Escarole and Brown Rice Minestrone

Escarole looks like it's destined for salad, and it could be, but its calling here is to your soup bowl. Those big, leafy greens soften to silky strands in a broth thickened by the starches of creamy beans and whole grain brown rice, which keeps a tiny bit of its chew through all that simmering. Inspired by the classic rustic Italian recipes for minestrone soup and escarole soup, this one is a simple dinner that's brimming with the nutrients you need from every ingredient it hosts.

Makes 6 servings

2 tablespoons extra-virgin olive oil

1 medium yellow onion, diced small

2 medium carrots, diced small

2 medium celery stalks, diced small

1 medium head escarole (about 1 pound/453 g)

3 garlic cloves, minced

1 (15-ounce/425 g) can diced fire-roasted tomatoes

1 (15-ounce/425 g) can cannellini beans, drained and rinsed, or

1¼ cups/284 g cooked beans

1 cup/170 g frozen lima beans (substitute shelled edamame or cut green beans)

¾ cup/170 g uncooked brown rice

4 cups/946 ml chicken stock (page 214, or low-sodium store-bought)

1 teaspoon fine sea salt

¼ teaspoon freshly ground black pepper (about 20 grinds)

Grated Parmigiano-Reggiano or Asiago cheese, for serving (optional)

Heat the olive oil in a large Dutch oven or saucepot over medium heat. Add the onion, carrot, and celery and sweat them for 10 minutes, stirring occasionally, or until the onions are translucent and showing the first signs of caramelization and browning around the edges.

Set the escarole leaves on a cutting board and slice them lengthwise two or three times. Then cut them crosswise into strips about ½ inch/1.3 cm thick.

Stir the garlic into the onions, carrots, and celery and cook for 30 seconds before adding the escarole by the fistful, stirring often for about 5 minutes to help the heat wilt the greens completely.

Add the tomatoes, cannellini beans, lima beans, and brown rice and stir to combine. Pour in the chicken stock and 3 cups/710 ml of water, season with the salt and pepper, cover the pot, and bring the liquid to a boil. Once you hear the rapid bubbles, cock the lid just slightly so the soup is partially covered, lower the heat to medium-low, and simmer for 45 minutes or more, stirring now and then, until the rice is tender (brown rice will retain a slight bite) and has thickened the soup along with the starch from the beans.

Serve immediately with a sprinkle of grated Parmigiano-Reggiano or Asiago cheese, if you like.

Refrigerate leftovers in an airtight container for up to 1 week. Add a splash of water per serving to reheat since the soup will thicken significantly as the rice continues to absorb liquid once chilled.

BELLY BONUS: When tomatoes are cooked, their cell walls break down and release lycopene, a phytonutrient, trapped behind them. Lycopene's antioxidant activity is enhanced then, and it becomes more available for our bodies to absorb. On top of antioxidant prowess lent by canned tomatoes, this soup offers a considerable amount of plant-based protein and pregnancy super nutrients vitamin A and folate.

NUTRITION PER SERVING (1^2/$_3$ CUPS/325 G)

Calories 289 | Total fat 7 g (Saturated 1 g, Poly 1 g, Omega-3 0.07 g, DHA 0.00 g, EPA 0.00 g, Mono 4 g) | Cholesterol 0 mg | Protein 11 g | Sodium 713 mg | Carbohydrates 46 g | Fiber 8 g | Sugars 5 g | Vitamin A 270 mcg | Vitamin B6 0 mg | Vitamin B12 0 mcg | Vitamin C 24 mg | Vitamin D 0 IU | Choline 30 mg | Folate 120 mcg | Calcium 109 mg | Iron 3 mg

Cranberry Pistachio Salad
with Chive Vinaigrette

This salad looks lovely and delicate, but it's got some chops! You might balk at the 29 g of fat per serving (in a salad?!), but wait! Remember, Mom, that you need fat to sustain that life in your belly. Fat is not a foe when it comes from reputable sources brimming with other benefits, like the cheese and pistachios (see the Belly Bonus below) in this recipe. Baby arugula and its trademark peppery flavor plays host to vitamins A and C and folate. It's also a good source of bone-building calcium.

Makes 4 servings

8 cups/170 g baby arugula	½ cup/113 g crumbled goat cheese
¼ cup/38 g shelled pistachios	¼ cup/59 ml Champagne vinegar
⅓ cup/42 g dried cranberries	1 teaspoon honey
2 medium celery stalks, sliced diagonally into ¼-inch/0.6 cm pieces	⅓ cup/79 ml extra-virgin olive oil
	1 tablespoon minced fresh chives

Put the arugula in a large, wide mixing bowl and scatter the pistachios, cranberries, celery, and goat cheese over it. Toss everything together several times to distribute.

In a small mixing bowl or jar, whisk the vinegar and honey thoroughly. Pour the oil in a slow, steady stream, whisking it into the vinegar. Once the oil and vinegar emulsify, becoming one glossy liquid, stir in the chives. Let the dressing sit for 15 minutes or so, to let the flavors come together. Whisk or shake the jar to re-emulsify everything again before pouring the vinaigrette over the salad and tossing to coat the arugula with it.

If you don't plan to serve the entire salad at once, store it and the vinaigrette separately, dressing each serving instead.

Undressed salad and the vinaigrette will keep in separate airtight containers for up to 2 days.

BELLY BONUS: A 1-ounce portion of pistachios provides 3 g of fiber, which is what you'd find in a bowl of oatmeal or a small apple. The nuts are also an excellent source of copper, which helps form red blood cells, and manganese, a trace mineral.

NUTRITION PER SERVING (1 SALAD)

Calories 353 | Total fat 29 g (Saturated 7 g, Poly 3 g, Omega-3 0.23 g, DHA 0.00 g, EPA 0.00 g, Mono 18 g) | Cholesterol 13 mg | Protein 8 g | Sodium 146 mg | Carbohydrates 17 g | Fiber 3 g | Sugars 11 g | Vitamin A 141 mcg | Vitamin B6 0 mg | Vitamin B12 0 mcg | Vitamin C 9 mg | Vitamin D 4 IU | Choline 18 mg | Folate 51 mcg | Calcium 130 mg | Iron 2 mg

Easy Being Green

DO YOU MOSEY ON PAST THAT WALL OF GREENERY IN THE PRODUCE SECTION AS IF IT'S LANDSCAPED shrubbery lining the path to the rest of the store? Wait! Leafy greens are a wellspring of pregnancy nutrients, including vitamins A, C, and K, folate, fiber, and even iron and calcium. Plus, they're an excellent way to bulk up your meals so you can pack in more of what your body needs without adding empty or less valuable calories. Kale, spinach, collard greens, mustard greens, arugula, lettuces, chard, and cabbage (including its cousin, broccoli) are some of the great options. Greens are incredibly versatile and easy to cook with. Use them in salads; sauté, stir-fry, braise, or stew them; or chop them and mix them into soups, stuffings, meatballs, or sauces. To help get you started, here are all the recipes in this book that call on the power of greens.

- Honeydew Kiwi Smoothie, page 88
- Frittata Florentine, page 46
- Spinach Cheese Dip, page 101
- Baked Potatoes with Broccoli and Bacon Vinaigrette, page 108
- Whole Wheat Couscous with Cherries, Almonds, and Arugula, page 114
- Ginger Bok Choy Stir-Fry, page 117
- Bulgur with Sausage, Kale, and Mushrooms, page 136
- Sweet Potato Black Bean Hash, page 142
- Linguine with Chard and White Beans, page 126
- One-Pot Pearl Couscous with Shrimp and Tomatoes, page 122
- Potato, Leek, and Broccoli Soup, page 168
- Everlasting Kale and White Bean Salad, page 167
- Cranberry Pistachio Salad with Chive Vinaigrette, page 162
- Alaskan Niçoise Salad with Lemon Vinaigrette, page 151
- Spicy Cabbage Crunch, page 176
- Escarole and Brown Rice Minestrone, page 160
- Apple Salad with Pepitas and Honey Cider Vinaigrette, page 153
- Green Grape and Avocado Salad with Lime Yogurt Dressing, page 166
- Steak and Orange Salad with Sesame Dressing, page 179
- Rainbow Farro Salad, page 171
- Red and Orange Sunflower Salad, page 172
- Spring Mix with Strawberries, Pine Nuts, and Goat Cheese, page 177
- Butternut Ragù Lasagna, page 199
- Braised Chicken and Collards with Noodles, page 196
- Slow Sweet Brisket with Vinegar Slaw, page 225
- White and Greens Chicken Chili, page 229
- Beefy Chopped Veggie Sloppy Joes, page 191

Curry Noodle Soup

There comes a time in these forty weeks when your tummy starts to cower behind that growing baby. Meals that accommodate the problem are the ones that are lighter and smaller, but still nutritious and comfortably filling. A bowl of this soup fits the bill. Noodles thicken the broth redolent with coconut and warmed with chili paste, and strips of vegetables soften into twirlable strands. If you don't have a mandoline, simply quarter the zucchini and carrots lengthwise and slice them into thin ¼-inch/0.6 cm pieces. If you have room, bulk up your bowl with a handful of chopped peanuts or cashews, or a small heap of shredded roasted or poached chicken (page 214).

Makes 4 servings

1 tablespoon coconut oil or vegetable oil

1 medium yellow zucchini, cut into ⅛-inch/0.3 cm strips on a mandoline

1 medium green zucchini, cut into ⅛-inch/0.3 cm strips on a mandoline

1 thick, large carrot, cut into ⅛-inch/0.3 cm strips on a mandoline

2 garlic cloves, thinly sliced

2 tablespoons red curry paste

1 tablespoon fish sauce

1⅔ cups/394 ml light coconut milk

6 cups/1.4 L chicken stock (page 214, or low-sodium store-bought)

4 to 6 ounces/113 to 170 g thin rice noodles or capellini pasta snapped in half

2 tablespoons freshly squeezed lime juice

½ cup/13 g packed fresh cilantro leaves, chopped

Heat the oil in a large Dutch oven or soup pot (at least 5 quarts) over medium-high heat. Sauté the zucchini, carrot, and garlic for about 2 minutes, just to soften them as they sweat. Add the curry paste and stir for about 30 seconds to help the paste melt into the vegetables. Add the fish sauce, coconut milk, and stock. Cover the pot until the liquid boils, 7 to 10 minutes, and then slip in the noodles. Reduce the heat to low, partially cover the pot, and simmer the soup for about 15 minutes, stirring two or three times to prevent the noodles from sticking, until the vegetables and noodles are tender.

Stir in the lime juice and cilantro and serve.

Cool leftovers and refrigerate for up to 5 days. The soup thickens considerably as it cools and as the vegetables and noodles absorb the liquid. To reheat, stir in 3 or 4 tablespoons of water per serving and warm in a saucepot over medium heat or in the microwave until hot. Adjust the seasoning to taste to compensate for the additional water, if necessary.

BELLY BONUS: Carrots deliver a wallop of vitamin A, important for the development of healthy skin and eyes. You can also find the nutrient in dark, leafy greens and sweet potatoes.

NUTRITION PER SERVING (2 CUPS/454 G)

Calories 309 | Total fat 12 g (Saturated 8 g, Poly 1 g, Omega-3 0.13 g, DHA 0.00 g, EPA 0.00 g, Mono 1 g) | Cholesterol 0 mg | Protein 12 g | Sodium 777 mg | Carbohydrates 44 g | Fiber 6 g | Sugars 10 g | Vitamin A 353 mcg | Vitamin B6 0 mg | Vitamin B12 0 mcg | Vitamin C 33 mg | Vitamin D 0 IU | Choline 27 mg | Folate 58 mcg | Calcium 71 mg | Iron 2 mg

Green Grape and Avocado Salad
with Lime Yogurt Dressing

Refreshing. I could leave it at that here, since the one word describes the combination of sweet, snappy grapes tossed with crisp lettuce, smooth avocado, and vibrant pops of scallion bits. All of it dressed in a tangy, creamy, bright dressing that won't weigh down the salad or you. A serving does the trick for a light lunch or even a midday snack. If you want to fill it out a little for a more substantial meal, add grilled and sliced flank steak, chicken, or pork tenderloin.

Makes 4 servings

⅓ cup/84 g plain whole milk yogurt (not Greek-style, which is too thick for these purposes)

1 tablespoon mayonnaise

Zest and juice of 1 lime (about 1 teaspoon lime zest and 2 tablespoons juice; see tip)

¼ teaspoon garlic powder

Pinch of fine sea salt

Pinch of granulated sugar

2 tablespoons fresh cilantro leaves, finely chopped

1 medium head butter lettuce or romaine, or 2 romaine hearts, cut or torn into bite-size pieces

1 large ripe avocado, pitted, peeled, and diced

1 cup/170 g green grapes, halved

2 scallions, white and green parts thinly sliced

In a small mixing bowl, whisk together the yogurt, mayonnaise, lime zest, lime juice, garlic powder, salt, and sugar until everything comes together in a smooth, thick, pourable dressing. Stir in the cilantro. Set the dressing aside or cover and refrigerate for up to 3 days.

In a large serving bowl, gently toss together the lettuce, avocado, grapes, and scallions. Drizzle the dressing over the surface of the salad and then toss to coat everything thoroughly. Dress each serving separately if you're not serving the salad all at once.

• • •

Tip: The juiciness of citrus fruits varies wildly, and there's no way to know what you're going to get until you cut in and start squeezing. If your lime doesn't offer the 2 tablespoons of juice the dressing requires and you don't have another lime on hand, supplement the amount missing with white wine vinegar or rice vinegar.

BELLY BONUS: Romaine is high in vitamin A and is a good source of folate, a nutrient needed to prevent neural tube defects. Avocados are packed with folate, potassium, and vitamins C and E. They are also a source of monounsaturated fat and fiber. Avocados make a great first solid food for babies.

NUTRITION PER SERVING (1 SALAD)

Calories 140 | Total fat 9 g (Saturated 2 g, Poly 2 g, Omega-3 0.18 g, DHA 0.00 g, EPA 0.00 g, Mono 5 g) | Cholesterol 4 mg | Protein 3 g | Sodium 111 mg | Carbohydrates 16 g | Fiber 4 g | Sugars 9 g | Vitamin A 111 mcg | Vitamin B6 0 mg | Vitamin B12 0 mcg | Vitamin C 12 mg | Vitamin D 1 IU | Choline 18 mg | Folate 87 mcg | Calcium 63 mg | Iron 1 mg

Everlasting Kale and White Bean Salad

In all their virtuousness, salads have one sticking point: they typically don't survive as leftovers. Day-old salad wilts like a woman at the end of her third trimester in the dead of summer. But kale is the leaf that keeps on giving to make a salad that lasts and lasts. Brimming with nutrients like folate, calcium, and vitamins A and C, this make-ahead mix of greens and beans sits pretty in your fridge for days. It's fast food of the healthiest kind.

Makes 4 servings

1 small bunch curly kale

1 (15-ounce/425 g) can cannellini, navy, or great Northern beans, drained and rinsed, or 1¼ cups/284 g cooked beans

½ cup/51 g shredded Parmesan cheese

3 tablespoons freshly squeezed lemon juice

1 teaspoon honey

¼ cup/59 ml extra-virgin olive oil

1 teaspoon lemon zest (from 1 small lemon)

½ teaspoon finely minced garlic

¼ teaspoon freshly ground black pepper (about 20 grinds)

¼ teaspoon fine sea salt

Pull the tough stems from the kale and discard them. Pile three or four pieces of the leaves on top of one another, roll them up onto themselves lengthwise, and slice crosswise into very thin strips. Repeat with all of the kale. Pile the shreds into a large mixing bowl and toss them with the beans and Parmesan.

In a small mixing bowl, whisk together the lemon juice and honey until completely incorporated. Add the olive oil in a slow steady stream, whisking constantly. Whisk in the zest, garlic, pepper, and salt. Pour the dressing over the salad and toss several times to distribute. While it's okay to eat this straight away, it really benefits from sitting at least 30 minutes, refrigerated or at room temperature, so the dressing softens the kale. Because kale is so sturdy, the salad dressed with the vinaigrette resists getting soggy for up to 5 days.

BELLY BONUS: Beans are a great source of plant-based protein. Low in fat, they also provide fiber (to get things moving), folate, and iron. Dried beans have a slight advantage over canned, as processing can diminish some nutrients and add sodium. Still, the canned variety can be convenient. Just be sure to drain and rinse to remove some added sodium.

NUTRITION PER SERVING (ABOUT 1½ CUPS/185 G)

Calories 286 | Total fat 19 g (Saturated 4 g, Poly 2 g, Omega-3 0.23 g, DHA 0.00 g, EPA 0.00 g, Mono 12 g) | Cholesterol 9 mg | Protein 11 g | Sodium 399 mg | Carbohydrates 20 g | Fiber 5 g | Sugars 3 g | Vitamin A 259 mcg | Vitamin B6 0 mg | Vitamin B12 0 mcg | Vitamin C 60 mg | Vitamin D 3 IU | Choline 3 mg | Folate 18 mcg | Calcium 261 mg | Iron 2 mg

Potato, Leek, and Broccoli Soup

For a bowl of something as straightforward as this simple soup, the nutrient quotient is surprisingly high. All told, a single serving spills over with calcium, potassium, folate, and more of what's high on the list of good-for-you-and-baby vitamins and minerals. The smoothness of the final soup depends on a buzz in the blender or, ideally, the powerful whir of a handheld immersion blender.

Makes 6 servings

2 large leeks

3 tablespoons extra-virgin olive oil

3 garlic cloves, minced

4 small russet potatoes, peeled and cut into ½-inch/1.3 cm cubes (about 2½ cups/679 g)

1 pound/454 g broccoli, cut into bite-size pieces of stems and florets (about 5 cups)

4 cups/946 ml chicken stock (page 214, or low-sodium store-bought)

½ teaspoon fine sea salt

¼ teaspoon freshly ground black pepper (about 20 grinds)

Cut off and discard the tough dark green tops and the stringy root bottom of the leeks. Slice the light green and white cylindrical end in half and then into skinny ¼-inch-/0.6 cm-thick half moons. Fill a large bowl with cold water, scrape the leeks into the water, and swish them around with your fingers a bit to agitate the water. Change the water a couple of times, until it runs clean. Leave the leeks to soak while you prep the other ingredients, freeing them of any dirt naturally stuck in the layers.

Skim the leeks off the surface of the water and either dry them in a salad spinner or set them atop a clean kitchen towel, dabbing them of excess water. They don't have to be completely dry, but dry enough to prevent complete steaming and to promote some browning when they cook.

Heat the oil in a large Dutch oven or saucepot over medium-high heat. Shake the leeks into the oil and sauté them for about 5 minutes, stirring often with a wooden spoon, until they soften and wilt a bit as they begin to brown just slightly. Add the garlic and cook for another minute, pushing it around in the leeks to prevent burning.

Dump in the potatoes and broccoli and cook them for 3 minutes, stirring often. A starchy crust will start to stick to the bottom of the pot. Drizzle in ½ cup/118 ml of water and scrape up some of the crust as the water hits the pot and sizzles a bit. Pour in another 1½ cups/355 ml of water plus the chicken stock. Season with the salt and pepper and bring the liquid to a boil, which will take about 5 minutes.

Lower the heat and simmer, partially covered, for 40 minutes, or until the potatoes and broccoli are completely tender when poked with a fork. Turn off the heat. Blend the soup until completely smooth, either using a handheld immersion blender or by scooping the soup into the blender in two batches, taking care to hold the lid down with a towel to prevent soup or hot steam from pushing it off. Pour the puréed soup back into the pot to warm through before serving.

BELLY BONUS: Fluids don't only come from glasses of water. Soup is a great way to meet your needs during pregnancy (see "General Pregnancy Guidelines" on page 15 for more information). Besides a subtle oniony flavor, leeks offer up vitamins A and C and folate, all important nutrients for pregnancy. They're also low in sodium, which helps if you're worried about fluid retention. Broccoli is high in vitamin C and folate and a good source of fiber and potassium.

NUTRITION PER SERVING (ABOUT 2 CUPS/473 ML)

Calories 198 | Total fat 8 g (Saturated 1 g, Poly 1 g, Omega-3 0.12 g, DHA 0.00 g, EPA 0.00 g, Mono 6 g) | Cholesterol 0 mg | Protein 7 g | Sodium 263 mg | Carbohydrates 26 g | Fiber 4 g | Sugars 3 g | Vitamin A 51 mcg | Vitamin B6 0 mg | Vitamin B12 0 mcg | Vitamin C 77 mg | Vitamin D 0 IU | Choline 32 mg | Folate 75 mcg | Calcium 70 mg | Iron 2 mg

Rainbow Farro Salad

I love the way grains bulk up a salad, adding texture and substance for sustenance. Farro is an ancient grain that's rich in fiber, magnesium, and vitamins A, B, C, and E. Flecks of color from the stems of rainbow chard keep their crunch for several days, and the leaves soften pleasantly under the influence of a simple vinaigrette. Because leftovers keep nicely, you can add this to your list of excellent portable lunches or quick meals that require no extra effort.

Makes 6 servings

1 cup/198 g farro

1 tablespoon Dijon mustard

1 tablespoon honey

2 tablespoons white balsamic or white wine vinegar

1/4 cup/59 ml extra-virgin olive oil

1/2 teaspoon red curry powder

1/4 teaspoon fine sea salt

1/8 teaspoon freshly ground black pepper (about 10 grinds)

1 small bunch rainbow chard

1 small yellow zucchini, diced small (about 1 cup/184 g)

1 small orange bell pepper, diced small (about 1 cup/167 g)

1/2 small shallot, minced

1/4 cup/42 g slivered almonds, toasted

Bring 2½ cups/591 ml of water to a boil in a small saucepot over high heat. Add the farro, lower the heat to medium, partially cover the pot, and simmer for 25 minutes, or until the farro is tender but not mushy and all of the water has been absorbed. Drain any remaining water from the cooked farro and let it cool to room temperature.

While the farro cooks, whisk together the mustard, honey, and vinegar in a small bowl or spouted measuring cup. Add the olive oil in a slow, steady stream, whisking briskly. Stir in the curry powder, salt, and pepper. Set the dressing aside.

Trim the bottom edges off the chard stems and then fold the leaves onto themselves lengthwise. Cut the leaves crosswise into thin strips, about 1/4 inch/0.6 cm thick. Cut the stems into small pieces, about 1/4 inch/0.6 cm wide. Add the chard to a large mixing bowl along with the zucchini, pepper, and shallot and toss to combine. Scrape the farro into the bowl, drizzle the mustard dressing over the top, and toss again to coat all the ingredients.

Sprinkle the almonds over the top of each serving for maximum crunchiness (or fold into the salad along with the dressing if you don't expect leftovers). Refrigerate in an airtight container up to 3 days.

BELLY BONUS: Calcium doesn't only come from dairy. Most of the 71 mg of the nutrient in this dish comes from the farro, chard, and almonds.

NUTRITION PER SERVING (ABOUT 1½ CUPS/180 G)

Calories 281 | Total fat 14 g (Saturated 2 g, Poly 2 g, Omega-3 0.09 g, DHA 0.00 g, EPA 0.00 g, Mono 9 g) | Cholesterol 0 mg | Protein 8 g | Sodium 276 mg | Carbohydrates 35 g | Fiber 6 g | Sugars 7 g | Vitamin A 215 mcg | Vitamin B6 0 mg | Vitamin B12 0 mcg | Vitamin C 55 mg | Vitamin D 0 IU | Choline 18 mg | Folate 35 mcg | Calcium 71 mg | Iron 2 mg

Red and Orange Sunflower Salad

Is your mind preoccupied by pink and blue? Forget them both and go with *red* and *orange*. They say babies prefer bright colors anyway, and not just on the walls of their nursery. The brighter your diet (*naturally* brighter . . . put down the king-size bag of jelly beans), the better your diet by virtue of all of the extra nutrients housed in colorful foods, like the red cabbage and juicy oranges that make up this salad.

Makes 4 servings

1 medium navel orange	2 tablespoons white wine vinegar
1 small head green-leaf lettuce, torn into bite-size pieces	½ teaspoon honey
2 cups/142 g shredded red cabbage	3 tablespoons extra-virgin olive oil
⅓ cup/42 g thinly sliced red onion	¼ cup/35 g roasted, salted sunflower seeds

Using a microplane, zest the orange and reserve the zest for the vinaigrette. Then peel the orange, pull the segments apart, and cut each segment in half or thirds. Put the segments into a large serving bowl.

Add the lettuce, cabbage, and onion to the orange segments and toss everything together to combine.

In a small mixing bowl or glass jar, whisk together the vinegar and honey. Slowly drizzle the oil into the vinegar and whisk briskly until the liquids emulsify into a vinaigrette. Mix in the reserved zest and pour the dressing over the salad, tossing to coat. Sprinkle the sunflower seeds on top and serve immediately.

To enjoy one serving at a time, reserve the dressing and sunflower seeds and then add about 1 tablespoon of each to the single serving of salad.

BELLY BONUS: The orange and the sunflower seeds in the salad are sources of folate, an important vitamin that helps with cell growth and division and prevents neural tube defects in a growing embryo. Red cabbage gets its distinctive color from plant pigments called anthocyanins. Emerging research suggests that anthocyanins may help protect against cancer and improve brain function—great news for the gestating body!

NUTRITION PER SERVING (1 SALAD)

Calories 203 | Total fat 15 g (Saturated 2 g, Poly 4 g, Omega-3 0.13 g, DHA 0.00 g, EPA 0.00 g, Mono 9 g) | Cholesterol 0 mg | Protein 4 g | Sodium 27 mg | Carbohydrates 17 g | Fiber 4 g | Sugars 9 g | Vitamin A 239 mcg | Vitamin B6 0 mg | Vitamin B12 0 mcg | Vitamin C 69 mg | Vitamin D 0 IU | Choline 25 mg | Folate 73 mcg | Calcium 76 mg | Iron 1 mg

Seriously Speedy Homemade Chicken Soup

For the same reasons chicken soup is the most suggested natural cold remedy, a pot of it is an excellent recipe for pregnancy. Whether or not you're feeling run-down, chicken soup ranks high on the comfort-food rating scale. Homemade versions don't require an entire chicken, a giant stockpot, and hours of simmering. Smaller cuts of chicken, like the split breasts used here, cook fast, and low-sodium prepared stocks (organic brands don't contain MSG, an additive you'll want to avoid now and in general) work fine if you don't have a stash of homemade stock. Balance a bowl on your belly for a really well-rounded lunch or dinner.

Makes 4 servings

1 tablespoon vegetable or olive oil

1 medium yellow onion, diced small

2 large carrots, cut into ½-inch/1.3 cm rounds

3 medium celery stalks, cut into ¼-inch/0.6 cm pieces

2 large garlic cloves, thinly sliced

1 medium zucchini, diced

4 cups/946 ml chicken stock (page 214, or low-sodium store-bought)

1 dried bay leaf

2 sprigs fresh thyme

2 large, full bone-in, skin-on chicken breasts (about 1¼ pounds/680 g)

1 (15-ounce/425 g) can navy or great Northern beans, drained and rinsed, or 1½ cups/233 g cooked beans

1 cup/105 g ditalini or other small tubular pasta

Coarse sea salt and freshly ground black pepper to taste

Heat the oil in a large Dutch oven or wide saucepot over medium-high heat. Add the onion, carrots, and celery and sauté for about 5 minutes, or until the vegetables just begin to soften. Add the garlic and zucchini and sauté 2 minutes more.

Pour in the stock and 3 cups/710 ml water and add the bay leaf and thyme. Pull off and discard the skin of the two chicken breast halves and add the chicken to the pot. Bring the liquid to a boil. Cover the pot and reduce the heat to medium low. Gently simmer the chicken and vegetables for 20 minutes, or until the chicken is cooked through.

Remove the chicken from the pot and transfer to a cutting board. Let it rest for about 5 minutes, or until it is cool enough to handle.

Meanwhile, return the pot to high heat and boil the liquid for 2 minutes. Reduce the heat to medium and stir in the beans and the pasta. Simmer until the pasta and vegetables are tender, about 10 minutes.

While the soup simmers, cut or pull all of the chicken from the bones. Discard the bones. Cut the chicken into cubes or shred it by hand. Add the cooked chicken back to the pot and season the soup with salt and pepper to your liking. Fish out the bay leaf and thyme sprig and discard. Serve immediately.

Cool any leftovers and refrigerate in an airtight container for up to 5 days.

BELLY BONUS: Courtesy of the veggies, good old chicken soup is a great source of vitamin C and fetus-fostering folate. A few ladles provide slurp after slurp of potassium, a mineral that helps maintain electrolyte balance that sometimes tilts a bit during pregnancy. Plus, a bowlful holds a healthy dose of vitamin A, which in addition to being important for your growing baby, may also help with postpartum tissue repair and recovery!

NUTRITION PER SERVING (ABOUT 1$\frac{2}{3}$ CUPS/304 G)

Calories 463 | Total fat 10 g (Saturated 2 g, Poly 3 g, Omega-3 0.47 g, DHA 0.00 g, EPA 0.00 g, Mono 3 g) | Cholesterol 91 mg | Protein 45 g | Sodium 318 mg | Carbohydrates 50 g | Fiber 11 g | Sugars 6 g | Vitamin A 328 mcg | Vitamin B6 1 mg | Vitamin B12 1 mcg | Vitamin C 19 mg | Vitamin D 7 IU | Choline 152 mg | Folate 181 mcg | Calcium 118 mg | Iron 4 mg

Spicy Cabbage Crunch

Around the beginning of your third trimester, you'll probably read the odd, albeit demonstrative comparison of your growing baby's size to that of a medium head of cabbage. These week-by-week food comparisons, which made me laugh and raise an eyebrow at once, often stirred a hankering for whatever my baby was measuring against that week. Luckily, cabbage packs a solid share of folate, the nutrient that is critical to your growing baby's development and that has been associated with significantly reduced risks of neural tube defects in newborns. You'll need an uptick in intake right from the beginning, well before your baby is the size of a blueberry, so enjoy this robust salad throughout the trimesters. Eat it just as it is, add grilled or roasted chicken for protein, or pile the slaw on top of a roasted turkey (page 216) sandwich or a burger (page 111).

Makes 6 servings

1 small head green cabbage, shredded (see tip)

3 medium celery stalks, sliced diagonally into ¼-inch-/0.6 cm-thick pieces

1 small cucumber, peeled, quartered, and sliced diagonally into ¼-inch-/0.6 cm-thick pieces

¼ cup/59 ml rice vinegar

3 tablespoons mayonnaise

1 tablespoon reduced-sodium soy sauce

1 teaspoon Sriracha, or more to taste

1 teaspoon sesame oil

1 teaspoon dark brown sugar

2 tablespoons sesame seeds, toasted

In a large, wide bowl, toss the cabbage together with the celery and cucumber.

In a spouted measuring cup or small mixing bowl, whisk together the vinegar, mayonnaise, soy sauce, Sriracha, sesame oil, and brown sugar until the sugar dissolves and everything is completely combined. Drizzle the mixture over the cabbage and toss to coat it with the dressing. Cover the bowl and refrigerate for at least 30 minutes. Sprinkle the sesame seeds over the salad before serving.

Store leftovers in an airtight container for up to 5 days.

Tip: To shred the cabbage, cut the head in quarters through the core. Cut out the tough core stem that runs up through the center. Set each quarter down on a flat side and cut the cabbage lengthwise into ¼-inch/0.6 cm or thinner strips.

BELLY BONUS: Cabbage is so often dismissed simply as fodder for summer coleslaw or an annual corned beef feast and overlooked as the nutrient-rich leafy green that it is! A serving of this slaw delivers craving-quenching flavors and textures plus a whole bunch of vitamin C, folate, and fiber.

NUTRITION PER SERVING (4 CUPS/340 G)

Calories 104 | Total fat 5 g (Saturated 1 g, Poly 2 g, Omega-3 0.15 g, DHA 0.00 g, EPA 0.00 g, Mono 2 g) | Cholesterol 2 mg | Protein 3 g | Sodium 204 mg | Carbohydrates 14 g | Fiber 5 g | Sugars 7 g | Vitamin A 16 mcg | Vitamin B6 0 mg | Vitamin B12 0 mcg | Vitamin C 58 mg | Vitamin D 0 IU | Choline 20 mg | Folate 73 mcg | Calcium 78 mg | Iron 1 mg

Spring Mix with Strawberries, Pine Nuts, and Goat Cheese

I added this recipe to the book because I made it often when my daughter was a baby. With the exception of quartering the strawberries and slicing the scallions, I could pull it off one-handed while I held her on my hip with my other arm. Eating it made me feel much more civilized than shoveling in snack food while standing up, which is typical for parents. The spring mix and strawberries are both good sources of folate, which so many of us think of first when we ponder what our growing babies need from our diet. Pine nuts are a source of magnesium, a mineral that helps maintain blood pressure, but almonds, pistachios, or sunflower seeds taste great in this mix, too.

Makes 4 servings

2 teaspoons honey	6 ounces/170 g spring mix
¼ cup/59 ml balsamic vinegar	3 scallions, white and green parts thinly sliced
Pinch of coarse sea salt	10 large strawberries, quartered
Pinch of freshly ground black pepper	½ cup/255 g crumbled goat cheese
⅓ cup/79 ml extra-virgin olive oil	¼ cup/35 g pine nuts, toasted

In a small bowl, whisk the honey, vinegar, salt, and pepper thoroughly. Pour the oil into the bowl in a slow, steady stream, whisking briskly until it's incorporated into the vinegar mixture and the vinaigrette thickens. Set aside and assemble the salad.

Toss the spring mix, scallions, and strawberries together in a wide serving bowl. Scatter the goat cheese and pine nuts across the top. Drizzle the vinaigrette over the salad, toss several times to distribute, and serve immediately. If you plan on leftovers, assemble and dress only as much as you want now and refrigerate the components and vinaigrette separately up to 3 days to make another time.

BELLY BONUS: In addition to folate, strawberries are a good source of vitamin C, which helps the body absorb iron and promotes healthy gums and teeth.

NUTRITION PER SERVING (1 SALAD)

Calories 328 | Total fat 29 g (Saturated 6 g, Poly 5 g, Omega-3 0.17 g, DHA 0.00 g, EPA 0.00 g, Mono 17 g) | Cholesterol 10 mg | Protein 7 g | Sodium 186 mg | Carbohydrates 13 g | Fiber 2 g | Sugars 8 g | Vitamin A 202 mcg | Vitamin B6 0 mg | Vitamin B12 0 mcg | Vitamin C 43 mg | Vitamin D 3 IU | Choline 11 mg | Folate 20 mcg | Calcium 78 mg | Iron 3 mg

Steak and Orange Salad
with Sesame Dressing

This salad is a balanced meal with protein and B vitamins from iron-rich red meat, plus oranges dripping with vitamin C (which helps with iron absorption) and fiber and folate from lettuce and carrots. The crisp crunch kissed by ginger and sesame and the umami intensity of soy-marinated steak is the real lure. If you don't have to serve four, make the full recipe anyway and dress only the portion of salad you plan to eat immediately. Refrigerate the rest and enjoy an already assembled quick meal without any additional effort.

Makes 4 servings

FOR THE STEAK

1 tablespoon rice vinegar

1 teaspoon reduced-sodium soy sauce

¼ teaspoon sesame oil (light or dark)

¼ teaspoon garlic powder

¼ teaspoon finely grated fresh ginger

1 pound/453 g flank steak

FOR THE SALAD

2 medium navel oranges (or your favorite variety)

3 tablespoons rice vinegar

½ teaspoon honey

½ teaspoon reduced-sodium soy sauce

¼ teaspoon sesame oil (light or dark)

¼ teaspoon garlic powder

¼ teaspoon finely grated fresh ginger

3 tablespoons extra-virgin olive oil or vegetable oil

1 medium head romaine lettuce, cut into bite-size pieces

1 large carrot, cut into thin rounds

1 small cucumber, peeled, quartered, and diced

2 large scallions, white and green parts thinly sliced

1 heaping teaspoon sesame seeds, toasted

Start by making a marinade for the steak. In a small mixing bowl, combine the rice vinegar, soy sauce, sesame oil, garlic powder, and ginger and whisk thoroughly. Set the steak in a wide, shallow bowl or a large resealable plastic bag. Pour the marinade over the steak and flip it around a few times, or if it's in a bag, squeeze the marinade up around the steak to distribute it over the meat. Let the steak marinate for 30 minutes at room temperature, or longer refrigerated, up to overnight.

For the salad, use a microplane to zest one of the oranges and collect the zest in a small mixing bowl. Cut the tops and bottoms off the oranges and set them on one end. Use a sharp paring knife to cut the white pith away from the orange pulpy fruit beneath, working from top to bottom with your knife. Now hold one orange in the palm of your hand and position your hand over the mixing bowl with the zest to collect falling juices as you proceed. Follow along the white membranes with

{Recipe continues on next page}

the blade of the knife to cut the segments out of the orange. Collect the segments in a large bowl from which you plan to serve the salad. Repeat with the other orange. Wring the juice out of the remaining orange membranes into the bowl with the zest.

Add the rice vinegar, honey, soy sauce, sesame oil, garlic powder, and ginger to the bowl with the zest and juice. Whisk everything thoroughly. Then slowly drizzle the olive oil into the bowl, whisking briskly as you do, until a thickened, glossy dressing comes together. Set this aside.

Heat the grill to medium high. Set the steak on the hot grates and discard the marinade. Grill the steak for 3 minutes and then shift it 90 degrees, for nice grill marks, and grill for another 3 minutes. Flip the steak over and cook 3 minutes, shift the meat 90 degrees, and cook for an additional 3 minutes for medium doneness. Remove the steak to a plate and let it rest for 10 minutes before slicing it into very thin strips against the grain.

While the steak rests, toss the lettuce, carrots, cucumbers, and scallions with the orange segments in the serving bowl. Drizzle the dressing over the salad and toss to coat everything. Divide the steak among four servings of the salad, setting the slices over the top. Sprinkle the sesame seeds over each serving.

BELLY BONUS: Most of the fat in this salad comes from healthy monounsaturated fats, which are known to reduce the risk of heart disease. Each serving is brimming with vitamins and minerals like vitamins A and C, calcium, and iron, in addition to lots of protein and fiber.

NUTRITION PER SERVING (1 SALAD)

Calories 360 | Total fat 19 g (Saturated 5 g, Poly 2 g, Omega-3 0.35 g, DHA 0.00 g, EPA 0.00 g, Mono 11 g) | Cholesterol 78 mg | Protein 28 g | Sodium 138 mg | Carbohydrates 20 g | Fiber 6 g | Sugars 11 g | Vitamin A 849 mcg | Vitamin B6 1 mg | Vitamin B12 1 mcg | Vitamin C 61 mg | Vitamin D 3 IU | Choline 131 mg | Folate 272 mcg | Calcium 141 mg | Iron 4 mg

Where's the Good Beef?

CHATTING ABOUT THE CONDITIONS OF MEAT PROCESSING TODAY CAN BE A REAL BUZZKILL TO THE JOY of tucking into a juicy burger dripping with the works. But if you're taking the time to tune into healthful eating for you and your baby, you'd be remiss to skip over a quick reality check about factory-farmed meat and safer alternatives. In short, animals raised in enormous Confined Animal Feeding Operations (CAFOs) are literally knee-deep in unappetizing and potentially dangerous environs. The vast majority of meat in America comes from these facilities, and food safety measures don't guarantee safekeeping during processing. The results can be devastating cases of food-borne illness from bacteria like *E. coli*, which manifest not only in frightening recalls but also in sickness and death.

I like beef and crave it on occasion (I ate significantly more than usual during my pregnancies). In light of what I've learned, though, I opt to pay more for better-quality meat from sources equipped to maintain safer, cleaner methods of raising and slaughtering animals. If possible, I buy grass-fed beef instead of meat from cows fed a predominantly grain- or corn-based diet. (Research shows that cows and other ruminant animals like deer, buffalo, and sheep are not meant to eat corn, and their systems react in opposition to it over time, requiring antibiotics and possibly churning a vicious cycle of illness for animals and humans alike.) Besides supporting the environment and the health and welfare of cattle, eating pastured animals is more nutritious, making it well worth the extra cost. In studies, grass-fed beef tends to be higher in antioxidants, vitamins A and E, and healthy fats like omega-3 fatty acids and conjugated linoleic acid (CLA). The meat also tends to be lower in calories, cholesterol, and saturated fat and have a grassier flavor. The increased demand for grass-fed meat these days has made it easier to buy. You can find it at some supermarkets, butchers, and farmers' markets. Look for "100% grass-fed" on the labels.

Since red meat is such a significant source of iron and other important nutrients, consumers, especially pregnant women, can rest assured that quality meat from trustworthy sources is worth the trouble and cost. With a little extra attention, you should have no trouble seeking out better products from supermarkets, butchers, specialty stores, and local farmers' markets. Good ingredients are the stuff of the happiest meals.

Tomato-Basil Bread Soup

A *panade* is a sponge of crusty, toasted bread dunked in hot soup. Its origins are rustic and survivalist, an attempt to make much out of not much at all. This soup takes its cue from *panade* but tastes far from desperate times. It is comforting and filling without any heaviness, and it boasts the nutrients that make tomatoes prized for their good-for-you worth. A bowlful also offers a considerable amount of iron and folate.

Makes 4 servings

¼ cup/59 ml extra-virgin olive oil, plus more as needed for serving

1 medium Vidalia or sweet yellow onion, diced small

4 garlic cloves, smashed and thinly sliced

3 tablespoons all-purpose flour

4 cups/946 ml chicken stock (page 214, or low-sodium store-bought) or vegetable stock

28 ounces/780 g crushed tomatoes

½ teaspoon dried oregano

¼ teaspoon smoked paprika

¼ teaspoon smoked salt or fine sea salt

¼ teaspoon freshly ground black pepper (about 20 grinds)

8 ounces/227 g crusty Italian bread, cut into 1-inch/2.5 cm cubes (about 4 cups)

⅓ cup/8 g fresh basil leaves, sliced into very thin strips (see tip)

Grated Parmigiano-Reggiano cheese, for serving (optional)

Heat the oil in a Dutch oven or large pot over medium-high heat. Add the onions and sweat them for 5 minutes, stirring once or twice, until they turn translucent and start to soften slightly. Add the garlic and sauté for 30 seconds.

Sprinkle the flour across the surface of the onions and garlic and then stir it in, creating a pasty mixture. Cook the flour for about 3 minutes, or until it turns golden in color and fragrant, like baking bread. Slowly pour in ½ cup/118 ml of the stock and stir continuously to fight off any clumps of flour from forming. Add 2 cups/473 ml of the stock in ½-cup/118 ml increments, stirring well. Once a thick paste forms, and the mixture is smooth with the exception of the onions and garlic, pour in the rest of the stock, stirring continuously to prevent lumps. Now add the tomatoes, oregano, paprika, salt, and pepper. Bring the liquid to a boil and then reduce the heat to medium low. Simmer for 30 minutes, stirring occasionally.

While the soup simmers, toast the bread cubes. Preheat the oven to 375°F/190°C/Gas 5. Spread the bread out in a single layer on a baking sheet and bake the cubes for 10 to 15 minutes.

After the soup has simmered, stir in the basil and adjust the seasoning to your tastes. Divide the soup among four bowls, about 1⅔ cups/394 ml per serving. Divide the bread cubes between the four servings and float them on top of the soup, letting them absorb the hot liquid as they sit, or stirring them in to soften immediately. Drizzle a few teaspoons of extra-virgin olive oil and sprinkle grated Parmigiano-Reggiano cheese over each serving, if you like.

• • •

Tip: To *chiffonade* the basil, or slice it very thinly, stack the leaves up and roll them tightly lengthwise into a tube. Now slice across the rolled-up leaves, creating tiny strips as thin as you can cut.

BELLY BONUS: The majority of the fat in this dish comes from olive oil, a monounsaturated fat that is preferred over saturated or poly. About 25 to 35% of the calories you consume a day should come from fat.

NUTRITION PER SERVING (1²/₃ CUPS/394 ML)

Calories 433 | Total fat 18 g (Saturated 3 g, Poly 3 g, Omega-3 0.20 g, DHA 0.00 g, EPA 0.00 g, Mono 12 g) | Cholesterol 0 mg | Protein 15 g | Sodium 799 mg | Carbohydrates 57 g | Fiber 7 g | Sugars 12 g | Vitamin A 32 mcg | Vitamin B6 0 mg | Vitamin B12 0 mcg | Vitamin C 24 mg | Vitamin D 0 IU | Choline 46 mg | Folate 158 mcg | Calcium 149 mg | Iron 5 mg

Watermelon Salad with Muddled Mint Vinaigrette

Fresh, crunchy, cool, and light—descriptors that pacify many a pregnant palate—tumble over each other under a drizzle of bright, herbal vinaigrette. A sprinkle of salty, firm ricotta salata cheese rounds out the amalgam of tastes and textures. Watermelon is a great source of lycopene, an anti-oxidant compound that gives the fruit its color. Since watermelon and cucumbers hold plenty of H2O (watermelon is about 90% water by weight), several scoops of this salad help with hydration for pregnancy and breastfeeding.

Makes 4 servings

3 tablespoons freshly squeezed lemon juice	4 cups/623 g bite-size watermelon cubes
2 teaspoons white balsamic vinegar or white wine vinegar	1½ cups/200 g bite-size peeled cucumber cubes (from about 1 medium cucumber)
½ teaspoon honey	1 cup shelled, blanched edamame (thawed if frozen)
⅛ teaspoon fine sea salt	
3 tablespoons safflower, canola, or vegetable oil	⅓ cup/38 g very thinly sliced red onion
	2 ounces/57 g ricotta salata cheese, grated (about ½ cup)
¼ cup/7.5 g fresh mint leaves (about 24)	

In a small bowl, whisk together the lemon juice, vinegar, honey, and salt. Slowly drizzle in the oil, whisking constantly for about 10 seconds. Tear the mint leaves into two or three small pieces each and drop them into the vinaigrette. Use a spoon to gently press the leaves into the side of the bowl several times. Set the vinaigrette aside while you prepare and assemble the salad.

Gently toss the watermelon, cucumbers, edamame, and red onion together in a large, wide bowl. Divide the salad into four servings. Sprinkle 2 tablespoons of the cheese and drizzle about 1½ tablespoons of the vinaigrette over each serving (the mint can be added to the salad or strained and discarded if you prefer).

Refrigerate leftovers separately in airtight containers for up to 3 days. The fruit and vegetables will continue to release plenty of water as they sit, so use a slotted spoon to scoop out servings and add the vinaigrette and cheese to each serving, rather than tossing everything together before storing.

BELLY BONUS: Edamame, or soybeans, have been called "miracle beans" or "super vegetables" because they contain the nine essential amino acids, which we can't make and need to obtain through food. Amino acids are the building blocks of protein and help us grow and repair body tissue. A half-cup serving of edamame also offers up 9 g of fiber.

NUTRITION PER SERVING (ABOUT 2 CUPS/337 G)

Calories 253 | Total fat 17 g (Saturated 3 g, Poly 2 g, Omega-3 0.00 g, DHA 0.00 g, EPA 0.00 g, Mono 8 g) | Cholesterol 15 mg | Protein 10 g | Sodium 308 mg | Carbohydrates 22 g | Fiber 4 g | Sugars 15 g | Vitamin A 54 mcg | Vitamin B6 0 mg | Vitamin B12 0 mcg | Vitamin C 23 mg | Vitamin D 0 IU | Choline 8 mg | Folate 9 mcg | Calcium 92 mg | Iron 2 mg

Belly-to-Belly

On mindful eating for pregnancy and parenthood . . .

Cathy B: "I try to eat healthy to set a good example and to set myself up for a long healthy life with these amazing kids."

Karin M: "It is the parents' responsibility to educate children on building a healthy lifestyle as much as to be advocates for their safety, their education, and their religious and moral upbringings."

Alison G: "I definitely feel like I need to set an example for my kids, and I also need to eat healthy foods so I can have the energy to keep up with them."

Carrie S: "I was cognizant of the fact that my food choices—good and bad—would impact not only me but also my little one. I thought it was unfair to make bad choices since she could not protest."

Christine V: "I wanted my baby to have the healthiest start possible. I also had to continue my healthy eating since I breastfeed. I often think of myself as a 'food processor' or 'juicer.' What goes in, comes out in the milk, so I have to remain mindful of my eating. It is a very big responsibility, but it is worth it."

Danielle M: "The biggest change I made was eliminating artificial sweeteners and preservatives as much as possible. It was an easy choice to make based solely on the fact I was doing it for myself and baby—since baby had no say in the matter!"

Laurie F: "I never felt like I was 'Eating for Two.' I felt like I was eating for me, to be healthy, and to keep my body as healthy as I could so it was a healthy place for my baby to grow and thrive."

Jess T: "I feel a huge sense of responsibility to be a good role model for my child. I think that now, as he's learning to make his own food choices, it's important for him to know the difference between 'grow' food and food that isn't as useful for his body, but I think, more importantly, it's good for him to see me eating healthy food. I totally eat cookies in private."

Julie S: "I wanted everything to count and to be beneficial for the baby. But I also trusted that my body would get the important nutrients to the baby. Food was the first real, tangible way for me to take care of the baby."

Joelle G: "When I was pregnant I took extra steps to make sure I was putting good things into my body. Except Hot Tamales and fruit snacks. It was either eat those or throw up all the good food I was managing to consume."

Dina V: "I want my son to have a sense that food is fuel, but also that a four-hour dinner with people you love can become one of the fondest memories of your lifetime. So can Friday night pizza night with your dad after a softball game."

CHAPTER 5

For Now and Later

Nesting is loosely defined as an expectant mother's intense urge to prepare and organize before the birth of a baby. Supposedly, pregnant female animals also exhibit nesting behaviors. The instinct, which is said to be prompted by both biological and emotional cues, is explained as a survival mechanism in some way: if everything is in order when the baby arrives, the shipshape environment will give him or her the best shot at healthy growth and survival.

I'm fascinated by the commonality and consistency of the urges described. Women confess hanging out of windows to clean the outside panes, frantically scrubbing toilets and floors, flipping out on partners to finish home improvements, obsessively laundering and compulsively cleaning.

My nesting instinct manifested in lots of activity in the kitchen and a stockpile of frozen prepared food for the initial weeks of newborn exhaustion when cooking would fall off the priority list. I hoped the reserves of homemade food would help us feel remotely sane or exhibit some semblance of normal as we struggled through sleep deprivation and the inevitable bewilderment of early parenthood.

The recipes in this chapter are designed so that you can cook and stash them for another day, either in the refrigerator or freezer as indicated. If you plan ahead this way, you just need enough energy to thaw and/or reheat what's already cooked when the time comes.

RECIPE	VITAMIN A	VITAMIN C	VITAMIN D	B6	B12	FOLATE	CHOLINE	CALCIUM	IRON	DHA	FIBER	PROTEIN
Baby Bundle Burritos				**	*		*		*		*	**
Beefy Chopped Veggie Sloppy Joes	**	**		**	**		*	*	*		**	**
Bowl of Iron Beef Stew	**	**		**	**		**		**		**	**
Braised Chicken and Collards with Noodles	*	**		**	**	*	**		*		*	**
Butternut Ragù Lasagna	**	**		**	**	*	*	**	*		*	**
Cauliflower Chickpea Curry		**							*		**	*
Golden Split Pea and Pumpkin Stew	**	*			*				*		**	**
Hearty Meat and Bean Chili		**		**	**		*	*	**		**	**
Indian Spice Chicken in Yogurt Sauce		*		**	**		**	*	*	*	*	**
Lentil Ratatouille with Baked Polenta	*	**		**		*	*		**		**	**
Poached Chicken				*	*					*		**
Chicken Stock												
Roasted Turkey Breast				**	**					*		**
Roasted Vegetable Enchilada Pie	**	**		**				*	*		**	*
Simple Fish Stew		**	*	**	**		**	*	*	**	*	**
Simpler Sunday Meatballs and Spaghetti		**		**	**	**	**	*	**		**	**
Slow Sweet Brisket with Vinegar Slaw	**	**		**	**	*	**	*	**		**	**
Vegetable Stew	**	**		**		*					**	
White and Greens Chicken Chili		**		**	**		**	*	*		**	**

Key:
* = Good Source (10 to 19%)   ** = Excellent Source (>20%)
Note: DHA is based on 200 mg recommendation

Baby Bundle Burritos

Shortly after our twin sons were born, the editor of this book, Kristen, dropped on my doorstep a care package complete with homemade burritos and a refrigerator magnet clip that held the critical instructions for reheating. The burritos were all wrapped up and frozen and were a splendid stash that became quick, protein-packed, sustaining meals in minutes with virtually no cleanup. Just good food fast that we didn't have to order, or wait for, or spend any more time on aside from enjoying. They won a place in my lineup of excellent make-ahead meals and became an obvious addition to this chapter. Kristen's burritos were made with tender pulled pork and bacony lentils. I followed her lead on flavors and construction to develop a streamlined recipe that yields ten burritos (five servings of two burritos each) for eating now and later. You can follow this one to the T, or customize as you like with chicken, vegetables, more beans, or different grains. Generally, you'll need 2 cups of cooked grains and 3 cups of the other filling for this serving size. However you make them, a little time cooking and bundling now means quick meals when you can really use them.

Makes 5 servings

½ cup/85 g quinoa (white, red, black, or multicolored)

2 tablespoons tomato paste

1 cup/237 ml chicken stock (page 214, or low-sodium store-bought)

½ teaspoon ground cumin

½ teaspoon ancho chili powder

½ teaspoon garlic powder

½ teaspoon fine sea salt

¼ teaspoon freshly ground black pepper (about 20 grinds)

2 strips thick-cut bacon, cut into ¼-inch/0.6 cm pieces

1 pound/454 g pork tenderloin, cut into ½-inch/1.3 cm cubes

1 (15-ounce/425 g) can pinto beans, drained and rinsed, or 1½ cups/257 g cooked beans

10 (8-inch) flour tortillas, at room temperature

Bring 1 cup/237 ml water to a boil in a small saucepot over high heat. Stir in the quinoa, cover, and reduce the heat to low. Simmer for 15 minutes. Remove the pot from the heat and let it sit for 10 minutes. Uncover, fluff the quinoa, and let it cool completely.

While the quinoa cooks, combine the tomato paste and 2 tablespoons of the chicken stock in a small mixing bowl or spouted measuring cup. Stir it together to loosen the paste a little and then add the rest of the stock slowly, whisking away any lumps into a smooth sauce. Add the cumin, chili powder, garlic powder, salt, and pepper. Set aside.

Heat a large skillet over medium heat. Add the bacon to the dry, hot pan and cook it, pushing it around the pan every now and then, for about 7 minutes, or until the bits are dark and crisp. Lift the bacon from the pan with a slotted spoon and set it on a paper towel–lined plate.

Drop the pork cubes into the pan with the bacon grease, raise the heat to medium high, and cook away most of the pink for about 3 minutes, stirring often. Dump in the beans and then pour the spiced tomato sauce mixture over everything, stirring to distribute. Raise the heat to simmer for

15 minutes, uncovered. Turn off the heat and let the pork and beans cool completely. The sauce will thicken considerably while it does.

Refrigerate the pork and beans and the quinoa for several hours or overnight, until cold. (This step is optional but makes for neater assembly.)

Make sure the tortillas are at room temperature before assembling (or warm them slightly in the microwave or in a warm oven, stacked and wrapped in foil).

Set a tortilla on a clean surface. Pile 3 tablespoons of the cooked quinoa in a horizontal line in the center of the tortilla, leaving about 1½ inches/4 cm of space to the left and right. Top the quinoa with ¼ cup/about 60 g of the pork and beans, leaving the same space on the sides. Fold the left and right sides over the ends of the pile and then tuck the half of the tortilla closest to you up over the pile and snugly down on the other side. Continue to roll the tortilla over onto itself, tucking the seam underneath. (All this folding and tucking is excellent practice for swaddling.) Wrap the tortilla tightly in a small piece of plastic wrap. Repeat this process with the remaining ingredients to yield ten wrapped burritos. These will keep well refrigerated up to 3 days. Otherwise, pack the individually wrapped tortillas in an airtight container or in a resealable plastic freezer bag and freeze up to 3 months. Follow the instructions for reheating from frozen in the box below.

Baby Bundle Burritos Reheating Instructions
(adjust instructions as needed for multiple burritos)

I must eat 5 minutes ago.
Microwave loosely wrapped in plastic wrap until hot throughout, about 2 minutes. Eat immediately.

I can wait 5 minutes. Maybe.
Microwave loosely wrapped in plastic wrap until thawed, about 1 minute. Remove plastic, rewrap in foil. Lay in a hot, dry pan to crisp for 2 minutes on each side. Eat immediately.

I have the wherewithal for garnishes.
Heat through using either method, or in a warm oven. Melt grated cheese over the top. Adorn with sliced scallions. Stir together pinches of cumin, salt, and plain yogurt or sour cream and dip repeatedly. Eat with hot sauce or salsa.

BELLY BONUS: Compared to white rice, quinoa packs in a wider variety of nutrients, including protein, fiber, potassium, folate, calcium, iron, magnesium, and vitamin A. Plus, it's a complete protein, supplying all the essential amino acids you need. A serving of this dish provides more than half of the protein you'll need a day to sustain growth.

NUTRITION PER SERVING (2 BURRITOS)

Calories 593 | Total fat 16 g (Saturated 6 g, Poly 1 g, Omega-3 0.07 g, DHA 0.01 g, EPA 0.00 g, Mono 1 g) | Cholesterol 73 mg | Protein 41 g | Sodium 1,701 mg | Carbohydrates 74 g | Fiber 4 g | Sugars 4 g | Vitamin A 9 mcg | Vitamin B6 1 mg | Vitamin B12 1 mcg | Vitamin C 1 mg | Vitamin D 7 IU | Choline 90 mg | Folate 43 mcg | Calcium 52 mg | Iron 3 mg

Curing Your Bacon Hankerin'

SODIUM NITRATE IS A NATURALLY OCCURRING COMPOUND, A TYPE OF SALT FOUND IN WATER, SOIL, and lots of foods that grow up from the ground, like celery, arugula, beets, and more. It is also used in foods such as bacon, hot dogs, fish products, and deli meats to prevent spoilage and enhance flavor and color and to combat dangerous bacteria like *C. botulinum* in products like cured hams and sausages. When it is consumed, sodium nitrate is converted in the body to sodium *nitrite*. Some studies have identified a possible link between cured meats and cancer due to nitrites and high-heat cooking, but there still is uncertainty about the issue. Brands labeled "uncured" or "nitrate and nitrite-free" are increasingly available, but these products simply call on ingredients that are naturally high in sodium nitrate, like celery, instead of synthetic nitrates to do the same curing job. Some argue the labels are suggestive of a healthier alternative, and, thus, misleading. In general, eating bacon is probably not going to harm you and your baby if you do so in moderation. Eating it all day every day might be more problematic for your general health than anything else, whether you are pregnant or not, because it is high in sodium and saturated fat. Since the jury is still out on the topic of nitrates in food, I use very minimal amounts of bacon and other types of cured meats in *Full Belly* for flavor and texture, and encourage eating them in moderation. It's important to understand, however, that the potential harm to our bodies from sodium nitrate is very different from the threat of listeriosis from bacteria that can be harbored in deli meats and cured meats like salami, soppressata, and prosciutto (see page 31). Bacon may (or may not) have a negative cumulative effect on health, but bacteria can have a sudden and serious impact after just one exposure. So enjoy your bacon . . . sparingly.

Beefy Chopped Veggie Sloppy Joes

Somewhere along the way of my thirty-seven weeks pregnant with twins, I scribbled down in my food journal, "I wanted sloppy Joes." Maybe it was the richness of the sauce and the softness of the bun. Or maybe a more scientific explanation about my body wanting the iron in the beef explains it. Regardless of what drove the craving, the fix was easy. Typically, sloppy Joes are a straight-up meat sandwich, save for the tomato product in the sauce. But this version takes advantage of the Joes' malleability and forgivable untidiness and cooks a small garden of vegetables with lean beef into a sandwich that's not only satisfying but also very nutritious. And very, very sloppy. Go ahead and put a bib right over that baby bump and enjoy the mess. The mixture freezes nicely for a quick, effortless meal another time.

Makes 8 servings

1 tablespoon extra-virgin olive oil or vegetable oil

½ cup/80 g minced shallot (about 2 large shallots)

2 garlic cloves, minced

1 medium bunch rainbow chard, stem cut into ¼-inch/0.6 cm pieces and leaves cut lengthwise and then crosswise into very small pieces

2 cups/255 g finely chopped cauliflower florets (about ¼ of a medium head)

1 large carrot, grated (about 1 cup/110 g)

1 pound/454 g lean (90%) ground beef

1 (14-ounce/411 g) can crushed tomatoes (about 1½ cups/363 g)

2 tablespoons malt vinegar or cider vinegar

1 tablespoon Dijon mustard

1 tablespoon blackstrap molasses

1 tablespoon soy sauce

1 teaspoon garlic powder

¼ teaspoon fine sea salt

¼ teaspoon freshly ground black pepper (about 20 grinds)

8 small whole wheat burger buns

Heat the oil in a large, high-sided sauté pan or skillet over medium heat. When the oil is hot, add the shallot and garlic and sauté for 1 minute, or just until the shallot starts to release some of its water. Add the chard stems and sauté for another minute before adding the cauliflower. Cook the vegetables for 10 minutes, stirring often, or until they start to soften slightly. Add the carrot and the chard leaves and let them sweat until the chard is completely wilted, about 5 minutes, stirring now and again.

Add the beef to the mix and break it up in the pan with a wooden spoon. Then cook it into the veggies for 10 minutes, stirring often and continuing to break it apart into little bits, making sure no lumps cook into small meatballs.

Pour in ½ cup/118 ml water and scrape up any browned bits from the bottom as it sizzles and cooks away slightly. Add the tomatoes, vinegar, mustard, molasses, soy sauce, garlic powder, salt, and pepper and stir very well to combine thoroughly and to distribute the veggies and meat throughout the sauce.

{Recipe continues on next page}

Let the sauce come up to a steady simmer. Then cover the pan, reduce the heat to medium low, and simmer for 15 minutes or more so the veggies and meat become even more tender and infused with the sauce.

Toast the buns, if you like. Then scoop ⅔ cup/170 g of the sloppy Joe mixture to build the sandwich and serve hot.

Cool any leftovers completely and transfer to an airtight container. Refrigerate up to 5 days and freeze up to 3 months. Thaw the mixture completely in the refrigerator or just enough to tap it out of the container in a frozen block. Put the block in a small saucepot over medium heat with 1 tablespoon of water. Cover the pot and cook until the sloppy Joe mix is thawed and heated completely through. Alternatively, spoon individual servings into small containers for single sandwiches to order! Microwave until heated through and serve on a toasted bun.

BELLY BONUS: Sneaking veggies into this meal bumps up its vitamin A, vitamin C, folate, fiber, calcium, and iron content. Plus, they meld so well, you might forget those little bits aren't meat. Chard is an excellent source of vitamins A and C. It's also a good source of magnesium.

NUTRITION PER SERVING (ABOUT ⅔ CUP/170 G EACH ON 1 BUN)

Calories 320 | Total fat 10 g (Saturated 3 g, Poly 2 g, Omega-3 0.12 g, DHA 0.00 g, EPA 0.00 g, Mono 5 g) | Cholesterol 37 mg | Protein 19 g | Sodium 759 mg | Carbohydrates 41 g | Fiber 7 g | Sugars 11 g | Vitamin A 253 mcg | Vitamin B6 1 mg | Vitamin B12 1 mcg | Vitamin C 34 mg | Vitamin D 2 IU | Choline 72 mg | Folate 40 mcg | Calcium 130 mg | Iron 5 mg

Bowl of Iron Beef Stew

Of the many things pregnancy bestows upon us, extra blood to fuel our expanding system is a big one. Its role is supplying oxygen to the entire body, and to do that effectively, blood needs to be iron-rich. Our bodies absorb iron most efficiently from animal sources such as red meat, so dig into a bowl of beef stew thickened by the starches of potatoes and barley. Big bites of tender veggies make a serving a balanced meal, but go ahead and treat yourself to a hunk of soft bread for dunking into the substantial broth.

Makes 6 servings

1 tablespoon vegetable oil

1 pound/475 g chuck-roast beef cubes (stew beef)

1 large yellow onion, cut into ½-inch/1.3 cm pieces

3 medium carrots, cut into 1-inch/2.5 cm chunks

2 large celery stalks, cut into 1-inch/2.5 cm pieces

2 tablespoons tomato paste

2 large garlic cloves, thinly sliced or chopped

1 (15-ounce/425 g) can whole peeled or crushed tomatoes

2 medium russet potatoes, unpeeled and cut into large cubes (about 3 cups/454 g)

8 ounces/231 g green beans, cut into 1-inch/2.5 cm pieces

3 cups/710 ml beef stock

4 cups/946 ml chicken stock (page 214, or low-sodium store-bought)

½ cup/80 g pearled barley

2 teaspoons dried oregano

1½ teaspoons fine sea salt

½ teaspoon freshly ground black pepper

Heat the oil in a large Dutch oven or saucepot over medium-high heat. Sear the beef cubes on two sides until a dark crust forms, 3 minutes per side. Do this in batches, removing the browned pieces to a plate before adding the next batch. Overcrowding causes steaming, which prevents browning.

Once the meat cubes are browned, remove them all to the plate and set aside. Reduce the heat to medium, add the onion, carrots, and celery and sweat them, stirring occasionally and scraping any browned bits from the bottom as the vegetables release their water, about 5 minutes.

Add the tomato paste and garlic and stir for about 30 seconds to help melt the tomato paste into the vegetables. Stir in the tomatoes, potatoes, green beans, beef and chicken stock, barley, oregano, salt, and pepper. Return the meat to the pot. Increase the heat to high to bring the liquid to a boil. Then partially cover the pot and maintain a gentle simmer over low heat for 3 hours, stirring every 30 minutes or so until the vegetables and beef cubes are very tender.

Season the stew with more salt and pepper to taste and serve.

Refrigerate leftovers for up to 5 days, or freeze in an airtight container for up to 6 months.

{Recipe continues on next page}

NUTRITION PER SERVING (2 CUPS/611 G)

Calories 384 | Total fat 10 g (Saturated 3 g, Poly 2 g, Omega-3 0.26 g, DHA 0.00 g, EPA 0.00 g, Mono 3 g) | Cholesterol 79 mg | Protein 36 g | Sodium 1281 mg | Carbohydrates 39 g | Fiber 7 g | Sugars 7 g | Vitamin A 289 mcg | Vitamin B6 1 mg | Vitamin B12 2 mcg | Vitamin C 24 mg | Vitamin D 4 IU | Choline 129 mg | Folate 46 mcg | Calcium 98 mg | Iron 7 mg

Iron Deficiency

ANEMIA OR IRON DEFICIENCY IS COMMON DURING PREGNANCY AND IS CHARACTERIZED BY LOW RED blood cell count. A woman can enter pregnancy already iron-deficient, or it can be induced by pregnancy, due to the increase in blood volume to support mom and the baby. Because iron is necessary to produce red blood cells, which carry oxygen around the body, a deficiency in the mineral can leave you feeling weak or extremely run-down. Severe iron deficiency during pregnancy can lead to premature birth. Your healthcare provider may recommend a supplement in addition to eating more iron-rich foods if your blood tests show a deficiency. Iron supplements can have side effects such as constipation, making fiber an even better friend than it already is. The daily recommendation of iron for pregnant women is 27 mg.

There are two types of iron available in food: heme iron, which is found in animal protein sources (meat, poultry, fish), and non-heme iron, which is found in both plant and animal food sources. Our bodies absorb heme iron much more efficiently than non-heme iron. Eating sources of the two in combination, and eating foods rich in vitamin C along with iron sources, helps the body absorb the nutrient even better.

Refer to the recipes and nutrients chart after the introduction to each chapter to find iron-rich recipes throughout the book.

Some iron-rich foods

- Red meat
- Spinach
- Chard
- Blackstrap molasses
- Eggs

- Lentils
- Dried beans
- Tomatoes
- Grains and cereals fortified with iron

Braised Chicken and Collards with Noodles

You could sit upright and civilized at a table with a napkin on your lap tending to a wide bowl of tender chicken, greens, and noodles, or you could put your feet up on the couch, propped up by pillows, with a napkin 'round your neck, and dig happily into this comforting combo. It's filling without being heavy, and brimming with the nutrients you need. If you haven't cooked much with collards, give them a go! They are a member of the cancer-fighting cabbage family (cruciferous), an excellent source of vitamin A, vitamin C, and folate, and a good source of fiber and non-dairy calcium.

Makes 8 servings

1 tablespoon olive oil or canola oil

1 teaspoon fine sea salt, divided

½ teaspoon freshly ground black pepper, divided

3 pounds/1.4 kg boneless, skinless chicken thighs

2 tablespoons all-purpose flour

1 medium yellow or white onion, halved and thinly sliced

1 medium red bell pepper, cut into strips

1 medium green bell pepper, cut into strips

1 small bunch collard greens (about 320 g), tough stems pulled and discarded

3 garlic cloves, thinly sliced

2 tablespoons cider vinegar

2 cups/473 ml chicken stock (page 214, or low-sodium store-bought)

½ teaspoon smoked paprika

8 ounces/227 g egg noodles

Heat the oil in a large Dutch oven or high-sided sauté pan over medium-high heat. Sprinkle half of the salt and half of the pepper over one side of each of the chicken pieces, and then sprinkle the flour across the surface of the same side. Pick up each piece and shake off any excess flour, then set it into the hot oil, flour-side down. Brown the pieces on one side for 5 to 7 minutes. If your pan will not accommodate all the pieces at once, do this in batches. Overcrowding promotes steaming, which prevents browning. Remove the browned chicken to a plate and set aside.

Add the onions and peppers to the pan and sauté for 5 minutes, or just until the vegetables begin to soften. While the onions and peppers cook, cut the collards across the leaves into ½-inch-/1.3 cm-thick strips. Add the greens and garlic to the onions and peppers and cook for 5 minutes, stirring occasionally until the greens begin to wilt. Add the cider vinegar and scrape any brown bits from the bottom as the liquid sizzles and evaporates. Pour in the stock and sprinkle in the smoked paprika and the remaining ½ teaspoon salt and ¼ teaspoon pepper, stirring to incorporate. Return the chicken to the pan, nestling it into the stock and vegetables. Reduce the heat to low, cover the pan, and braise the chicken until it pulls apart easily with a fork, about an hour.

Cook the noodles according to the package directions and drain. Divide them among individual bowls. Serve the chicken, vegetables, and stock over top of the hot noodles.

Refrigerate any leftovers for up to 5 days or freeze the chicken and greens mixture in an airtight container for up to 2 months. (Do not freeze the noodles.)

BELLY BONUS: White meat chicken contains less fat and calories than dark meat, but the latter has more iron, zinc, and B vitamins. This is because dark meat contains myoglobin, a compound needed for activity. Body parts that move a lot, like legs, will have more myoglobin than the breast.

NUTRITION PER SERVING (ABOUT 2 THIGHS AND 1 CUP/336 G OF THE VEGETABLES AND NOODLES)

Calories 367 | Total fat 11 g (Saturated 2 g, Poly 2 g, Omega-3 0.16 g, DHA 0.01 g, EPA 0.01 g, Mono 4 g) | Cholesterol 185 mg | Protein 39 g | Sodium 452 mg | Carbohydrates 27 g | Fiber 3 g | Sugars 2 g | Vitamin A 107 mcg | Vitamin B6 1 mg | Vitamin B12 1 mcg | Vitamin C 41 mg | Vitamin D 5 IU | Choline 124 mg | Folate 118 mcg | Calcium 93 mg | Iron 3 mg

Butternut Ragù Lasagna

Next to blankets and onesies, lasagna is the item most commonly gifted to new parents by friends and family bestowing help—and for good reason. It freezes and reheats beautifully, it's a one-dish meal, it's filling, and it's some of the best comfort food of all time. This particular lasagna recipe is like one of those fancy multifunction apparatuses that rocks, swings, serenades, and shushes the baby (if only it changed diapers). It yields a robust ragù for pasta if you want to stop there (serve it over rigatoni, linguini, or any other type that holds up to a weighty sauce), or it goes on to create lasagna that does all the aforementioned things (except for the swing jobs) and packs way more nutrients than its more traditional brethren. Consider assembling a recipe's worth in two or three separate dishes: one for eating as soon as it emerges bubbly hot from the oven, and the others for freezing and reheating some night when you just need to put up your feet, or for later when motherhood prevents you from getting around to making dinner.

Makes 10 servings

FOR THE RAGÙ

1 tablespoon extra-virgin olive oil

8 ounces/228 g ground turkey (thigh meat)

1 medium yellow onion, diced small

4 garlic cloves, roughly chopped

1 small bunch Swiss chard, leaves and stems cut crosswise into ½-inch-/1.3 cm-thick pieces

1 large butternut squash, peeled and cut into small ¼-inch/0.6 cm cubes (if you buy the squash already peeled and cut, you'll need 2 pounds/906 g)

4 large fresh sage leaves, thinly sliced

½ teaspoon fresh thyme leaves, chopped (from about 4 sprigs)

1 (28-ounce/794 g) can crushed tomatoes

1 teaspoon fine sea salt

¼ teaspoon freshly ground black pepper (about 20 grinds)

FOR THE LASAGNA

1 large egg, beaten

16 ounces/454 g ricotta

¼ cup/45 g grated Parmesan cheese

1½ cups/170 g grated mozzarella cheese, divided

4 large fresh sage leaves, minced

½ teaspoon fresh thyme leaves, chopped

⅛ teaspoon freshly ground black pepper (about 10 grinds)

12 ounces/340 g no-boil lasagna noodles

For the ragù: Heat the oil in a large Dutch oven or saucepot over medium-high heat. Add the turkey and cook it for about 3 minutes, stirring with a wooden spoon to break it up, until it's no longer pink and just beginning to brown. Add the onion and cook for 2 minutes, stirring once or twice. Drizzle ¼ cup/59 ml of water into the pan and scrape up the browned bits from the bottom as the water sizzles and steams. Add the garlic and sauté for 30 seconds.

{Recipe continues on next page}

Add the chard and squash and stir to incorporate all of the ingredients. Cover the pot partially and cook for 8 minutes, stirring once, or until the chard wilts to half of its original volume and the squash starts to soften slightly.

Add the sage, thyme, tomatoes, salt, and pepper, stir well, and then reduce the heat to low. Simmer the ragù uncovered for 30 minutes, stirring occasionally. (Note: If you are only making the ragù, the recipe ends here. Serve with pasta, as suggested above, or cool completely and refrigerate up to 5 days. Store portions in airtight containers or resealable plastic freezer bags and freeze up to 6 months.)

For the lasagna: While the ragù simmers, combine the egg, ricotta, Parmesan, 1 cup of the mozzarella, sage, thyme, and black pepper in a large mixing bowl.

Preheat the oven to 350°F/175°C/Gas 4.

Put 1 heaping scoop of the ragù at the bottom of a 13 x 9-inch/33 x 23 cm baking dish and start assembling the lasagna. Set a single layer of noodles in the saucy bottom of the pan. Drop several dollops of the ricotta mixture across the noodles. Don't fuss much with spreading it out across the noodles. It will melt and spread as it bakes. Pour a heaping scoop of ragù over this layer and use a rubber spatula or the back of the ladle or measuring cup to spread it out to cover. Repeat the layers—noodles, ricotta, ragù—until you reach nearly the top of the baking dish, ending with noodles. Depending on the width of the noodles, you may need to snap them into pieces to fill spaces in each layer as you build. Top the last layer of noodles with the remaining ragù, no ricotta mixture, and the remaining ½ cup/57 g of mozzarella.

Cover the dish with aluminum foil and bake for about 45 to 50 minutes, or until the noodles are tender. If you like the cheese on the top layer of your lasagna to be a little bit browned, remove the foil during the last 10 minutes of baking.

Let the lasagna sit for about 10 minutes before cutting into pieces and serving.

If you plan to freeze any of it, let the lasagna cool to room temperature and then refrigerate overnight. Cut the lasagna into chunks or individual portions and wrap each tightly in plastic wrap and then foil. Freeze for up to 6 months. To reheat, unwrap the lasagna, remove and discard the plastic and foil, and set the pieces in an oven-safe dish and cover the dish with foil. Bake in a 350°F/175°C/Gas 4 oven for 30 minutes, or until hot through to the center.

BELLY BONUS: Take comfort in knowing that a solid square of this lasagna serves up a whopping amount of vitamins A and C, calcium, iron, and folate. Swiss chard is considered a power food because it's nutrient dense. Most notably, carotenoids (precursors to vitamin A) help with the growth and health of cells and tissues in the body, which is important for the development of the baby. Butternut squash contains essentials like folic acid for brain and spinal cord development, magnesium for bone integrity and blood pressure, and vitamin A, fiber, and potassium for blood pressure maintenance, too.

NUTRITION PER SERVING (1 PIECE/334 G)

Calories 404 | Total fat 16 g (Saturated 8 g, Poly 2 g, Omega-3 0.21 g, DHA 0.00 g, EPA 0.00 g, Mono 5 g) | Cholesterol 75 mg | Protein 21 g | Sodium 568 mg | Carbohydrates 46 g | Fiber 5 g | Sugars 8 g | Vitamin A 665 mcg | Vitamin B6 0 mg | Vitamin B12 1 mcg | Vitamin C 34 mg | Vitamin D 15 IU | Choline 53 mg | Folate 111 mcg | Calcium 300 mg | Iron 4 mg

Cauliflower Chickpea Curry

Homely as it might appear, cauliflower is a powerhouse. It's got nutrients out the wazoo that matter to you, not the least of which is choline, which plays an important role in your baby's brain development. Despite its cabbage relations, cauliflower's flavor is mild and adaptable. Here it takes a warm bath in spiced coconut milk and finds balance with protein from chickpeas and cashews. Enjoy it as is or on top of cooked rice or couscous. Reheat leftovers or freeze them for another time.

Makes 4 servings

1 tablespoon extra-virgin olive oil

1 teaspoon cumin seeds

1 large Vidalia onion or other sweet onion, halved and very thinly sliced

3 garlic cloves, sliced

1 small head cauliflower, cut into bite-size pieces of florets and stems (or about 2¼ pounds/1 kg already cut)

2 tablespoons tomato paste

1⅔ cups/394 ml light coconut milk

1½ teaspoons red curry powder

½ teaspoon fine sea salt

1 (15-ounce/425 g) can chickpeas, drained and rinsed, or 1½ cups/256 g cooked beans

½ cup/57 g roasted, salted cashews, chopped

Heat the oil in a large, high-sided sauté pan over medium-high heat. Add the cumin seeds and let them sizzle in the hot oil for about 1 minute. Add the onions and garlic and cook them, stirring often, for about 3 minutes, or until the onions turn translucent and soften into strands. Add the cauliflower and sauté for 5 minutes, or just enough to take the edge off its rawness.

While the cauliflower cooks, put the tomato paste into a small mixing bowl. Slowly add the coconut milk a few tablespoons at a time, stirring to loosen the paste into a smooth liquid. Once the paste is a lumpless liquid, add the rest of the coconut milk and ½ cup/118 ml of water, and then sprinkle in the curry powder and salt, whisking to combine everything.

Pour the coconut milk mixture into the pan with the cauliflower, add the chickpeas, and stir to combine. Bring the liquid to a boil and then reduce the heat and simmer for 10 minutes, stirring often, or until the cauliflower is tender but not mushy.

Sprinkle 2 tablespoons of the cashews over each serving just before eating.

Refrigerate leftovers in an airtight container for up to 1 week or freeze for up to 3 months. Thaw completely in the refrigerator before reheating. Warm through in the microwave or in a small saucepot with a few splashes of water over medium heat.

BELLY BONUS: Thanks mostly to the cauliflower and chickpeas, this dish has 10 g of fiber per serving, helpful in moving things through your system (if you know what I mean).

NUTRITION PER SERVING (ABOUT 2 CUPS/380 G)

Calories 342 | Total fat 17 g (Saturated 6 g, Poly 1 g, Omega-3 0.05 g, DHA 0.00 g, EPA 0.00 g, Mono 7 g) | Cholesterol 0 mg | Protein 11 g | Sodium 749 mg | Carbohydrates 41 g | Fiber 10 g | Sugars 12 g | Vitamin A 7 mcg | Vitamin B6 0 mg | Vitamin B12 0 mcg | Vitamin C 110 mg | Vitamin D 0 IU | Choline 17 mg | Folate 23 mcg | Calcium 87 mg | Iron 3 mg

Golden Split Pea and Pumpkin Stew

A scoop of stew warmed with spices and ginger and thickened with its own healthful ingredients is the perfect kind of meal for a hungry tummy that's losing out to a growing belly. When space is at a premium, a bowlful will fill you without stuffing you. If you have some extra room, toasted naan is excellent with this stew, and a dollop of plain yogurt spiked with a little freshly grated ginger adds extra richness. And for still more sustenance, I can confirm that a smoked Gouda grilled cheese sandwich on crusty whole grain bread is just right. The stew itself packs in nourishing nutrients including plant protein, potassium, and plenty of fiber, all of it good for you and your own growing pumpkin.

Makes 6 servings

2 tablespoons extra-virgin olive oil

1 teaspoon cumin seeds

1 large shallot, minced

4 garlic cloves, minced

1 (2-inch/5 cm) chunk fresh ginger, peeled and finely grated on a microplane (1½ teaspoons)

1 medium Yukon gold potato, unpeeled, diced small

1 large carrot, diced small

8 cups/1.9 L chicken stock (page 214, or low-sodium store-bought)

1 (15-ounce/425 g) can puréed pure pumpkin (not pumpkin pie filling) (or 1¾ cups/429 g fresh pumpkin purée)

1 cup/226 g golden split peas

½ teaspoon ground coriander

½ teaspoon ground cumin

½ teaspoon fine sea salt

½ teaspoon freshly ground black pepper

½ cup/15 g loosely packed fresh cilantro leaves, chopped

Heat the oil in a large Dutch oven over medium heat. When the oil is hot, add the cumin seeds and fry them for about 30 seconds. Scrape in the shallot, garlic, and ginger and sauté for 2 minutes, or until the shallot softens just slightly and everything is very fragrant.

Add the potato and carrot and cook them for 5 minutes, stirring now and again and using a wooden spoon to scrape up the crust that forms on the bottom from the potato starches.

Slowly drizzle in 1 cup/237 ml of water and scrape up any bits on the bottom of the pot as the water sizzles and cooks away. Stir in the stock and pumpkin. If necessary, use a whisk to break up lumps of pumpkin. Add the peas, coriander, cumin, salt, and pepper.

Increase the heat to medium high and bring the liquid to a boil, which will take about 10 to 15 minutes. Then reduce the heat to medium and simmer gently for 60 to 90 minutes, or until the peas are tender and have thickened the stew significantly. Be sure the soup doesn't get caught in a rapid boil, which will cook away too much of the liquid before the vegetables and peas have time to soften.

Stir in the cilantro, adjust the seasoning to your taste, and serve.

{Recipe continues on next page}

Cool leftovers and then refrigerate them in an airtight container up to 5 days, or freeze for up to 6 months. Thaw in the refrigerator overnight, or just enough to tip out the frozen block into a saucepot. Add a few tablespoons of water, cover the pot, and set it over medium heat. Simmer until warmed completely through.

BELLY BONUS: The combo of protein and fiber makes this soup filling and satisfying for those ravenous times. It doesn't hurt that you'll also get a huge boost of vitamin A (thanks to the pumpkin), vitamin C, and iron. Split peas belong to the family of pulses (legumes), along with chickpeas and lentils. They've been recognized for promoting good health and may reduce the risk of chronic disease. Per cooked cup, split peas offer more fiber than chickpeas or lentils, a significant amount of protein, and vitamin A, calcium, and iron.

NUTRITION PER SERVING (1¹/₂ CUPS/360 G)

Calories 306 | Total fat 8 g (Saturated 1 g, Poly 1 g, Omega-3 0.07 g, DHA 0.00 g, EPA 0.00 g, Mono 5 g) | Cholesterol 0 mg | Protein 18 g | Sodium 295 mg | Carbohydrates 44 g | Fiber 16 g | Sugars 5 g | Vitamin A 543 mcg | Vitamin B6 0 mg | Vitamin B12 0 mcg | Vitamin C 13 mg | Vitamin D 0 IU | Choline 13 mg | Folate 6 mcg | Calcium 51 mg | Iron 3 mg

Hearty Meat and Bean Chili

Homemade chili joins the ranks of other soups and stews that are well-rounded meals in a single bowl. Made with lean meat (or none at all, if you prefer), beans, and tomatoes, chili is low in fat, overflowing with nutrients, and full of flavor. This chili is velvety rich with a bit of almond butter, which melts into the sauce, adding its nuttiness just behind the scenes. The chipotle spikes the finished product with smoky notes. It's only mildly spicy, but if you are exceptionally spice-averse, leave the chipotle out. If you love chili but are battling pregnancy heartburn, try the White and Greens Chicken Chili (page 229) instead. It's made without tomatoes, which often aggravate agita because of high acidity.

Makes 6 servings

1 pound/454 g lean ground meat (turkey breast or thighs, buffalo or beef)

1 large yellow onion, diced small

1 large chipotle, dried or canned in adobo sauce, seeded and chopped (optional)

4 large garlic cloves, minced

2 tablespoons creamy almond butter

2 tablespoons chili powder

2 tablespoons unsweetened cocoa

2 tablespoons granulated sugar

1 tablespoon ground cumin

2 teaspoons dried oregano

1 teaspoon coarse sea salt

1/4 teaspoon freshly ground black pepper (about 20 grinds)

2 tablespoons cider vinegar

1 (15-ounce/425 g) can dark red kidney beans, drained and rinsed, or 1 1/4 cups/230 g cooked beans

2 (28-ounce/792 g) cans crushed tomatoes

Heat a large Dutch oven or pot over medium-high heat. Drop small clumps of the ground meat into the hot pot to keep it from cooking into a clump. Stir constantly with a wooden spoon, breaking up the meat into bits as it begins to brown. Continue to brown the meat for about 5 minutes. Add the onion and sauté with the meat, scraping up browned bits off the bottom as the onion releases some water. Continue cooking for about 5 minutes, or until the onion begins to soften. Add a tablespoon or two of water to the pan to help scrape up additional brown bits if necessary.

Stir in the chipotle, garlic, and almond butter and cook for about 1 minute, or until the almond butter melts into the mixture.

Add the chili powder, cocoa, sugar, cumin, oregano, salt, pepper, vinegar, beans, tomatoes, and 1 cup/237 ml of water and stir well to combine all of the ingredients. Bring the chili to a simmer, cover the pot, and reduce the heat to medium low. Simmer for at least 1 hour, stirring occasionally.

Serve immediately or cool to room temperature and store in portions in the refrigerator or in a freezer-safe container.

To reheat from frozen, run the sealed container of chili under water until the chili releases from the bottom and sides. Put the frozen chunk of chili in a pot over medium-high heat and add

{Recipe continues on next page}

½ cup/118 ml or more of water. Cover and simmer until the chili is completely thawed, breaking up the chunk as it melts. Simmer about 15 minutes more before serving.

BELLY BONUS: Even more than raw tomatoes, cooked tomatoes (like those of the canned variety) offer lycopene, a powerful antioxidant that is protective against cancer and heart disease. That's because cooking breaks down the cell walls where the antioxidant is trapped, allowing it to become more available for our bodies to absorb.

NUTRITION PER SERVING (ABOUT 1⅔ CUPS/430 G)

Calories 300 | Total fat 5 g (Saturated 1 g, Poly 1 g, Omega-3 0.11 g, DHA 0.00 g, EPA 0.00 g, Mono 1 g) | Cholesterol 60 mg | Protein 26 g | Sodium 1 I076 mg | Carbohydrates 47 g | Fiber 13 g | Sugars 18 g | Vitamin A 41 mcg | Vitamin B6 1 mg | Vitamin B12 2 mcg | Vitamin C 30 mg | Vitamin D 10 IU | Choline 86 mg | Folate 57 mcg | Calcium 176 mg | Iron 7 mg

If You Can't Handle the Meat, Get Out of the Kitchen

A GOOD FRIEND WHO IS AN AVID COOK AND MEAT EATER COULD HARDLY BE IN THE SAME ROOM AS raw meat when she was pregnant. She would set out to make dinner and invariably end up gagging, running from the kitchen to the bathroom as soon as she unwrapped uncooked chicken, pork, or beef. Her aversion isn't an isolated case. Lots of women report repugnance toward raw meat during pregnancy, most often in the first trimester or first half. It usually fades away as the weeks stretch on.

Since meat is such a valuable source of complete protein, vitamin B12, and other important nutrients for pregnancy, find another way to get it if you can't cook it yourself. Ask your partner to take over or try a grocery store or market that offers rotisserie chicken or roasted turkey or beef that you can eat without any prior interaction with the food in its raw state!

If your distaste for meat doesn't pass, or you're a vegetarian, you'll need to find other sources of complete proteins or combinations of non-meat and plant proteins that glue together all the essential amino acids to be sure you're covered. Some good non-meat sources of protein include the following:

- Whole grains, especially amaranth and quinoa
- Beans
- Peas
- Lentils
- Nuts and nut butters
- Seeds

- Milk
- Cheese
- Yogurt (especially Greek-style)
- Fish, including canned
- Eggs
- Soybeans and tofu
- Some leafy greens and vegetables

Can We Use Cans?

WE ALL CAME TO KNOW AND FEAR BISPHENOL A, OR BPA, WHEN CONSUMER GROUPS REPORTED THAT THE plastic additive, which is seemingly everywhere, poses health risks. BPA is a compound used to make hard plastics (think: water and baby bottles) and epoxy resins, the stuff that lines the insides of metal food cans. When BPA comes in contact with the foods and beverages we consume, it can get absorbed and enter our bloodstreams.

In short order, reusable water bottles we'd bought to be environmentally respectful ended up in landfills, and trusted companies scrambled to make new BPA-free versions. Since manufacturers pledged to keep our littlest ones safe from the stuff, a stroll through the baby bottles and pacifiers section of any baby superstore guarantees at least 300 sightings of the term "BPA-FREE!"

But the canned food industry is still playing catch-up on the cleanup. Only a few companies can claim their can linings are BPA-free, which means that most of our trusty convenience products—everything from canned peaches to tomatoes, and canned beans of every variety—may be laced with BPA. Pregnant women are considered especially vulnerable, with possible impact ranging from miscarriage to reproductive complications for the developing baby, so it's important to educate yourself on the current BPA research and on your options for avoiding it if you are concerned that your lifestyle is exposing you to high levels.

In the case of beans, some companies are packaging in aseptic boxes, but the best alternative is cooking dried beans. In addition to being a painless task, it is cheaper and yields an even more abundant supply than any Can Can Sale will. A single one-pound bag of dried black beans, for example, yields 6 cups of cooked beans and will run you about $2. Plus, you can freeze the cooked beans in portions comparable to the amount in a 15-ounce/425 g can (roughly 1¼ to 1½ cups/about 250 to 290 g), run hot water over them to quickly thaw, and toss them into whatever you're cooking. Cooking dried beans promises the convenience of cooked beans without the potential for BPA contamination.

Canned tomatoes pose a considerable challenge to manufacturers trying to create a BPA-free can. The acidity of the tomatoes requires a resilient coating between it and the aluminum can, lest the contents corrode the metal. Aseptic boxes, like the ones that store shelved stocks and broths, are BPA-free packages coming to market for prepared tomato products.

BPA warnings are based on ever-evolving evidence. The FDA has said that BPA is safe at current human exposures, but recent studies have raised concerns about its effects as an endocrine disruptor in children and adults. Enough concern has been raised by researchers to warrant seeking out safe options and especially to support cooking from scratch instead of with processed food whenever possible.

Indian Spice Chicken in Yogurt Sauce

A friend said that she and her husband ate spicy Indian food the night before she delivered her twin sons, and so they decided to make a tradition of enjoying it on the night before the boys' birthday forevermore. Whether driven by a hankering or a quest to ingest spicy food to induce labor, as instructed by folklore, Indian food makes it into the rotations of pregnant women far and wide. This recipe is inspired by infamous and well-loved recipes for butter chicken, but it takes it easy on the richness and spice. If you are a heat seeker, add more red pepper flakes than the amount prescribed here, which lends just a touch of fire behind the creamy, thick tomato-based yogurt sauce spiked with spices. Chicken legs braise to tender perfection without drying out in a way chicken breasts just won't, and they offer a few extra nutrients, too.

Makes 6 servings

1 teaspoon red curry powder

1 teaspoon dried oregano

½ teaspoon garam masala

½ teaspoon fine sea salt

¼ teaspoon freshly ground black pepper (about 20 grinds)

6 whole chicken legs, skinless (or 6 legs and 6 thighs)

1 tablespoon vegetable oil

1 medium yellow onion, quartered and thinly sliced crosswise

4 large garlic cloves, minced

¼ teaspoon crushed red pepper flakes

⅔ cup/170 g tomato paste

1 (15-ounce/425 g) can crushed tomatoes

1 cup/255 g low-fat or whole milk plain yogurt

Preheat the oven to 350°F/175°F/Gas 4.

Mix the curry powder, oregano, garam masala, salt, and pepper in a small bowl. Rub half of the spices into one side of all the chicken pieces. Set the rest aside.

Pour the oil into a Dutch oven or high-sided oven-safe sauté pan that will accommodate all of the chicken and sauce eventually. Set the pan over medium-high heat. When the oil is hot, add several pieces of chicken, but do not stuff too much in at once, forcing the chicken to steam with little breathing room. Instead, do this in batches to give the chicken space to brown. Cook the chicken for about 3 minutes per side, so a light-brown crust forms on the meat. Set the browned pieces on a plate.

Drop the onions and garlic into the pan and sauté them for 5 minutes, or just enough to lift the brown bits that stuck to the bottom while the chicken browned. Scatter the red pepper flakes in and sauté for another minute. Pour in 2 tablespoons of water and give the bottom of the pan one last scrape while the water sizzles and evaporates.

Stir the tomato paste into the onions, and let it melt down in the heat. Add the rest of the reserved spices, the crushed tomatoes, and ½ cup/118 ml water. Stir thoroughly to combine everything. Turn off the heat and stir in the yogurt, turning the sauce an orangey-pink color. Nestle the chicken down into the sauce and pour in any juices that gathered on the plate.

{Recipe continues on next page}

Cover the pan either with a tight-fitting lid or a piece of aluminum foil. Put the chicken in the oven and roast for 1 hour, or until the meat starts to fall from the bones.

Serve the chicken and several spoonfuls of the thick sauce over cooked basmati rice and with sautéed garlic chard or kale.

BELLY BONUS: Dark leg meat has more iron, zinc, and B vitamins than chicken breasts because it contains myoglobin, a compound needed for movement. Yogurt adds protein, as well as bone-building calcium, while its creaminess helps tame fiery foods.

NUTRITION PER SERVING (1 LEG PLUS ABOUT $\frac{1}{2}$ CUP/127 G SAUCE)

Calories 419 | Total fat 14 g (Saturated 3 g, Poly 4 g, Omega-3 0.35 g, DHA 0.03 g, EPA 0.01 g, Mono 5 g) | Cholesterol 244 mg | Protein 56 g | Sodium 768 mg | Carbohydrates 15 g | Fiber 3 g | Sugars 10 g | Vitamin A 62 mcg | Vitamin B6 1 mg | Vitamin B12 2 mcg | Vitamin C 14 mg | Vitamin D 3 IU | Choline 156 mg | Folate 31 mcg | Calcium 145 mg | Iron 4 mg

Lentil Ratatouille with Baked Polenta

Polenta is the soft, creamy cornmeal gruel that infamously calls for an extended stay on the stove-top, complete with regular stirring. It's a nice alternative to pasta but is sometimes faulted for its hands-on prep time. This oven-baked version turns out supple spoonfuls just the same, leaving you with some extra time to put up your feet. Tender veggies and lentils spill over the polenta mounds in this warm, comfort-food meal that packs in iron and protein despite being completely meat-free. Lentils are an ancient superfood that provides impressive amounts of fiber and protein. A cooked half-cup serving of them packs in 9 g of protein and 8 g of fiber. Lentils are also a good source of iron and an excellent source of folate, two essential nutrients for pregnancy. The ratatouille freezes nicely for a few months and would be equally delicious over pasta, rice, or even served on baked potatoes.

Makes 4 servings

1 cup/170 g stone-ground coarse yellow cornmeal

½ teaspoon fine sea salt, plus more as needed

¼ teaspoon garlic powder

⅛ teaspoon freshly ground black pepper (about 10 grinds)

2 medium bell peppers, red and yellow, cut into 1-inch/2.5 cm pieces

1 small eggplant, unpeeled, cut into medium chunks

1 medium zucchini, cut into large chunks (about 340 g)

Freshly ground black pepper

¼ cup/59 ml olive oil, divided, plus more for coating the baking pan

1 small yellow onion, diced small

4 garlic cloves, minced

1 cup/199 g green lentils

1 (15-ounce/425 g) can diced tomatoes, preferably fire-roasted

½ teaspoon dried oregano

⅓ cup/27 g grated Asiago cheese

Preheat the oven to 375°F/190°C/Gas 5. Position a rack in the lower part of the oven and set a baking sheet on the middle rack in the oven as it gets hot. Coat the bottom and sides of an 8-inch/20 cm square baking dish with olive oil (enameled dishes make cleaning up stubbornly stuck-on polenta easy).

Pour 4 cups/946 ml of water into the baking dish and then whisk in the cornmeal along with the salt, garlic powder, and black pepper. Carefully set the dish on the lower rack and bake for about 45 minutes, stirring once halfway through, or until the mass of polenta is thick and smooth and the grains are tender and creamy.

In a large mixing bowl, combine the peppers, eggplant, and zucchini. Season with a pinch of fine sea salt and a few grinds of black pepper. Drizzle 2 tablespoons of the olive oil over the vegetables and toss to coat them. Take the hot baking sheet out of the oven and spill the oiled

{Recipe continues on next page}

veggies out across it. Push them into a single layer and roast for 30 minutes, or until soft, sweet, and slightly browned.

Meanwhile, heat the remaining 2 tablespoons of olive oil in a Dutch oven or large saucepot over medium high. Add the onions and garlic and sauté for 5 minutes, or until the onions are translucent and starting to soften. Pour in 3 cups/710 ml of water and bring it to a boil. Add the lentils, reduce the heat to medium, and simmer them until they are completely tender and about two thirds of the water has been absorbed and evaporated, at least 20 minutes. Stir in the tomatoes and oregano and continue simmering over medium low.

When the vegetables have finished roasting, carefully scrape them into the pot with the lentils. Reduce the heat to low and keep warm.

Stir the polenta, scraping up any that might be baked on the bottom with a wooden spoon. Sprinkle the cheese over the surface and stir it in or let it melt across the top.

Serve heaping scoops of polenta topped with ladlefuls of the lentil ratatouille.

Refrigerate leftovers in an airtight container up to 5 days. Freeze the lentil ratatouille for up to 2 months. To reheat, thaw in the refrigerator and then warm through in a saucepot with a splash of water. To freeze any leftover polenta, cool it completely to room temperature and then either wrap it tightly with plastic wrap or store it in an airtight container. Thaw completely before reheating with a few tablespoons of water.

BELLY BONUS: Good news for your digestive system: a serving packs in 17 g of the 28 g per day of fiber recommended, and almost a quarter of your iron needs. Plus, it offers up plenty of vitamin A, vitamin C, calcium, iron, and folate to nourish you and the little one. Cornmeal is considered a whole grain, as long as it hasn't been de-germinated to preserve the shelf life. To get the benefits of whole grain corn, which has vitamin A, fiber, and antioxidants, look for "whole grain" on the label.

NUTRITION PER SERVING (ABOUT 1 CUP POLENTA AND 1½ CUPS RATATOUILLE/521 G)

Calories 584 | Total fat 20 g (Saturated 4 g, Poly 2 g, Omega-3 0.20 g, DHA 0.00 g, EPA 0.00 g, Mono 11 g) | Cholesterol 6 mg | Protein 20 g | Sodium 594 mg | Carbohydrates 86 g | Fiber 17 g | Sugars 13 g | Vitamin A 122 mcg | Vitamin B6 1 mg | Vitamin B12 0 mcg | Vitamin C 191 mg | Vitamin D 0 IU | Choline 29 mg | Folate 93 mcg | Calcium 137 mg | Iron 6 mg

Poached Chicken and Chicken Stock

Protein is always a critical nutrient for humans, especially during pregnancy when it serves the maintenance of one human and the creation of another. It is also known to keep pregnancy nausea at bay because it helps you feel full longer. If you take the time to poach a whole chicken, you'll have plenty of adaptable protein on hand for several days, making it easy to prepare quick meals and snacks (see the list of ideas below). This recipe converts the poaching liquid into a simple chicken stock, one of the most useful ingredients in a kitchen! When I was sick in the first trimester of my twin pregnancy, I called on chicken stock, adorned with not much more than a few noodles and a couple shreds of chicken, if I could handle them, to steady my faltering stomach. When I wasn't able to cook because it aggravated my symptoms, I found all the restaurants in my neighborhood that made good, homemade chicken soup to soothe me until I could get back in the kitchen myself.

Makes 1 poached chicken and about 2 quarts stock

1 small whole chicken (about 3½ pounds/1 kg)

2 medium carrots, cut into large chunks

2 celery stalks, cut into large chunks

1 small onion, cut into large chunks

4 large garlic cloves, smashed

1 teaspoon fine sea salt

¼ teaspoon freshly ground black pepper (about 20 grinds)

Set the chicken in a large stockpot along with the carrots, celery, onions, and garlic. Fill the pot with cold water to cover the chicken by about ½ inch/1.3 cm. Add the salt and pepper. Set the pot over high heat to bring the water to a boil, which will take about 15 minutes with the pot covered. As soon as the water starts to boil, reduce the heat to medium low (keep the cover on), barely simmering the chicken for about 1 hour and 45 minutes, or until the meat is very tender. You should be able to pull the legs off with an easy twist using tongs, and the meat should register 165°F/74°C on an instant-read thermometer. While the chicken simmers, don't fiddle with it, but do use a ladle to skim off some of the foam now and then.

Once the chicken is fully poached, very carefully lift it out of the hot water using tongs and another sizable utensil, like a carving fork or serving spoon. Let any excess liquid drain back into the broth in the pot, which should remain simmering. Set the chicken in a large bowl and let it cool for 15 to 20 minutes, or until you can handle it without burning yourself.

When the chicken is cool enough, peel the skin off and pull the meat from the bones (legs, thighs, breast and tenders, and back meat, too). The meat will come off without much effort. Put the skin and bones back into the pot with the poaching liquid. Let the meat continue to cool to room temperature and then refrigerate it in an airtight container for up to 5 days.

Continue simmering the vegetables, skin, and bones for another 2 hours. Strain the stock into a clean pot or storage container(s) to cool down to about room temperature and discard all of the solids. Refrigerate the stock overnight. Skim off the fat that solidifies on top of the stock and discard it. Keep the stock refrigerated up to 1 week, or transfer it to freezer-safe containers and freeze for up to 6 months.

Use the stock

- In soups
- To cook rice for extra flavor and nutrients
- To sauce pasta
- For baby food!

Use the poached chicken for

- Chicken salad
- Sliced chicken and cheese sandwiches
- Pulled chicken tacos
- Chicken soup
- Chicken enchiladas and burritos
- Salads for added protein

NUTRITION PER SERVING (3 OUNCES/84 G OF CHICKEN)

Calories 93 | Total fat 2 g (Saturated 1 g, Poly 1 g, Omega-3 0.06 g, DHA 0.03 g, EPA 0.01 g, Mono 1 g) | Cholesterol 54 mg | Protein 17 g | Sodium 63 mg | Carbohydrates 0 g | Fiber 0 g | Sugars 0 g | Vitamin A 11 mcg | Vitamin B6 0 mg | Vitamin B12 0 mcg | Vitamin C 0 mg | Vitamin D 0 IU | Choline 0 mg | Folate 6 mcg | Calcium 8 mg | Iron 1 mg

Chicken Stock

BELLY BONUS: Homemade stock is better than store-bought or canned stock because it's fresh, it's more flavorful, and it doesn't contain additives and preservatives, or nearly as much sodium. Listen to your grandma on its restorative properties and virtues, too.

NUTRITION PER SERVING (ABOUT 1$\frac{1}{2}$ CUPS/355 ML)

Calories 81 | Total fat 3 g (Saturated 1 g, Poly 0 g, Omega-3 0.00 g, DHA 0.00 g, EPA 0.00 g, Mono 1 g) | Cholesterol 7 mg | Protein 6 g | Sodium 324 mg | Carbohydrates 8 g | Fiber 0 g | Sugars 4 g | Vitamin A 2 mcg | Vitamin B6 0 mg | Vitamin B12 0 mcg | Vitamin C 0 mg | Vitamin D 0 IU | Choline 0 mg | Folate 11 mcg | Calcium 7 mg | Iron 0 mg

Roasted Turkey Breast

You always want what you cannot have. Pregnancy might be the perfect living example of the phrase. I had a regular hankering for turkey sandwiches with the works, but most places make them with processed deli turkey, which is on the pregnancy foods blacklist. Anytime I came across an establishment making sandwiches with fresh roasted turkey, I had to get one. Since unprocessed turkey is tough to come by outside of Thanksgiving leftovers, roasting a whole breast at home and storing leftovers for several days afterward guarantees a sandwich made-to-order, without the food-safety doubt associated with processed meat. The truth is, deli turkey should earn a space on life's food blacklist, too, given its sodium content and additives. Real roasted turkey, though, is very low in fat and sodium, and it's kind to the temperamental palate of pregnancy with its mild flavor and inherent association with the notion of comfort food. Roasting one requires less effort than deciding which condiments you want on your sandwich when it's done. See the tip for a list of other great uses for roasted turkey breast, too.

Makes 10 to 12 servings

1 (4 to 6 pound/1.8 to 2.7 kg) fresh skin-on, bone-in turkey breast

½ teaspoon coarse sea salt

½ teaspoon freshly ground black pepper

1½ tablespoons extra-virgin olive oil

Zest of 1 lemon

1 small yellow onion, quartered

1 small carrot, cut into 2-inch/5 cm pieces

2 celery stalks, cut into 2-inch/5 cm pieces

Preheat the oven to 375°F/190°C/Gas 5.

Put the turkey breast in a roasting pan (rack optional) skin-side up. In a small bowl, stir together the salt, pepper, olive oil, and lemon zest.

Slip your fingers under the skin at the top of the breast and spread some of the olive oil mixture around on the meat. Rub the remaining mixture on top of the skin. Stuff the onion, carrot, and celery under the turkey breast. Transfer the pan to the oven and roast for 1½ to 2 hours, rotating the pan once, or until an instant-read thermometer registers 165°F/74°C.

Remove the turkey from the oven and let it rest for 15 minutes before slicing. Carefully peel off the browned skin and discard.

Slice all of the meat from the bone and wrap tightly to store or refrigerate the entire bone-in breast and slice as needed.

• • •

Tip: What to do with an entire roasted turkey breast:

Slice thin and stack on toasted bread with cheese, tomatoes, lettuce, and your favorite condiments (try Chickpea Guacamole, page 86; Eggplant and Red Pepper Dip, page 84; Hummus as You Like It, page 89; Spinach Cheese Dip, page 101).

Enjoy with potatoes and green beans any time of year.

Cut meat into cubes for turkey soup.

Add to any salad for extra protein.

Make turkey potpies with vegetables, stock, and pie crust.

Toss chunks with chopped apples, celery, and Buttermilk Dip (page 83) for turkey salad.

Shred and wrap in flour tortillas with black beans, lettuce, and Lime Salsa (page 91).

Stir into Linguine with Chard and White Beans (page 126) for a protein boost.

BELLY BONUS: A 6-ounce serving of skinless roasted turkey breast registers minimal fat and saturated fat, plus a quarter of a day's protein requirements.

NUTRITION PER SERVING (6 OUNCES/170 G)

Calories 221 | Total fat 3 g (Saturated 1 g, Poly 1 g, Omega-3 0.05 g, DHA 0.02 g, EPA 0.00 g, Mono 2 g) | Cholesterol 112 mg | Protein 45 g | Sodium 197 mg | Carbohydrates 0 g | Fiber 0 g | Sugars 0 g | Vitamin A 0 mcg | Vitamin B6 1 mg | Vitamin B12 1 mcg | Vitamin C 0 mg | Vitamin D 0 IU | Choline 0 mg | Folate 15 mcg | Calcium 19 mg | Iron 2 mg

Belly-to-Belly

On rules, guidelines, and (unsolicited) input from others . . .

Amy M: "I love coffee—the taste, the smell, the warmth, the social nature. I was a by-the-book kind of pregnant lady, but I missed coffee so much, I started having a half cup, then a cup a day during my second trimester. Bliss."

Dina V: "I drank coffee (less than I normally do) the entire pregnancy and never felt badly or guilty about it, but I stopped using artificial sweeteners in my coffee."

Laurie: "I am a communicable disease medical epidemiologist with *way* too much knowledge about food-borne illness, so I tended to be really freaked out about undercooked meats, undercooked eggs, and the general cleanliness of food. But in general I figured, pregnancy is hard. I am going to have a damn cup of coffee, and these babies are going to be just fine. And they are."

Nicole R: "I heard apples were good for brain development. I am not a huge fan, but I tried really hard to shove one down my throat every day for all three pregnancies."

Tara H: "I always took my prenatal vitamin because I was petrified that even if I ate a balanced diet, I wouldn't get enough folate and my kid would have nine heads or whatever folate is supposed to prevent. Also, I took DHA/omega-3 supplements during both pregnancies out of fear that my salmon aversion would lead to children who could not do higher math."

Jill R: "At a coffee shop a few times, people would say something about caffeine and pregnancy. My OB actually prescribed me to drink two coffees to help with migraines. One time when someone was 'surprised' a pregnant person would drink coffee, I jokingly replied, 'It's less harmful than the wine I drink at night!'"

Cathy B: "For everything I did—activity, eating, whatever—I asked myself, if I found out whatever it was might cause a problem, would it have been worth it?"

Roasted Vegetable Enchilada Pie

My parents arrived the day before our twins were due to take good care of our first born while we welcomed our second and third. We all sat down to dinner that night and enjoyed enchiladas that my mother had made ahead and transported down in a baking dish from her New York kitchen to warm in mine in Philadelphia. I like to think my mom's home cookin' fueled me through the events of the next day, and so I'll remember those enchiladas always and with love. Aside from the serving of sentimentality though, enchiladas are an excellent make-ahead meal, and they freeze and reheat beautifully. This iteration overrides the filling and rolling of individual tortillas in favor of baked layers. The time saved later in the process frees it up for the steps of roasting a bumper of vegetables for the bulk of the pie and the heart of the homemade enchilada sauce.

Makes 6 servings

2 large poblano peppers, seeded and cut into ½-inch/1.3 cm pieces

1 medium red bell pepper, seeded and cut into ½-inch/1.3 cm pieces

1 medium yellow bell pepper, seeded and cut into ½-inch/1.3 cm pieces

1 small yellow onion, sliced into very thin half-moons

8 ounces/227 g sliced baby portobello mushrooms

4 garlic cloves, smashed

2 tablespoons extra-virgin olive oil or vegetable oil, divided

2 medium sweet potatoes, unpeeled and cut into ½-inch/1.3 cm cubes

1 teaspoon ancho chili powder

½ teaspoon ground cumin

½ teaspoon fine sea salt

¼ teaspoon freshly ground black pepper (about 20 grinds)

¼ teaspoon chipotle powder (optional, or more if you really want a kick)

1 (15-ounce/425 g) can crushed tomatoes

1 cup/237 ml chicken stock (page 214, or low-sodium store-bought) or vegetable stock

½ cup/15 g loosely packed fresh cilantro leaves

1 (15-ounce/425 g) can black beans, drained and rinsed, or 1½ cups/258 g cooked beans

6 (6-inch) corn tortillas, cut in half, at room temperature

½ cup/56 g grated sharp Cheddar cheese

Sliced scallions, for serving (optional)

Sour cream, for serving (optional)

Preheat the oven to 400°F/200°C/Gas 6. Place two baking sheets on two separate racks set on the middle and lower positions in the oven to get hot.

In a large mixing bowl, combine the poblanos, bell peppers, onion, mushrooms, and garlic with 1 tablespoon of the oil. Toss everything together to coat the vegetables with the oil. Take the baking sheet on the uppermost rack out of the oven and dump the vegetables out across it, pushing them into a single layer. Return the pan to the oven.

Immediately add the potato cubes to the large mixing bowl, drizzle them with the remaining tablespoon of oil and toss to coat. Spill the potatoes out across the second hot baking sheet, spread them into a single layer, and return the pan to the low rack in the oven. Roast the vegetables and potatoes for 30 minutes, or until the peppers are tender with only a bit of snap left, the mushrooms are shrunken, and the potatoes are sweet, completely tender, and starting to brown or even blacken slightly. Use a metal spatula to turn them over on their pans about halfway through the roasting. (Roasting the potatoes on their own pan helps them to roast into soft squares with caramelized edges and prevents them from steaming into soggy cubes.)

While the vegetables roast, mix together the chili powder, ground cumin, salt, pepper, and chipotle powder in a small bowl. Pour the tomatoes and stock into the carafe of a blender and add the cilantro and 2 teaspoons of the spice mixture.

When the vegetables and potatoes are done roasting, take them out of the oven and then reduce the oven temperature to 350°F/175°C/Gas 4. Scoop half of the roasted vegetables (not the sweet potatoes) into the blender with the other ingredients. Dump the beans onto the pan with the remaining veggies. Then divide the remaining spice mixture among the veggies and beans and the potatoes, tossing to coat them with the spices.

Blend the tomatoes, stock, cilantro, spices, and vegetables for a full minute into a smooth, thick brick-red-colored sauce.

Pour 1/2 cup/121 g of the sauce into the bottom of a 9-inch/23 cm pie dish. Situate four of the corn tortilla halves into a bottom layer that covers the sauce beneath it. Scatter a scoop each of the veggies/beans and the potatoes across the tortilla layer. Pour another 1/2 cup of the sauce all over the vegetables and potatoes. Situate another layer of four tortilla halves on top. Add the remaining vegetables, beans, and potatoes. Spoon another 1/2 cup of sauce on top of those and then top with four more tortilla halves. Spread the rest of the sauce over these tortillas and sprinkle the cheese on top. Cover the pie plate with foil, tenting it slightly so the cheese doesn't stick to it as it melts. Set the plate on one of the baking sheets and bake for 30 minutes. If you like the cheese to be a little bit browned, remove the foil and bake for 10 minutes more.

Let the pie sit for 10 minutes before slicing it into six wedges to serve. Top with sliced scallions and a dollop of sour cream, if you like.

Refrigerate leftovers for up to 5 days. To freeze all or some of the pie, cool it completely, and preferably overnight in the refrigerator. Cover the plate tightly with plastic wrap and then again with foil and transfer it to the freezer. Or cut the pie into six wedges and wrap each wedge in plastic and then foil. To reheat, thaw completely in the refrigerator and warm through in a 350°F/175°C/Gas 4 oven (remove plastic and then cover again with foil for the oven) until the center is hot, or microwave (without plastic or foil) until hot. You can warm from frozen in an oven-safe dish (including the pie plate in which it was frozen, if applicable) in a 350°F/175°C/Gas 4 oven, covered (with foil only, no plastic) for about 30 minutes. Alternatively, build the layers of the pie and freeze, wrapped, without baking. Remove the plastic wrap, replace the foil and bake according to the directions, adding 10 to 15 minutes to account for the frozen start.

{Recipe continues on next page}

BELLY BONUS: Instead of using canned enchilada sauce, which can be packed with sodium, blending roasted vegetables into seasoned tomatoes ups the nutrition factor of this pie several times (as evidenced by the amounts of vitamin A and vitamin C). In fact, blending vegetables into sauces, smoothies, or soups can be a great way of adding more veggies to your diet. Sweet potatoes add color, flavor, fiber, vitamin A, and potassium.

NUTRITION PER SERVING (1 WEDGE/255 G)

Calories 290 | Total fat 9 g (Saturated 3 g, Poly 1 g, Omega-3 0.06 g, DHA 0.00 g, EPA 0.00 g, Mono 4 g) | Cholesterol 8 mg | Protein 11 g | Sodium 525 mg | Carbohydrates 46 g | Fiber 10 g | Sugars 10 g | Vitamin A 645 mcg | Vitamin B6 1 mg | Vitamin B12 0 mcg | Vitamin C 79 mg | Vitamin D 4 IU | Choline 29 mg | Folate 49 mcg | Calcium 161 mg | Iron 4 mg

Simple Fish Stew

I had more trouble naming this recipe than coming up with four names for all the possible outcomes while pregnant with twins, gender unknown. First, I thought to call it Cioppino, in the likeness of the famous San Francisco stew of shellfish, seafood, tomatoes, and wine, but I wanted to minimize fuss by using fish that doesn't require special handling or bumbling with forks and spoons. I also aimed to avoid calling for wine, which, unless you have some on hand for others in your household, would require the purchase of a bottle that may or may not be put to use otherwise. This seemed wasteful (and frustrating if you are missing alcohol while you abstain). But "fish stew" doesn't quite do justice to the rich complexity of what comes from a short list of ingredients and good fish. There's much confusion about the consumption of fish during pregnancy (see "Safe Fish: What's the Catch?" on page 130), but the resounding consensus is actually that women should try their best to get plenty of it because the benefits for mother and baby far outweigh any risks associated with eating varieties that are considered safe. Regardless of what it's called, know that this recipe is an easy and delicious way to add fish and all of its virtues to your diet.

Makes 6 servings

2 tablespoons extra-virgin olive oil

1 medium yellow onion, quartered and thinly sliced crosswise (about 2 cups/230 g)

2 celery stalks, cut into 1/4-inch/0.6 cm pieces

2 canned sardine fillets packed in water, no salt added, chopped

5 garlic cloves, chopped

1/4 teaspoon crushed red pepper flakes (add more if you are fond of extra heat)

1 (28-ounce/792 g) can crushed tomatoes

8 ounces/237 ml bottled clam juice

1/2 cup loosely packed fresh flat-leaf or curly parsley, finely chopped

1 teaspoon dried oregano

1/2 teaspoon fine sea salt

1/2 teaspoon freshly ground black pepper

1 pound/454 g cod, cut into 6 pieces

8 ounces/227 g sea scallops, halved or quartered

8 ounces/227 g large shrimp (10/20), peeled and deveined

2 cups cooked farro, for serving (optional; see tip)

Lemon wedges, for serving (optional)

Heat the oil in a large Dutch oven or saucepot over medium heat. When the oil is hot, add the onion and celery and cook them, stirring often, for 10 minutes, or until the onion edges start to brown a bit and the celery's texture softens just slightly while its green becomes brighter. Scrape in the sardines and garlic, sprinkle in the pepper flakes, and sauté for another 2 minutes. Drizzle 1/3 cup/79 ml of water in, scraping up any browned bits from the bottom of the pot as the liquid sizzles and evaporates.

Pour in the tomatoes, 2 cups/473 ml of water, and the clam juice and stir to combine everything. Stir in the parsley, oregano, salt, and pepper. Let the stew base come to a slow boil where bubbles

{Recipe continues on next page}

lackadaisically pop up to the surface. Then partially cover the pot, propping the lid off just slightly, and lower the heat to medium low to simmer for at least 30 minutes or up to an hour, stirring now and then.

Take off the lid and nestle the cod, scallops, and shrimp into the stew base. Replace the lid and let the fish braise for about 7 minutes, or until all the pieces are cooked through. The cod will just begin to flake, the scallops will become opaque, and the shrimp will turn from gray to pink.

Ladle the stew into bowls, fishing out several pieces of the seafood per serving. If using, sprinkle cooked farro (see tip) and squeeze fresh lemon juice over each serving.

Note: If you plan to enjoy some of this stew now and freeze some for later, make the stew base all the way up to the point just before adding the fish. Reserve whatever you plan to freeze and cool that portion to room temperature before freezing it in one or more airtight containers (1 serving is about 2 cups/473 ml, plus seafood). Continue with the remainder of the recipe, using only as much seafood as you need for the amount you're serving now (about 5 ounces of seafood per serving). Buy fresh seafood per serving of the frozen stew base when you're ready to eat it. Thaw the stew base either in the refrigerator overnight or just enough to release it as a frozen block from the storage container. Put it in a saucepot, covered, over medium heat to thaw it and then simmer for 10 to 15 minutes, or until heated all the way through. Add the seafood as instructed by the recipe.

• • •

Tip: Farro adds wonderful chewy bits and even more substance to an already satisfying meal. To include it, cook the grains separate from the stew. Bring 2 cups/473 ml of water to a boil in a small saucepot over high heat. Stir in 1 cup/198 g of farro and calm the boil to a simmer (medium-high or medium heat). Cook it this way for about 15 minutes, or until the farro grains are tender and chewy, just slightly more al dente than readied pasta. Drain any water that hasn't been absorbed. Sprinkle several heaping spoonfuls of the grains into each serving of stew (about ¼ to ⅓ cup/50 to 60 g per serving). Cooked farro keeps well refrigerated for up to a week.

BELLY BONUS: Sardines are considered one of the best foods you can eat. These little fish are packed with omega-3s (EPA and DHA), calcium, and vitamin D, along with iron, magnesium, phosphorus, potassium, zinc, and copper. As an added benefit, sardines are low on the food chain, making them low in toxins. Opt for sardines with bones, if you can, for an extra boost of calcium.

NUTRITION PER SERVING (ABOUT 2 CUPS/355 G)

Calories 229 | Total fat 7 g (Saturated 1 g, Poly 1 g, Omega-3 0.45 g, DHA 0.23 g, EPA 0.12 g, Mono 4 g) | Cholesterol 94 mg | Protein 27 g | Sodium 947 mg | Carbohydrates 15 g | Fiber 3 g | Sugars 7 g | Vitamin A 66 mcg | Vitamin B6 1 mg | Vitamin B12 5 mcg | Vitamin C 20 mg | Vitamin D 70 IU | Choline 123 mg | Folate 45 mcg | Calcium 110 mg | Iron 3 mg

Simpler Sunday
Meatballs and Spaghetti

If your nonna delivers to you an enormous pot of meatballs that she molded with her own little hands, fried in multiple batches, and simmered all day, stirring ritualistically with her own mother's wooden spoon, then eat them happily and count your blessings that your baby might get to taste her great-grandmother's loving spoonfuls soon. But between visits or in lieu of them, make a simpler, lighter batch yourself. Freeze some for another time and then enjoy a hot bowl of spaghetti and meatballs that skips the frying and sneaks in an unexpected healthful twist. Whole grain millet fits into these meatballs without calling any attention to the added extra nutrients. Just like Nonna's, the longer the meatballs simmer in the sauce, the more tender they become, so sit down, relax, and update your registry while you wait.

Makes 6 servings

FOR THE MEATBALLS

¼ cup/48 g millet	¼ teaspoon smoked paprika
1 pound/454 g ground beef	¼ teaspoon garlic powder
¼ cup/7.5 g loosely packed fresh flat-leaf or curly parsley, minced, divided	¼ teaspoon fine sea salt
½ teaspoon dried oregano	⅛ teaspoon freshly ground black pepper (about 10 grinds)

FOR THE SAUCE AND SPAGHETTI

1 tablespoon extra-virgin olive oil	½ teaspoon granulated sugar
1 medium yellow onion, diced small	½ teaspoon fine sea salt
4 garlic cloves, chopped	¼ teaspoon freshly ground black pepper (about 20 grinds)
2 (28-ounce/794 g) cans crushed tomatoes	1 pound/454 g spaghetti
1 teaspoon dried oregano	

Combine the millet with ½ cup/118 ml of water in a small saucepot over high heat. Bring the water to a boil, cover the pot, reduce the heat to low, and let the millet simmer for 15 minutes. Turn off the heat and leave the pot covered for 5 minutes. Then uncover and fluff the cooked millet, which will be tender and fluffy, though the grains will stick to each other slightly.

Meanwhile, shape the meatballs. Put the ground meat in a large mixing bowl and break it up quite a bit with your hands. Sprinkle half of the parsley, the oregano, paprika, garlic powder, salt, and pepper across the surface of the meat and then gently work the seasonings into the meat with your fingers, turning and tossing without packing things together. Scrape the cooked, fluffed millet into the bowl and work it evenly into the mix with your hands. Now form about twenty meatballs the size of ping-pong balls (about 1½ inches/4 cm in diameter) and set them aside.

{Recipe continues on next page}

Heat the oil in a large Dutch oven or saucepot over medium heat. When the oil is hot, scrape the onions into it and sauté them for 5 to 7 minutes, or until they soften slightly and suggest that they'll start to brown around their edges soon. Add the garlic and sauté for a minute more. Stir in the tomatoes, reserved second half of the parsley, the oregano, sugar, salt, and pepper.

Gently deposit the meatballs into the sauce, mostly in a single layer. Bring the sauce up to a boil and then reduce the heat to low and partially cover the pot. Simmer the sauce and meatballs for at least 1 hour and up to 3, stirring gently now and again to ensure that none of the meatballs stick to the bottom of the pot.

Cook the spaghetti according to the package directions. Drain it and return the cooked pasta to the pot. Add about ½ cup/129 g of the sauce to the hot pasta and toss several times to coat the strands. Dole out about three meatballs plus around 1 cup/257 g of sauce with each serving.

If you plan to freeze some of the meatballs and sauce, let that portion cool to room temperature and then pack it in an airtight container and stash it in the freezer. (Cook only enough pasta for the number of servings you're planning at the moment.) Keep frozen for up to 6 months. To thaw, set the container in the refrigerator for a day and then push the meatballs and sauce into a saucepot to reheat over medium heat, about 15 minutes.

BELLY BONUS: The meatballs are an excellent source of iron, and mixing in millet with the beef adds extra protein, fiber, B vitamins, antioxidants, and minerals such as iron, magnesium, phosphorus, calcium, and zinc.

NUTRITION PER SERVING (ABOUT 1½ CUPS/460 G)

Calories 624 | Total fat 20 g (Saturated 7 g, Poly 2 g, Omega-3 0.12 g, DHA 0.00 g, EPA 0.00 g, Mono 9 g) | Cholesterol 54 mg | Protein 29 g | Sodium 677 mg | Carbohydrates 85 g | Fiber 9 g | Sugars 15 g | Vitamin A 36 mcg | Vitamin B6 1 mg | Vitamin B12 2 mcg | Vitamin C 28 mg | Vitamin D 4 IU | Choline 90 mg | Folate 232 mcg | Calcium 135 mg | Iron 8 mg

Slow Sweet Brisket
with Vinegar Slaw

Barbecue classics make plenty of lists of pregnancy cravings. Yours included? Here's an easy way to make beef brisket at home. I can't eat mine without crunchy, sour slaw, either on the side or piled high on top of the beef and between two sides of a bun. This quick slaw holds up very well in the fridge for days and days when made with particularly hardy green and red cabbages, and the recipe yields a little extra beyond what you might use for the sandwich. Use leftovers on other sandwiches or eat it as a salad all on its own. Flat-cut brisket is the leaner of the two cuts available ("point cut" is the other) and an excellent way to get the benefits of red meat, such as its iron content, without too much saturated fat.

Makes 6 servings

FOR THE BRISKET

1 tablespoon extra-virgin olive oil

½ teaspoon fine sea salt

½ teaspoon freshly ground black pepper

2 pounds/907 g flat-cut brisket (also called first cut)

1 large yellow onion, quartered and thinly sliced

1 large carrot, halved and then cut into 8 pieces

½ cup/168 g tomato paste

2 tablespoons dark brown sugar

1 cup/237 ml beef or chicken stock

2 tablespoons balsamic vinegar

1 tablespoon soy sauce

1 teaspoon Dijon mustard

1 teaspoon garlic powder

¼ teaspoon smoked paprika

¼ teaspoon ground coriander

Leaves from 4 sprigs of thyme

FOR THE SLAW

1 small cabbage (napa, green, red, or savoy), quartered, cored, and sliced into thin pieces across the leaf

2 medium carrots, grated

3 large scallions, white and green parts thinly sliced

⅓ cup/79 ml cider vinegar

1 tablespoon granulated sugar

1 teaspoon sea salt

Pour the oil into a large skillet and set the pan over medium-high heat. Sprinkle a few pinches of the salt and pepper over both sides of the brisket. Set the meat in the hot oil and sear for 5 minutes on each side, or until a dark crust starts to leave its mark. Lift the brisket out of the pan and set it aside on a plate.

Drop the onions and carrots into the hot pan and sauté them for 3 to 5 minutes, or just enough to lift up any of the browned bits left behind by the meat, and until the onions only start to soften.

{Recipe continues on next page}

Meanwhile, in a medium mixing bowl, mix the tomato paste and brown sugar together. Then slowly drizzle in the stock, whisking as you do, until all of it has been added and the liquid is thick and smooth. Add the vinegar, soy sauce, mustard, garlic powder, paprika, coriander, thyme, and the remaining salt and pepper. Whisk thoroughly to combine everything. Pour the sauce into a 5-quart slow cooker, dump in the onions and carrots, and then nestle the brisket down into the sauce (pour in any juices that collected on the plate while it sat), turning it over two or three times to coat it with the sauce.

Set the slow cooker to high and cook the brisket for 6 hours, or until it can be shredded easily by pulling at it with a fork against the grain.

While the brisket cooks, toss the cabbage, carrots, and scallions together in a 13 x 9-inch/ 33 x 23 cm glass baking dish. In a small bowl, whisk together the vinegar, sugar, and salt. Pour the vinegar mixture over the cabbage and toss with tongs to coat the vegetables.

Cut a piece of plastic wrap big enough to cover the dish and press it down across the surface of the cabbage. Marinate the slaw for at least 1 hour.

When the brisket is tender, lift it out of the slow cooker to a cutting board. Use two forks to pull the meat against the grain into shreds. If you prefer, slice the beef against the grain into thin strips instead. Scrape the beef back into the slow cooker and toss it with the sauce to coat it.

Eat the brisket the way you enjoy it: as a platter, on its own along with a heaping side serving of slaw, or as a sandwich, with about 1 cup/190 g of the brisket topped with 1/3 cup/28 g of the slaw on a toasted whole grain bun. Toss the slaw together again before serving, and store leftovers in an airtight container up to 1 week. Store leftover brisket in an airtight container up to 5 days or freeze for up to 6 months. Thaw in the refrigerator overnight before warming the meat and sauce thoroughly in a covered saucepot over medium heat.

BELLY BONUS: Beef brisket is available in two cuts. The flat half (also called thin, first, or center cut) is the leaner of the two with minimal fat. The point (or front, thick, or nose cut) is fattier. You can use either cut in this same method, and both, as with all red meat, offer significant amounts of iron and are good sources of B12 and protein as well.

NUTRITION PER SERVING (1 CUP/190 G BRISKET AND SAUCE PLUS 1¹/₃ CUPS/113 G SLAW)

Calories 467 | Total fat 15 g (Saturated 5 g, Poly 1 g, Omega-3 0.14 g, DHA 0.00 g, EPA 0.00 g, Mono 7 g) | Cholesterol 139 mg | Protein 54 g | Sodium 1,211 mg | Carbohydrates 28 g | Fiber 6 g | Sugars 17 g | Vitamin A 305 mcg | Vitamin B6 1 mg | Vitamin B12 4 mcg | Vitamin C 55 mg | Vitamin D 0 IU | Choline 219 mg | Folate 87 mcg | Calcium 121 mg | Iron 7 mg

Vegetable Stew

If you're having trouble knocking back enough vegetables, get out your biggest pot (at least 5.5 quarts) to accommodate a small garden's worth that surrender to tender after a long, hot bath in broth. It takes a few minutes to get all of the shapes and sizes situated, but when you do, you'll have a few meals' worth of stew, loaded with color, texture, and nutrients that help guarantee a well-balanced day for you and your kiddo. If you need a little extra to bulk up the meal, you will find the perfect pairing on page 120: Grilled Tomato, Red Onion, and Mozzarella Cheese Sandwiches.

Makes 6 servings

1 tablespoon extra-virgin olive oil

1 large yellow onion, diced small

2 medium carrots, sliced into ⅛-inch/0.3 cm rounds

3 medium celery stalks, cut into ¼-inch/0.6 cm pieces

1 large parsnip, quartered and cut into small ¼-inch/0.6 cm cubes

1 small fennel bulb, cored and diced small

4 garlic cloves, chopped

3 cups/255 g chopped cauliflower florets (about ¼ of a small head)

2 medium Yukon gold potatoes, unpeeled, cut into ¼-inch/0.6 cm cubes

2 small zucchini, quartered and cut into ½-inch/1.3 cm cubes

4 ounces/113 g green beans, cut into ½-inch/1.3 cm pieces

1 (15-ounce/425 g) can diced tomatoes, preferably fire-roasted

48 ounces/1.4 L vegetable or chicken stock (page 214, or low-sodium store-bought)

6 sprigs fresh thyme

½ teaspoon dried oregano

1 teaspoon coarse smoked salt or ½ teaspoon fine sea salt

½ teaspoon freshly ground black pepper

1 tablespoon red wine vinegar

Heat the oil in a large Dutch oven or stockpot over medium-high heat. Add the onion, carrots, celery, parsnip, and fennel and sauté for 10 minutes, stirring often, or until the onion and fennel start to brown around their edges. Slowly drizzle in ½ cup/118 ml water and scrape up any brown bits from the bottom as the water sizzles and evaporates.

Stir in the garlic and cook for a minute before adding the cauliflower, potatoes, zucchini, and green beans. Give all the vegetables several good turns and tosses so they are well combined. Add the tomatoes, stock, sprigs of thyme, oregano, salt, pepper, and vinegar.

Bring the liquid to a boil, which will take about 5 minutes or more if the stock was cold when added. Then reduce the heat to medium low, partially cover the pot, and simmer the stew for 45 minutes, or until the vegetables are tender (green beans that are soft with a slight bite remaining are a good gauge). Adjust the seasoning to your taste.

Cool leftovers and transfer them to an airtight container. Refrigerate up to 1 week or freeze up to 2 months.

{Recipe continues on next page}

BELLY BONUS: Vegetable soup is a comforting alternative to salads and an easy way to get the fiber and vitamins that veggies offer. A bowlful of this soup has more than a quarter of your fiber needs and is brimming with vitamins A and C and potassium. Soup is another way to meet your fluid needs during pregnancy.

NUTRITION PER SERVING (ABOUT 1²/₃ CUPS/550 G)

Calories 168 | Total fat 3 g (Saturated 0 g, Poly 0 g, Omega-3 0.08 g, DHA 0.00 g, EPA 0.00 g, Mono 2 g) | Cholesterol 0 mg | Protein 5 g | Sodium 1,439 mg | Carbohydrates 34 g | Fiber 8 g | Sugars 11 g | Vitamin A 234 mcg | Vitamin B6 0 mg | Vitamin B12 0 mcg | Vitamin C 57 mg | Vitamin D 0 IU | Choline 32 mg | Folate 84 mcg | Calcium 91 mg | Iron 2 mg

White and Greens
Chicken Chili

A good homemade chili can be a bowl brimming with vitamins, minerals, and nutrients that help to keep your system in balance. But tomato-based chili has the potential to set off the inner fire alarm with heartburn that will remind you of dinner way beyond bedtime. White chili takes the edge off but keeps the good-for-you bonuses in the stew. This one, strewn with threads of softened, silky baby spinach (feel free to substitute your green of choice, including chard, kale, or collards) scores bonus points on the nutrition scale. After a long, hot bath, tender chicken thighs shred with a pull of your fork. You can lift each out, pull the meat to pieces, and return it to the full pot, or you can ladle a full thigh or two per serving and cut into the meat with your spoon with almost no effort at all as you slowly make your way through the bowl.

Makes 6 servings

3 tablespoons all-purpose flour

¼ teaspoon fine sea salt, plus more for seasoning

⅛ teaspoon freshly ground black pepper (about 10 grinds), plus more for seasoning

2 tablespoons extra-virgin olive oil or vegetable oil

1½ pounds/680 g boneless, skinless chicken thighs (about 8 thighs)

1 medium yellow or white onion, diced small

1 medium green bell pepper, diced small

1 medium jalapeño, seeded and diced small

3 garlic cloves, minced

2 cups/56 g baby spinach

1 cup/155 g corn (frozen or fresh, cut from 1 cob)

4 cups/946 ml chicken stock (page 214, or low-sodium store-bought)

1 (15-ounce/425 g) can pinto beans, drained and rinsed, or 1½ cups/232 g cooked beans

1 (15-ounce/425 g) can cannellini beans, drained and rinsed, or 1¼ cups/284 g cooked beans

1 teaspoon ancho chili powder

½ teaspoon ground cumin

½ teaspoon dried oregano

¼ teaspoon ground coriander

Pinch of chipotle powder (optional)

¼ cup/7.5 g loosely packed fresh cilantro leaves, chopped

½ cup/56 g grated Monterey Jack cheese, for serving (optional)

2 scallions, white and green parts thinly sliced, for serving (optional)

Scatter the flour across a large plate and sprinkle the salt and pepper into it. Pour the oil into a Dutch oven or large saucepot set over medium-high heat.

Drop the chicken thighs into the flour to coat them all around. Shake off excess flour back onto the plate and set the thighs into the hot oil. Cook the chicken for 3 minutes on each side, or until lightly browned.

{Recipe continues on next page}

Nudge the flour left on the plate off to one side. Stack the chicken onto the cleared space and then scrape the flour into the pot. Set the chicken aside. Lower the heat to medium, whisk the flour into the oil, and cook it into a thickened paste for 1 minute, or until it starts to take on a pale golden color. Stir the onion, bell pepper, jalapeño, and garlic into the cooked flour roux. Sweat the vegetables, stirring often and scraping up brown bits from the bottom of the pot, for 5 minutes.

Drop in the spinach and cook for 2 minutes, or until it is almost completely wilted and softened. Add the corn and ¼ cup/59 ml of the stock and scrape up the bits as the liquid sizzles on the bottom. Add the remaining stock and 1 cup/237 ml of water, plus the beans, chili powder, cumin, oregano, coriander, and chipotle powder. Return the chicken to the pot. Cover the pot and bring the liquid to a boil. As soon as it boils, reduce the heat to medium low, tilt the lid so the pot is partially covered, and simmer the chili for about 45 minutes, stirring now and again, or until the chicken shreds without effort when you pull at it with a fork and the liquid has thickened a bit.

Taste the soup and add salt and pepper to taste. Stir in the cilantro.

To serve, scoop out one or two thighs per serving or shred the chicken with two forks in the pot (alternatively, pull the thighs out, shred them on a plate or cutting board, and return them to the pot). The chicken is so tender that it is easy to cut through with a spoon and scoop up as you eat the chili.

Top each serving with 2 tablespoons of grated cheese and a tablespoon of scallions, if you like.

BELLY BONUS: Chicken thighs are a great source of protein that helps support growth during pregnancy. A bowlful of this chili has 47 g of protein, which is more than half of the daily pregnancy needs. Frozen corn is a great option if you can't get fresh. Typically, frozen vegetables are picked at their peak and then flash-frozen to prevent aging and the loss of important nutrients. Canned corn, though, is often packed with sodium.

NUTRITION PER SERVING (1½ CUPS/647 G)

Calories 502 | Total fat 17 g (Saturated 3 g, Poly 3 g, Omega-3 0.18 g, DHA 0.01 g, EPA 0.01 g, Mono 9 g) | Cholesterol 162 mg | Protein 47 g | Sodium 540 mg | Carbohydrates 42 g | Fiber 6 g | Sugars 4 g | Vitamin A 58 mcg | Vitamin B6 1 mg | Vitamin B12 1 mcg | Vitamin C 36 mg | Vitamin D 2 IU | Choline 103 mg | Folate 58 mcg | Calcium 113 mg | Iron 5 mg

Belly-to-Belly

On help from family and friends after birth . . .

Amy M: "My mother and sister froze several meals for us when I was in the hospital, and a moms' club I joined when I was pregnant brought us dinner every day for a week."

Karin M: "When I was pregnant with my third, my good friends threw me a shower to update the baby supplies with current things. It was such an uplifter!"

Alison G: "I loved it when people brought premade food for us to eat! I found cooking so challenging with a baby, and I was always so hungry while nursing."

Carrie S: "A friend sent trays of cold cuts and side salads and bread. It saved us. We ate sandwiches every day for over a week, and everyone who visited that first week was fed."

Cathy B: "My aunt sent an Edible Arrangement, which I think we ate in one day. All the fruit was so refreshing after a few days of hospital food, sandwiches, and heavier dishes the people brought over."

Christine R: Three different women in my life, who were beyond child-bearing age but not ready to be grandmothers, offered me respite to do things like take a bath or go grocery shopping by myself. That kept me sane."

Danielle M: "My brother brought fruit salad to our house each time he visited, which was a wonderful treat! The thought of cutting and preparing the fruit was daunting, so having someone else do it was fantastic. I wish someone would do that for me now!"

Laurie F: "After I had my first baby, I suffered from what I now know was really significant post-partum depression. I will remember my neighbor Casey for the rest of my life for sending a community my way whether I was able to ask for it or not. She is a mother with a life of her own, and she found time to hold me up when I couldn't find the energy to do it on my own."

Jessica P: "I was struggling with juggling a toddler and twin newborns. My parents had both passed, and I didn't have any relatives nearby. My aunt and uncle came, and for a couple of nights, they stayed up continuously and took care of every need of my three children. They cared for me. For that, I am eternally grateful."

Jess T: "We spent four weeks with my son in the NICU. I had spent eleven days in the hospital as well and was exhausted and stressed out. Friends brought good homemade food. Although I remember the meals well, I was more impressed by *who* brought the food. It was the people I least expected to donate food who helped the most."

Jennifer M: "My favorite post-baby gift was having my house cleaned. I certainly didn't mind running a vacuum, but what a relief to have the bathrooms and kitchen cleaned for me!"

Lari R: "I had a very emergency C-section and so had a huge incision. A friend who also had a C gave me soap on a rope. You've no idea how painful it was to drop the soap in the shower and have to bend over and pick it up. So now I give soap on a rope to anyone I know who has had a C."

Tara H: "My mom is just incredibly helpful. I came home from the hospital both times to a sparkling clean, stocked fridge and a home-cooked meal."

Joelle G: "My mother bought me a water bottle with a straw and a blender. I had no idea how important they would be when I relied on smoothies and Luna bars for months while caring for and breastfeeding my colicky baby. With the twins, I needed a harness for that water bottle!"

CHAPTER 6

Sweets and Treats

Pregnancy's sweetest reward comes at the end, when you finally get to meet that little mystery who has been camped out inside. Before then, reward yourself for doing the work of taking good care of your body and that precious life.

I think treats are a requirement, yet I still try to be mindful about them so I can enjoy without feeling like I'm sabotaging overall good health. There was no way I was going to write a cookbook for pregnancy without wrapping it up on a sweet note. Every mother-in-waiting deserves dessert. So I developed a chapter full of goodies that qualify as indulgences but offer goodness and nutrients. Everything from brownies to a milkshake and a bunch of cookies in between uses whole grains, fruit, and unconventional ingredients and methods that make the most out of a splurge.

Trying your hand at more wholesome sweets is good practice for teaching your child how to look forward to treats as part of a healthy, happy life.

RECIPE	VITAMIN A	VITAMIN C	VITAMIN D	B6	B12	FOLATE	CHOLINE	CALCIUM	IRON	DHA	FIBER	PROTEIN
Almond Butter White Chocolate Blondies												
Apple Cranberry Cobbler		*						*			**	
Banana Bonbons				*							*	
BCPB (Banana Cocoa Peanut Butter) Whoopie Pies											*	
Berry Crumbles		*									**	
Brown Butter Fig Rice Pudding	*		*		**			**				
Cocoa Chewy Gem Drops												
Chocolate-Covered Strawberry Milkshake		**			**			*				
Double Chocolate Date and Cashew Cream Brownies											*	
Ginger Cookies												
Hot Chocolate	*		*		**			**				*
Chocolate Milk Syrup												
Lemon Ricotta Cake Cookies												
Lime Cornmeal Cookies												
Oat Nut Chocolate Chunk Cookies												

Key:
* = Good Source (10 to 19%)   ** = Excellent Source (>20%)
Note: DHA is based on 200 mg recommendation

Almond Butter White Chocolate Blondies

Every once in a while when I'm ogling a bakery case of treats chockablock with chocolaty things like fudgy brownies, chunky cookies, and cupcakes frosted high, something un-chocolate lures me to consider it. It's rare that I'll give in to something void of the sweet, dark richness of chocolate. But I'd pass up a chocolate chip cookie and all its cousins for this soft, chewy blondie kissed with almond and studded with bits of texture. Despite its definitive standing in the desserts category, these baked bars work in whole grains and sustaining protein while you're too busy enjoying them to care.

Makes 16 blondies

½ cup/151 g almond butter, at room temperature

¼ cup/56 g unsalted butter, at room temperature

⅔ cups/143 g packed dark brown sugar

¾ teaspoon almond extract

2 large eggs

½ cup/144 g whole wheat pastry flour

½ cup/34 g almond flour (also called almond meal)

¼ cup/37 g unbleached all-purpose flour

1 teaspoon baking powder

¼ teaspoon fine sea salt

½ cup/80 g white chocolate chips, chunks, or chopped whole bar

½ cup/74 g roasted unsalted almonds, chopped

Preheat the oven to 375°F/190°C/Gas 5. Line an 8-inch/20 cm square baking dish with a 12-inch/31 cm square piece of parchment paper, tucking in the corners so that the paper is flat against the bottom and up the sides.

Put the almond butter, butter, and brown sugar in a large mixing bowl. Use an electric mixer to beat at medium speed until soft and smooth, about 5 minutes. Add the almond extract and the eggs one at a time and beat until smooth, about 3 additional minutes.

In a medium mixing bowl, whisk together the whole wheat pastry flour, almond flour, all-purpose flour, baking powder, and salt. Sprinkle one third of the dry ingredients into the wet ingredients and mix for about 20 seconds. Repeat this twice with the remaining dry ingredients. Finally, add the white chocolate and almonds, mixing them in at low speed until incorporated, about 15 to 20 seconds.

Scrape the thick, dough-like batter into the parchment-lined baking dish and press it out evenly and into the corners. Bake for 25 minutes or more, checking often after about 20 minutes, or until the top and sides are light brown and a toothpick or fork stuck into the middle comes out clean. Take care not to overbake, which will dry them out. Let the blondies rest in the baking dish for about 5 to 10 minutes and then lift them out using the overhanging edges of the parchment paper. Set on a rack to cool completely before slicing into sixteen bars.

Store the blondies in an airtight container or wrapped tightly in plastic or parchment paper for up to 5 days.

BELLY BONUS: In comparison to other blondie recipes, which call for at least a stick of butter per batch, this recipe only calls for ¼ cup/56 g in the whole shebang, dropping the saturated fat total significantly. The remainder of the fat comes from almonds in the form of almond butter, almond flour, and whole almonds. Almonds are a source of monounsaturated fat, a heart-healthy fat that can help lower cholesterol. The nuts also contain bone-building calcium and magnesium.

NUTRITION PER SERVING (1 BLONDIE)

Calories 204 | Total fat 13 g (Saturated 4 g, Poly 1 g, Omega-3 0.02 g, DHA 0.00 g, EPA 0.00 g, Mono 3 g) | Cholesterol 32 mg | Protein 5 g | Sodium 78 mg | Carbohydrates 19 g | Fiber 2 g | Sugars 12 g | Vitamin A 35 mcg | Vitamin B6 0 mg | Vitamin B12 0 mcg | Vitamin C 0 mg | Vitamin D 7 IU | Choline 23 mg | Folate 10 mcg | Calcium 51 mg | Iron 1 mg

Apple Cranberry Cobbler

Simpler than a pie and not quite a cake despite a cakey crown, here is a cobbler kissed with orange and almond and baked together with whole grains. The fruit isn't weighed down by tons of sugar or fat, so the results are tart and only moderately sweet, making an obvious canvas for a scoop of vanilla ice cream. What's more, each serving supplies 6 g of fiber thanks to the unpeeled apples.

Makes 6 servings

3 medium apples (Honeycrisp, Granny Smith, Gala, or your favorite variety), unpeeled, cored, quartered, and thinly sliced

1 cup/113 g fresh cranberries

1½ tablespoons freshly squeezed lemon juice or orange juice

1 cup/128 g plus 1 tablespoon white whole wheat flour, divided

¼ cup/48 g plus 1 teaspoon granulated sugar, divided

⅓ cup/43 g almond flour

¼ cup/37 g corn flour or fine-grind cornmeal

1½ teaspoons baking powder

½ teaspoon fine sea salt

1 cup low-fat milk

¼ cup/59 ml extra-virgin olive oil

Zest of 1 medium orange

¼ teaspoon vanilla extract

¼ teaspoon almond extract

Preheat the oven to 350°F/175°C/Gas 4.

Dump the apples and cranberries into a 9-inch/23 cm pie plate and toss them about with each other a bit while you drizzle in the lemon juice. Sprinkle 1 tablespoon of the white whole wheat flour plus 1 teaspoon of the sugar over the fruit and toss everything together again, making sure the flour and sugar have settled on the fruit and not the bottom of the plate.

In a large mixing bowl, whisk together the remaining 1 cup of white whole wheat flour, the remaining ¼ cup of granulated sugar, the almond flour, corn flour, baking powder, and salt.

Whisk the milk, oil, orange zest, and vanilla and almond extracts in a spouted measuring cup. Pour the liquid ingredients into the dry ingredients and whisk everything together into a batter.

Pour the batter over the fruit in the pie dish and transfer the dish to the oven. Bake for 1 hour, or until the batter bakes into a cakey top with golden-tan speckles across it. A toothpick inserted in the center of the top of the cobbler should come out clean.

Let the cobbler rest for about 10 minutes before cutting into it. Slice into six wedges and top with a small scoop of vanilla ice cream.

BELLY BONUS: Apples are a source of soluble fiber, which lowers cholesterol, and insoluble fiber, which helps to "get stuff out" (much appreciated if you're having some trouble with your sluggish digestive system). A medium apple has about 4 g of fiber. Cranberries are rich in antioxidants such as vitamin C, which help neutralize free radicals in the body that can cause disease. The little red berries are also best known for their use in preventing (not treating) UTIs, a common irritation during pregnancy.

NUTRITION PER SERVING (1 WEDGE)

Calories 333 | Total fat 14 g (Saturated 2 g, Poly 1 g, Omega-3 0.08 g, DHA 0.00 g, EPA 0.00 g, Mono 7 g) | Cholesterol 2 mg | Protein 6 g | Sodium 323 mg | Carbohydrates 48 g | Fiber 6 g | Sugars 20 g | Vitamin A 27 mcg | Vitamin B6 0 mg | Vitamin B12 0 mcg | Vitamin C 9 mg | Vitamin D 20 IU | Choline 13 mg | Folate 5 mcg | Calcium 154 mg | Iron 2 mg

Banana Bonbons

These bonbons pass for dessert as well as a midday pick-me-up. Frozen bananas are meltingly smooth with a surprising resemblance to ice cream. Crowned with a dark chocolate cap and optional toppings, they're sweet enough to double as a treat as much as a nutritious snack. In fact, if you indulged in two servings' worth, you'd still beat out a candy bar in the good-for-you category, since these save face without even trying on account of potassium, natural sugars, flavanols, and a bit of iron.

Makes about 42 bonbons
(6 per serving)

½ cup/123 g dark chocolate chips or chopped dark chocolate

3 medium ripe bananas, peeled and sliced into ½-inch-/1.3 cm-thick rounds

¼ cup/35 g roasted, salted almonds, chopped (optional)

Line a baking sheet with waxed paper or parchment paper.

Put the chocolate into a small saucepot over medium heat and stir with a wooden spoon or rubber spatula until completely melted and smooth, about 2 minutes. Turn off the heat. (To melt in the microwave instead, put the chocolate in a microwave-safe bowl and heat on medium power for 1 to 2 minutes, stirring every 30 seconds until smooth.)

Dip one of the cut sides of each banana piece in the chocolate by hand and set the pieces chocolate-side up on the paper-lined baking sheet. Alternatively, use a spoon to spread a ½ teaspoon dollop of the chocolate across one side. Sprinkle the chopped almonds on top of the chocolate.

Set the bonbons in the freezer until completely firm, about 2 hours. Then transfer to an airtight container or resealable plastic freezer bag and freeze for up to 1 month.

BELLY BONUS: A banana contains about 422 mg of potassium, which helps control blood pressure and combat cramps. Pregnant women should have 4,700 mg a day. Chocolate contains flavanols (phytonutrients), which act like antioxidants and work to prevent cellular damage in our bodies. Flavanols can also help lower blood pressure and increase blood flow to brain and heart, which is a real boon to your pregnant body! Flavanol levels vary from chocolate to chocolate, with the highest amounts hiding out in darker chocolate.

NUTRITION PER SERVING (6 BONBONS)

Calories 151 | Total fat 7 g (Saturated 4 g, Poly 0 g, Omega-3 0.02 g, DHA 0.00 g, EPA 0.00 g, Mono 2 g) | Cholesterol 1 mg | Protein 2 g | Sodium 4 mg | Carbohydrates 21 g | Fiber 3 g | Sugars 11 g | Vitamin A 2 mcg | Vitamin B6 0 mg | Vitamin B12 0mcg | Vitamin C 5 mg | Vitamin D 0 IU | Choline 6 mg | Folate 12 mcg | Calcium 15 mg | Iron 2 mg

BCPB (Banana Cocoa Peanut Butter) Whoopie Pies

During my first pregnancy, whoopie pie mania was sweeping the food world. There were cookbooks dedicated to them, storefronts showing them off, and magazine centerfolds reserved for them. I think I could count on one hand the number of times in my life I'd eaten them before, and while the cake-like sandwich with fluffy filling doesn't have to try hard to sell itself, I would typically swoon over about a hundred other sweet treats first. But during that pregnancy, those soft little mounds put a dumbstruck look in my eye and a bit of drool on my lip. So I set out to make a whoopie pie that would make me feel good about . . . or at least not that bad about . . . giving in to the temptation. Compared with a popular recipe for a classic fluff-stuffed whoopie, this one has nearly 200 fewer calories, 7 less g of fat and only 1 g of saturated fat (as opposed to 8), no cholesterol (rather than 51 mg), and not an ounce less of oozy, messy, sticky indulgent goodness. This recipe's richness comes from raw cashew cream and light coconut milk, not butter or oils. The bananas and just ½ cup/110 g of granulated sugar supply the cake's sweetness. What's more, chocolaty peanut butter BCPBs beg to be washed down with a glass of cold milk, a perfect source of calcium.

Makes 1½ dozen whoopie pies

1½ cups/187 g whole wheat pastry flour

½ cup/47 g unsweetened cocoa powder (not Dutch processed)

1 teaspoon baking soda

½ teaspoon fine sea salt

½ cup/76 g raw cashews

½ cup plus 3 tablespoons/ 162 ml light coconut milk, divided

3 large over-ripe bananas

½ cup/110 g granulated sugar

1 tablespoon vanilla extract

½ cup/131 g creamy natural peanut butter

1 cup/117 g confectioners' sugar

Preheat the oven to 375°F/190°C/Gas 5. Line two baking sheets with parchment paper.

In a large mixing bowl, whisk together the flour, cocoa, baking soda, and salt. Set aside.

Put the cashews and ½ cup/118 ml of the coconut milk in the carafe of a blender. Blend until a thick cream forms, about 20 to 30 seconds. Add the bananas, granulated sugar, and vanilla and blend again until smooth, about 30 seconds.

Form a well in the center of the dry ingredients and pour in the wet ingredients. Fold everything together into a dense batter using a large rubber spatula.

Drop 36 heaping tablespoons of batter with about 1 inch/2.5 cm of space around each one on the parchment-lined baking sheets. Bake for 15 minutes, or until the cakes are dry but still soft to the touch. Transfer the cakes to a rack and cool completely.

{Recipe continues on next page}

While the cakes cool, make the filling. Using an electric mixer, beat the peanut butter and remaining 3 tablespoons of coconut milk in a large mixing bowl. Slowly add the confectioners' sugar a few tablespoons at a time, until all of it is incorporated and the peanut butter mixture is smooth and thick.

Once the cakes are cool, assemble the whoopie pies. Spread 1 tablespoon of the peanut butter filling on the flat side of one of the cakes. Sandwich it with another cake to complete the whoopie pie.

Refrigerate for up to 5 days in an airtight container.

BELLY BONUS: While most versions induce a sugar high that quickly deflates like a whoopee cushion, these whoopie pies actually offer sustaining energy with protein from nuts, natural sugars, and whole grain flour. Pack one as a to-go snack or an afternoon pick-me-up.

NUTRITION PER SERVING (1 WHOOPIE PIE)

Calories 190 | Total fat 7 g (Saturated 1 g, Poly 0 g, Omega-3 0.01 g, DHA 0.00 g, EPA 0.00 g, Mono 1 g) | Cholesterol 0 mg | Protein 5 g | Sodium 161 mg | Carbohydrates 31 g | Fiber 3 g | Sugars 16 g | Vitamin A 1 mcg | Vitamin B6 0 mg | Vitamin B12 0 mcg | Vitamin C 2 mg | Vitamin D 0 IU | Choline 3 mg | Folate 7 mcg | Calcium 13 mg | Iron 1 mg

Berry Crumbles

This fruit topped with just a bit of oaty crumble is a treat for sure, but I can't think why you couldn't have it for breakfast, too. Classic crisp and crumble recipes typically call for a significant amount of butter, but here a small quantity of olive and coconut oils bring the topping together nicely instead. You can use fresh or frozen berries, and any combination of them (I like to stash a frozen mix of strawberries, blueberries, raspberries, and blackberries for smoothies or simple desserts like this one), or a straight-up single variety, too. Sweet and tart, sticky and syrupy, crunchy and toasty, these crust-crowned berries stand on their own, but a scoop of ice cream that melts down into the molten mixture beneath is certainly called for under the circumstances.

Makes 4 crumbles

½ cup/58 g old-fashioned rolled oats	¼ teaspoon ground cinnamon
3 tablespoons oat flour or white whole wheat flour, divided	2 tablespoons extra-virgin olive oil or vegetable oil
2 tablespoons turbinado sugar, divided	2 tablespoons coconut oil, solid
1 tablespoon wheat germ	1 pound/456 g fresh or frozen berries (mixed or a single variety)
1 tablespoon dry millet	
1 tablespoon dark brown sugar	1 tablespoon orange juice or freshly squeezed lemon juice
Pinch of fine sea salt	

Preheat the oven to 375°F/190°C/Gas 5.

Pile up the oats, 2 tablespoons of the flour, 1 tablespoon of the turbinado sugar, wheat germ, millet, brown sugar, salt, and cinnamon in a medium mixing bowl. Whisk everything together really well. Now drizzle in the olive oil and drop in the coconut oil. Use your fingers to distribute the oils throughout the dry ingredients, squishing the coconut oil into the floury bits to create little lumps throughout.

Dump the berries into a separate medium mixing bowl, drizzle the juice in, and sprinkle the remaining tablespoon of flour and tablespoon of turbinado across the surface. Use a large rubber spatula to fold the berries, distributing the flour and the juice. Divide the fruit between four oven-safe bowls or large ramekins, about ¾ cup/113 g per bowl.

Scatter a heaping ¼ cup/35 g of the oat mixture across the berries in the bowls. Set the bowls on a baking sheet and transfer it to the oven. Bake the crumbles for 45 minutes, or until a thick, dark syrup bubbles up and sticks to the sides of the bowl and the crumbly oat mixture is a deep golden brown.

Let the crumbles rest for 10 minutes before digging in. It is highly advised that you top each serving with a small scoop of vanilla ice cream or cool, creamy yogurt. (Greek-style works especially nicely here, but any style will do.)

{Recipe continues on next page}

BELLY BONUS: Berries are low in calories but packed with antioxidants such as vitamin C, which help counter free radicals that can be harmful in the body. They are also rich in anthocyanins, pigments that give berries their brilliant red, blue, and purple colors. These powerful antioxidants may promote memory and heart and bone health. Berries also contain folate and fiber, which are musts for pregnancy. Frozen, minimally processed foods like berries are good choices when fresh is not available. They are picked at their peak and flash-frozen to prevent aging and loss of nutrients.

NUTRITION PER SERVING (1 CRUMBLE)

Calories 302 | Total fat 16 g (Saturated 8 g, Poly 1 g, Omega-3 0.05 g, DHA 0.00 g, EPA 0.00 g, Mono 6 g) | Cholesterol 0 mg | Protein 4 g | Sodium 68 mg | Carbohydrates 40 g | Fiber 6 g | Sugars 19 g | Vitamin A 0 mcg | Vitamin B6 0 mg | Vitamin B12 0 mcg | Vitamin C 16 mg | Vitamin D 0 IU | Choline 0 mg | Folate 17 mcg | Calcium 23 mg | Iron 1 mg

Brown Butter Fig Rice Pudding

Classic comfort foods rank high on the lists of pregnancy favorites, and luscious rice pudding certainly qualifies. This version couldn't be easier, and it skips the egg custard element of traditional recipes. Still, it's rich, thick, and creamy with deep dimension from just a bit of brown butter and sweet, earthy dried figs. Medium-grain white rice yields the best texture, but long grain will work, too. Short grains and brown rice tend to hold on to their bite, interrupting the trademark soft smoothness of rice pudding. Though the instructions advise letting the pudding set to cold for several hours in the refrigerator, I find it impossible to resist it warm, directly from the pot, and there's no good reason to not eat it that way. I also can't come up with any grounds for limiting this to dessert: it makes an indulgent breakfast, too.

Makes 6 servings

4 cups/946 ml whole milk

¼ cup/56 g turbinado sugar

¼ teaspoon fine sea salt

1 teaspoon vanilla extract

½ cup/112 g medium-grain white rice, uncooked

7 dried figs (golden or mission or a combo), chopped small (about ½ cup/99g)

2 tablespoons unsalted butter

Pour the milk into a medium saucepot and stir in the sugar, salt, vanilla, and rice. Bring the milk to a simmer, which will take about 10 minutes over medium heat. Once it reaches a steady simmer, lower the heat to medium low. Simmer for 45 to 50 minutes, stirring every 10 minutes or so, or until the rice is completely tender and has thickened the milk significantly to a pudding-like viscosity. Turn off the heat and stir in the figs.

Just before the rice is finished cooking, or right after you turn off the heat, melt the butter in a small saucepot or sauté pan set over medium heat. It will take about 3 minutes for the butter to melt completely and for white foam to float to the surface. Let it sit for another 30 seconds and keep an eye on it, watching for the milk solids throughout the melted butter to turn brown. As it does, it will start to smell like baking bread. Pour the browned butter over the hot rice and stir to combine.

Divide the pudding evenly among six ramekins or jelly jars, or scrape it all into a large glass mixing bowl. Cover and refrigerate for at least 2 hours, or until it is cold and has set up. Keep refrigerated for up to 5 days.

BELLY BONUS: Like prunes, figs are great for countering constipation. In fact, three to five figs provides 5 g of fiber. Figs are also sources of natural sugar (for a sugar fix), iron, vitamin B6, copper, and magnesium.

NUTRITION PER SERVING (ABOUT 6 OUNCES/191 G)

Calories 265 | Total fat 9 g (Saturated 6 g, Poly 1 g, Omega-3 0.14 g, DHA 0.00 g, EPA 0.00 g, Mono 2 g) | Cholesterol 26 mg | Protein 7 g | Sodium 162 mg | Carbohydrates 39 g | Fiber 1 g | Sugars 22 g | Vitamin A 107 mcg | Vitamin B6 0 mg | Vitamin B12 1 mcg | Vitamin C 0 mg | Vitamin D 86 IU | Choline 26 mg | Folate 53 mcg | Calcium 204 mg | Iron 1 mg

Cocoa Chewy Gem Drops

Chocolate and dried fruit have a natural affinity that shines in these soft cookies. Dark cherries and, that's right, prunes are studs of chewy sweetness that brighten each bite. Never mind the added fiber, the whole grain goodness of oat flour, and a rather judicious measure of butter for three dozen cookies, compared with other classic recipes. These are still the type for which you willingly run the risk of getting your hand caught in the jar.

Makes 3 dozen cookies

1 cup/131 g all-purpose flour	⅔ cup/138 g dark brown sugar
1 cup/107 g oat flour	2 large eggs
½ cup/43 g unsweetened cocoa powder	2 teaspoons vanilla extract
1 teaspoon baking soda	½ cup/84 g bittersweet chocolate chips (about 60 to 70% cacao)
½ teaspoon baking powder	
½ teaspoon fine sea salt	½ cup/85 g dried cherries
½ cup/113 g unsalted butter	7 pitted prunes, chopped into small pieces (about ¼ cup/57 g)
¾ cup/165 g granulated sugar	

Preheat the oven to 350°F/175°C/Gas 4. Line two baking sheets with parchment paper.

Whisk together the all-purpose flour, oat flour, cocoa powder, baking soda, baking power, and salt in a medium mixing bowl. Set aside.

Drop the butter, granulated sugar, and brown sugar into a large mixing bowl. Cream the butter into the sugars for about 5 minutes using an electric mixer, or until the mixture is fluffy and light in texture. Stop to scrape down the sides with a rubber spatula and incorporate any pockets of butter or sugar hiding toward the bottom of the bowl. Crack one of the eggs into the mixture and beat it in. Add the vanilla and the remaining egg and beat again until they are completely incorporated.

Whisk the dry ingredients again and then sprinkle one third of them into the butter mixture. Run the machine on low for about 30 seconds, just to work it into the butter. Repeat this addition twice more, mixing until everything is completely blended together. Add the chocolate chips, cherries, and prunes and beat one last time on low to work it all into the cookie dough.

Drop heaping tablespoons of the cookie dough onto the prepared baking sheets about 2 inches/5 cm apart. Depending on how many baking sheets or oven racks you have, you will likely have to bake in batches to accommodate the three dozen cookies the recipe yields. Bake for 12 minutes, or until the cookies have spread into circles and their bottoms are lightly browned. If you touch the top of a cookie, it will still give in to the pressure a little. Baking them too long will dry them out. Let the cookies sit on the hot pan out of the oven for 2 minutes before lifting with a spatula to cool on a rack.

{Recipe continues on next page}

Alternatively, bake some of the cookies and freeze some of the dough to bake later. Refrigerate the portion you plan to freeze for at least 30 minutes or up to overnight. Scoop tablespoons of the cold dough and roll them into balls. Place the balls onto a baking sheet (or any surface that will house the cookie dough balls in a single layer and fit in your freezer) and set it in the freezer until the dough is very firm, at least 30 minutes. Transfer the frozen dough balls to an airtight container or a resealable plastic freezer bag. Store them in the freezer for up to 3 months.

To bake the frozen dough, set the balls on a parchment-lined baking sheet about 2 inches/5 cm apart and bake in a 350°F/175°C/Gas 4 oven for about 15 minutes.

BELLY BONUS: For many pregnant women, prunes (or dried plums) are their best friends. Not only do they help with constipation because of their fiber and sorbitol, they also provide iron, potassium, vitamin A, and phytochemicals that act like antioxidants (advantages over laxatives). Oat flour has the same benefits as whole grain oats. It's a good source of soluble fiber, which has been shown to lower cholesterol, and it's also higher in protein than many other whole grains.

NUTRITION PER SERVING (1 COOKIE)

Calories 111 | Total fat 4 g (Saturated 2 g, Poly 0 g, Omega-3 0.01 g, DHA 0.00 g, EPA 0.00 g, Mono 1 g) | Cholesterol 17 mg | Protein 1 g | Sodium 79 mg | Carbohydrates 19 g | Fiber 2 g | Sugars 11 g | Vitamin A 27 mcg | Vitamin B6 0 mg | Vitamin B12 0 mcg | Vitamin C 0 mg | Vitamin D 4 IU | Choline 9 mg | Folate 8 mcg | Calcium 12 mg | Iron 1 mg

Chocolate-Covered
Strawberry Milkshake

During my first pregnancy, my husband and I always left successful visits to our obstetrician wishing we could treat our growing baby to an ice cream cone for doing such a good job in there. We did the next best thing and treated ourselves! This version of a smooth, creamy, thick shake is more likely to win nutrition points and satisfy the ice cream urge. It's made mostly of fruit and milk, blended with a bit of rich chocolate sorbet. Choose a good-quality sorbet void of additives or extra sugar. If you want to substitute ice cream, scoop a "gourmet" brand without gums and preservatives. These tend to be higher in fat, but natural fats are better than fillers of artificial ingredients. During the peak of early summer strawberry season, fresh, hulled berries are optimal. Otherwise, frozen berries add body and chill to the finished shake.

Makes 4 servings

2 cups/255 g frozen unsweetened strawberries (or fresh)

1 cup/190 g chocolate sorbet

2 cups/473 ml low-fat milk

Combine the berries, sorbet, and milk in the carafe of a blender. Blend until smooth, scraping down the sides and stirring a bit if necessary. Serve immediately.

BELLY BONUS: It's always nice when a treat delivers quality nutrients while satisfying an intense craving. This shake does just that. One cup of strawberries delivers 110% of your daily recommendation for vitamin C, plus fiber and folate. Milk is one of the best sources of calcium, a nutrient both the baby and you need for good bone, heart, and muscle health. An 8-ounce glass of the shake adds to the total tally.

NUTRITION PER SERVING (8 OUNCES/237 ML)

Calories 139 | Total fat 2 g (Saturated 1 g, Poly 0 g, Omega-3 0.02 g, DHA 0.00 g, EPA 0.00 g, Mono 0 g) | Cholesterol 6 mg | Protein 5 g | Sodium 90 mg | Carbohydrates 26 g | Fiber 2 g | Sugars 19 g | Vitamin A 72 mcg | Vitamin B6 0 mg | Vitamin B12 1 mcg | Vitamin C 26 mg | Vitamin D 59 IU | Choline 25 mg | Folate 17 mcg | Calcium 163 mg | Iron 1 mg

We All Scream for Ice Cream

WHILE IT MAY FEEL TONGUE-IN-CHEEK TO DECLARE, "THIS ICE CREAM IS FOR THE BABY!" IT'S ACTU-ally not too much of a stretch. A serving of ice cream is a good source of calcium, and grow-ing babies need calcium for bones, teeth, and healthy hearts and muscles. If you don't take in enough during pregnancy, the baby will simply draw it from your own reserves, putting you at risk for deficiency. Take aim at 1,000 mg of calcium each day. Enjoy a small bowl of your favorite flavor on occasion, but be considerate of the fact that a half-cup serving of ice cream can also scoop on more than half a day's worth of saturated fat.

Calcium-rich alternatives to a daily dish:

- Milk
- Yogurt
- Cheese
- Fortified products including tofu, non-dairy milks, juice, cereals, breads
- Almonds
- Salmon
- Dark leafy greens

Double Chocolate Date
and Cashew Cream Brownies

Dark, dense, cakey, and richly chocolaty, these are serious brownies. I love to pair a thick rectangle with a glass of cold milk, but my husband warms up his at the bottom of a bowl and tops it with a small scoop of vanilla ice cream. Either way, one is the antidote to infamous chocolate hankerings that can only be quelled by the real deal. There's more than a single route to indulgent treats, as the ingredients and method for this recipe prove. Sticky dates, nutty sweet cashews, and whole grain flours shed a bright light on the way good ingredients can lend nutritive value and impressive complexity well beyond what's baked from a box.

Makes 1 dozen brownies

¼ cup/56 g unsalted butter, cut into small pieces, plus 1 teaspoon for the baking dish

½ cup/48 g unsweetened cocoa powder

⅓ cup/36 g oat flour

⅓ cup/48 g whole wheat pastry flour

1 teaspoon baking powder

¼ teaspoon fine sea salt

½ cup/75 g roasted cashews (unsalted or lightly salted)

2 large eggs

8 dates (about 112 g), pulled in half and pitted (be sure to trim away and discard any hard stem shells that may remain on the ends)

⅓ cup/70 g dark brown sugar

½ cup/118 ml low-fat or whole milk

1 teaspoon vanilla extract

½ cup/85 g bittersweet chocolate chips, or a 3-ounce/85 g chunk (60 to 70% cacao) chopped into pieces

Preheat the oven to 350°F/175°C/Gas 4. Spread the teaspoon of butter over the bottoms and sides of an 8-inch/20 cm square baking dish.

Whisk the cocoa, oat flour, whole wheat pastry flour, baking powder, and salt in a medium mixing bowl. Set aside.

Put the cashews in a standard-size food processor and process for about 1 minute, or until they have been chopped into tiny bits and the sound goes from loud smashing of the larger nuts against the bowl to just the hum of the processor's blade against the pulverized pieces. Continue for another 30 seconds to 1 minute, or until tiny clusters of cashew butter forms (if you squeeze a little of the substance together, it will be like dry, gritty nut butter between your fingers).

Scrape down the sides and inner edges of the processor bowl. Add the eggs and process them for 30 seconds, or until a thick, pale yellow, creamy liquid forms. Drop in the dates and blend for a full minute, or until very small bits of the sticky fruit are distributed throughout the cashew egg cream. Add the brown sugar, milk, and vanilla and buzz the mixture together one last time for 30 seconds, or until thoroughly combined into a thick liquid. Scrape the liquid into a large mixing bowl.

{Recipe continues on next page}

Melt the chocolate and the butter together either in a small mixing bowl in the microwave (1 minute at 70% power, stirring halfway through) or in a double boiler (fill the bottom pot one third of the way up with water and combine the chocolate and butter up top in the upper pot) over medium heat. Stir the melted chocolate rapidly to cool just slightly. Pour the chocolate into the cashew cream liquid and stir thoroughly, turning the cream chocolaty throughout.

Sift the cocoa and flour mixture over the surface of the wet ingredients in three additions, folding in the dry with a large rubber spatula between each to create a thick dark chocolate batter. (In lieu of sifting, whisk the dry ingredients with fervor and then sprinkle them in three helpings over the liquid.)

Scrape the batter into the buttered baking dish and smooth it out into an even layer. Bake for 20 to 25 minutes, or just until a toothpick inserted into the center comes out mostly clean. Take care not to overbake these brownies, which will dry them out.

Let the brownies cool at least to barely warm before cutting into twelve rectangles (three rows of four brownies each). The flavors become more intense as they cool completely. Cover the baking dish tightly with plastic wrap and store at room temperature for up to 1 week (they won't last, but . . .).

> **BELLY BONUS:** The fact that these tasty rectangles pack in protein, fiber, folate, iron, calcium, and vitamin A makes them a godsend. When compared to a store-bought double chocolate brownie of the same weight, these brownies have fewer calories (70), less fat (5 g), less cholesterol (25 mg), and more fiber (1 g). This is because I substitute nutrient-dense foods like sweet dates and rich cashews for the sugar and butter in conventional brownies. A mix of whole grain flours also improves the nutrition profile by providing more vitamins and minerals.

NUTRITION PER SERVING (1 BROWNIE)

Calories 211 | Total fat 11 g (Saturated 6 g, Poly 1 g, Omega-3 0.04 g, DHA 0.00 g, EPA 0.00 g, Mono 3 g) | Cholesterol 42 mg | Protein 4 g | Sodium 112 mg | Carbohydrates 28 g | Fiber 3 g | Sugars 17 g | Vitamin A 54 mcg | Vitamin B6 0 mg | Vitamin B12 0 mcg | Vitamin C 0 mg | Vitamin D 14 IU | Choline 31 mg | Folate 10 mcg | Calcium 58 mg | Iron 1 mg

Ginger Cookies

During my first pregnancy, a friend gifted me a big bag of her perfect gingersnap cookies for snacking on a coast-to-coast flight en route to our "babymoon" getaway. She baked hers in little rounds the size of quarters, and their sweet crunchiness redolent of ginger's warm spiciness tasted so good on my tongue. I took my cue from her recipe but experimented with a mixture of whole grain flours that complement the flavors and textures of classic snaps. Instead of butter, melted coconut oil lends its mellow aroma and signature flavor to these cookies with a crisp exterior and soft interior. A combination of ground and freshly grated ginger offers its soothing properties to the treat.

Makes 3 dozen cookies

½ cup/67 g all-purpose flour	½ teaspoon ground cinnamon
⅓ cup/46 g whole wheat pastry flour	1 large egg
¼ cup/28 g rye flour	⅓ cup/84 g coconut oil, melted if solid and cooled slightly
1 teaspoon baking soda	
¼ teaspoon fine sea salt	¼ cup/59 ml molasses (not blackstrap)
1½ teaspoons ground ginger	⅓ cup/71 g turbinado sugar
	1 teaspoon finely grated fresh ginger

Preheat the oven to 375°F/190°C/Gas 5. Line two baking sheets with parchment paper.

In a large mixing bowl, whisk the all-purpose flour, whole wheat pastry flour, rye flour, baking soda, salt, ground ginger, and cinnamon.

In a large, spouted measuring cup, beat the egg into the oil, molasses, sugar, and fresh ginger.

Pour the wet ingredients over the dry ingredients and fold everything together with a large rubber spatula into a dough that seems closer in nature to a batter. Make sure there are no pockets of dry ingredients hiding throughout the dough or at the bottom of the bowl.

Cover the dough and refrigerate it for at least 2 hours, or until it is cold and firm. Scoop out heaping teaspoons and roll the dough into balls. Set the balls on the parchment-lined pans, about 2 inches/5 cm apart, and bake for 10 to 15 minutes, depending on how soft or crisp you like your cookie. At 10 minutes, the cookies will have a crisp exterior and a soft interior once they cool. After 15 minutes' bake time and cooling completely, they will be crisp throughout. Let the cookies rest on the baking sheets for 2 minutes after you take them out of the oven. Then transfer them to a rack to cool completely.

Alternatively, bake some of the cookies and freeze some of the dough to bake later. This comes in handy if you're having an especially queasy day and you've found ginger to be an antidote. After you roll the dough into balls, place them on a baking sheet (or any surface that will house the cookie dough balls in a single layer and fit in your freezer) and set it in the freezer until the dough is very

{Recipe continues on next page}

firm, at least 30 minutes. Transfer the frozen dough balls to an airtight container or a resealable plastic freezer bag. Store them in the freezer for up to 3 months.

To bake the frozen dough, set the balls on a parchment-lined baking sheet about 2 inches/5 cm apart and bake in a 350°F/175°C/Gas 4 oven for about 15 minutes.

Store in an airtight container for up to 2 weeks.

BELLY BONUS: Ginger lends an aromatic and pungent flavor to the cookies and can provide some relief from first-trimester nausea.

NUTRITION PER SERVING (1 COOKIE)

Calories 49 | Total fat 3 g (Saturated 2 g, Poly 0 g, Omega-3 0.00 g, DHA 0.00 g, EPA 0.00 g, Mono 0 g) | Cholesterol 5 mg | Protein 1 g | Sodium 53 mg | Carbohydrates 6 g | Fiber 0 g | Sugars 3 g | Vitamin A 2 mcg | Vitamin B6 0 mg | Vitamin B12 0 mcg | Vitamin C 0 mg | Vitamin D 1 IU | Choline 5 mg | Folate 4 mcg | Calcium 6 mg | Iron 0 mg

Prenatal Vitamins

FOR YOUR HEALTH AND YOUR BABY'S, IT'S IMPORTANT TO EAT A HEALTHY DIET. AT TIMES, THOUGH, A well-balanced diet can have nutritional gaps or you may have dietary restrictions or health conditions that make supplementation with a prenatal vitamin more important. Prenatal vitamins differ from multivitamins primarily because of folic acid and iron, two nutrients that most pregnant women don't get enough of from food alone.

There are plenty of over-the-counter brands to choose from, but your healthcare provider may recommend or prescribe a specific one that suits your needs. Look for a vitamin that includes omega-3s, or a combination pack of prenatal vitamin plus DHA supplement tablet. DHA is a type of omega-3 fatty acid that can benefit the baby's brain and eye development.

Prenatal vitamins are not a substitute for a healthy diet. In fact, they should be taken in conjunction with a healthy diet to ensure that you are getting all your recommended vitamins and minerals. Talk to your healthcare provider about taking supplements or if you have any concerns.

Hot Chocolate

Pregnant or not, I turn to hot chocolate for a treat, a pick-me-up, even a dose of nutrition. If you do, too, take a gander at the ingredients on a package of hot chocolate mix before you reach for one next time. It has nothing good to say. Homemade cups taste better because they don't include any artificial this-or-that. Keep a box of good cocoa in the cabinet so you can whip up a quick cup to curb a craving.

Makes 1 serving

2½ teaspoons granulated sugar

2 teaspoons unsweetened cocoa powder

1 cup/237 ml low-fat or whole milk

Spoon the sugar and cocoa into the bottom of a coffee mug. Mix them together. Add about 2 tablespoons of the milk and stir until the powders turn into a thick, smooth, shiny paste. Add the remainder of the milk and stir well, until the milk is tinted with the chocolate and there are no lumps. Microwave for 1 minute. Stop to stir, and then microwave for another 40 to 60 seconds, keeping an eye on the milk, which will foam and overflow the cup quickly if it gets too hot. Stir again before sipping.

In lieu of a microwave, heat the chocolaty milk in a small pot over medium heat until hot, about 2 minutes. Then pour back into the mug to drink.

BELLY BONUS: Flavanols are chemical compounds in foods like chocolate that have antioxidant powers and can benefit our vascular health, including lowering blood pressure and improving blood flow to the brain and heart. Different forms of chocolate have varying levels of flavanols. In general, the more processed the chocolate is, the fewer flavanols it will contain. If you're looking to maximize the health benefits of your cocoa, stick with natural cocoa, which is simply ground-up roasted cocoa beans.

NUTRITION PER SERVING (8 OUNCES/237 ML)

Calories 143 | Total fat 3 g (Saturated 1 g, Poly 0 g, Omega-3 0.01 g, DHA 0.00 g, EPA 0.00 g, Mono 1 g) | Cholesterol 11 mg | Protein 8 g | Sodium 100 mg | Carbohydrates 24 g | Fiber 1 g | Sugars 22 g | Vitamin A 132 mcg | Vitamin B6 0 mg | Vitamin B12 1 mcg | Vitamin C 0 mg | Vitamin D 109 IU | Choline 40 mg | Folate 11 mcg | Calcium 284 mg | Iron 0 mg

Chocolate Milk Syrup

A glass of chocolate milk is just enough of an indulgence for a hankering, and you sip up the nutritional worth of the milk while you're enjoying it. Most shelf-stable squeeze bottles of chocolate "flavored" syrup depend on far more than the three familiar ingredients used to make this homemade version. Keep a jelly jar of the syrup (one recipe makes eight servings) in the fridge so you can treat yourself as quickly as you would with the artificial stuff. And trust me, this trick will come in very handy as your baby (or babies) becomes a treat-enthused child.

Makes ½ cup plus 1½ tablespoons/143 ml

⅓ cup/85 g granulated sugar

¼ cup/20 g unsweetened cocoa powder

¼ cup/59 ml low-fat or whole milk

In a small saucepot, whisk together the sugar and cocoa. Add about half of the milk and stir the powdery ingredients into the milk vigorously until a thick paste forms. Turn the heat to medium and add the remaining milk, whisking to avoid lumps. Continue whisking for about 1½ minutes, or until the sugar has dissolved, which you'll know by tasting or touching a tiny dab of the chocolate syrup. When the sugar has melted into a liquid, you won't feel any tiny, grainy crystals in the chocolate. Pour the syrup into a glass container and let it cool completely. Then cover it with a tight-fitting lid or plastic wrap and refrigerate (it will keep this way for up to 2 weeks).

To make chocolate milk, spoon 1 tablespoon plus 1 teaspoon of the chocolate syrup into a glass and pour 8 ounces/237 ml of cold milk on top. Stir or whisk thoroughly, distributing the syrup and tinting the milk with the chocolate.

BELLY BONUS: This homemade syrup is void of ingredients like high-fructose corn syrup and artificial flavors, which are included in popular bottled chocolate syrups. Enjoy a better tasting glass of chocolate milk knowing that it's also a smarter nutritional choice.

NUTRITION PER SERVING (1 TABLESPOON PLUS 1 TEASPOON)

Calories 50 | Total fat 0 g (Saturated 0 g, Poly 0 g, Omega-3 0.00 g, DHA 0.00 g, EPA 0.00 g, Mono 0 g) | Cholesterol 0 mg | Protein 1 g | Sodium 4 mg | Carbohydrates 12 g | Fiber 1 g | Sugars 11 g | Vitamin A 4 mcg | Vitamin B6 0 mg | Vitamin B12 0 mcg | Vitamin C 0 mg | Vitamin D 4 IU | Choline 2 mg | Folate 1 mcg | Calcium 13 mg | Iron 0 mg

Lemon Ricotta Cake Cookies

My friend tells an endearing story of being rather pregnant at a little one's first birthday party, which featured a food truck doling out irresistible jumbo cupcakes. She's almost positive the tots got their share of those treats before she waddled back up for her second. If your indulgence hankering also falls squarely into a cake pan, look no further. I developed these cakey little cookies to cure that craving. These are a treat, but they pack in a little protein and use a balance of whole grain whole wheat pastry flour plus a conservative measure of sugar. Two of these are a much better choice than two visits to the cupcake truck, and you still get to have a bit of cake and eat it, too.

Makes about 2 dozen cookies

1 large egg	¼ cup/57 g unsalted butter, melted and cooled slightly
1 cup/241 g whole milk ricotta cheese	
¾ cup/165 g granulated sugar	¾ cup/104 g whole wheat pastry flour
1 teaspoon lemon zest (from 1 lemon)	¾ cup/103 g all-purpose flour
1 tablespoon freshly squeezed lemon juice (about ¼ of a lemon)	½ teaspoon fine sea salt
	½ teaspoon baking powder
½ teaspoon vanilla extract	¼ teaspoon baking soda

Preheat the oven to 350 °F/175°C/Gas 4. Line two baking sheets with parchment paper.

In a large mixing bowl, beat the egg completely and then whisk it together with the ricotta. Add the sugar, lemon zest, lemon juice, and vanilla and mix thoroughly. Drizzle in the butter and whisk vigorously again.

In a separate medium mixing bowl, thoroughly whisk together the whole wheat pastry flour, all-purpose flour, salt, baking powder, and baking soda. Sift the dry ingredients into the wet ingredients in two steps, stopping to fold the flour mixture into the cheese mixture after the first addition. Continue folding after the second addition, taking care to incorporate any hidden pockets of dry ingredients into the cookie dough.

Situate heaping tablespoons of the dough onto the parchment-lined baking sheets about 2 inches/5 cm apart, since the cookies spread significantly as they bake.

Bake the cookies for 15 to 20 minutes. These don't take on much color, but their edges tan a bit and they should feel soft but sturdy when you touch their domed tops. Transfer them to a rack to cool completely (feel free to nibble one while still warm!).

Store the cookies in an airtight container using the parchment paper from the baking sheets to keep the layers of cookies separate, lest they stick together. The cookies keep at room temperature or in a cool, dry spot for up to 1 week. Refrigerate in warmer, humid weather.

{Recipe continues on next page}

NUTRITION PER SERVING (1 COOKIE)

Calories 96 | Total fat 4 g (Saturated 2 g, Poly 0 g, Omega-3 0.02 g, DHA 0.00 g, EPA 0.00 g, Mono 1 g) | Cholesterol 18 mg | Protein 2 g | Sodium 80 mg | Carbohydrates 14 g | Fiber 1 g | Sugars 7 g | Vitamin A 32 mcg | Vitamin B6 0 mg | Vitamin B12 0 mcg | Vitamin C 0 mg | Vitamin D 4 IU | Choline 8 mg | Folate 10 mcg | Calcium 32 mg | Iron 0 mg

Whole Lotta Whole Grains

WHOLE GRAINS ARE THE WHOLE SEEDS OF PLANTS WITH ALL THREE LAYERS INTACT: THE BRAN, GERM, and endosperm. Much of the fiber, vitamins, minerals, and phytonutrients of grains are stripped out when they are processed to remove the bran and germ for products such as all-purpose flour. In addition to their high scores for nutrition, whole grains get a gold star for flavor and texture, too. Carbohydrates are important for pregnancy, and choosing whole grain complex carbs maximizes their worth in your diet.

Whole grains are becoming increasingly mainstream and available in all types of markets, not just "natural food stores." If you're lucky, your favorite grocery store has a bulk foods section where you can pick up specific amounts of ingredients at reasonable prices and without the packaging costs.

To store them, fold down opened bags and wrap a rubber band around them, then tuck them into a resealable plastic bag or a container with a tight-fitting lid and stash them in the refrigerator or freezer. Storing them this way spares them of grain bugs that inevitably invade kitchen pantries and cabinets, and it prevents the grains from potential rancidity of their natural oils.

When it comes to using whole grain flours in baked goods, it's important to know that they are much denser and will more readily absorb moisture, so they can't be substituted one for one for refined flours, lest you end up with tough, dry treats. Sometimes a combination of whole grain and all-purpose flours yields the best structure and flavor results. Every baked good in this book, including waffles and pancakes, calls for whole grains.

Aside from making satisfying crusty breads, whole grains like quinoa, bulgur, farro, and millet are excellent alternatives to white rice, potatoes, and pasta. Swapping them in now and then adds variety and nutrients to your rotations. Cooked whole grains also store very well and are terrific in hearty grain salads for portable lunches.

Whole grains get put to good use in every chapter of this cookbook. Start with the Seven-Grain Pancakes Make-Ahead Mix, which gives you good reason to stock up on a whole bunch of whole grains you may have never tried. You can scan this list of all the recipes that call on whole grains to work through your stash and experiment with lots of others.

Lime Cornmeal Cookies

You deserve a cookie. One that begs you to sit down, put your feet up, and nibble a while. This one. Whole grain flours lend nutritive value to just-sweet-enough dough that bakes up crunchy. Be sure to use pastry flour, whose lower protein content promises enough softness to bump them out of the biscotti category. (Cookies made with regular whole wheat flour, including softer white whole wheat, can be too tough.) Still, their sturdiness says, "Dunk me in tea!" and their zesty personality reminds you that there's more to the world than chocolate chip.

Makes 2 dozen cookies

⅓ cup/84 g coconut oil, solid

⅓ cup/74 g granulated sugar

⅓ cup/76 g packed dark brown sugar

Zest of 1 lime (about 1 teaspoon)

1 large egg

1 teaspoon vanilla extract

1 cup/129 g whole wheat pastry flour

⅔ cup/94 g yellow cornmeal (fine or medium grind) or corn flour

¾ teaspoon baking powder

½ teaspoon fine sea salt

Preheat the oven to 350°F/175°C/Gas 4. Line two baking sheets with parchment paper.

Combine the coconut oil, sugars, and lime zest in a medium mixing bowl. Using an electric mixer, beat on medium speed for 5 minutes, or until the mixture is soft and light. Stop once or twice to scrape down the sides of the bowl with a rubber spatula. Add the egg and vanilla and beat again to incorporate.

In a separate medium mixing bowl, whisk together the pastry flour, cornmeal, baking powder, and salt. Sprinkle the dry ingredients into the oil mixture in thirds and beat between each addition for about 30 seconds to incorporate. Be sure to include any flour sitting at the bottom of the bowl that hasn't been swept up into the dough.

Scoop out 24 heaping tablespoons of the dough, roll into balls, and set on the parchment-lined pans about 1 inch/2.5 cm apart. Use a fork to press a crosshatch into each ball, pushing the dough down into a disc shape.

Bake for 15 to 20 minutes, or until the cookies just begin to brown around the bottom edges. Switch the trays halfway through baking.

Remove from the oven and let the cookies cool on a rack. Store in an airtight container for up to 1 week.

> **BELLY BONUS:** Compared to refined grains, whole grains like whole wheat pastry flour and cornmeal contain more nutrients, including fiber, selenium, potassium, and magnesium, which are found in the bran and endosperm.

NUTRITION PER SERVING (1 COOKIE)

Calories 82 | Total fat 3 g (Saturated 3 g, Poly 0 g, Omega-3 0.00 g, DHA 0.00 g, EPA 0.00 g, Mono 0 g) | Cholesterol 8 mg | Protein 1 g | Sodium 65 mg | Carbohydrates 12 g | Fiber 1 g | Sugars 5 g | Vitamin A 4 mcg | Vitamin B6 0 mg | Vitamin B12 0 mcg | Vitamin C 0 mg | Vitamin D 2 IU | Choline 7 mg | Folate 2 mcg | Calcium 13 mg | Iron 0 mg

Oat Nut
Chocolate Chunk Cookies

If your food processor is hiding away someplace rather than sitting pretty on a spacious counter-top, ask someone to lug it out for you and tell him or her you'll reward them with a cookie. Nuts and oats add fiber, protein, good fats, and more to these flourless cookies that stay crisp with a bit of chew. They bake flat and wide with bumps of chocolate chunks dotting their landscape.

Makes 2 dozen cookies

1½ cups/169 g old-fashioned rolled oats

½ cup/58 g pecans

½ cup/58 g walnuts

½ teaspoon fine sea salt

½ teaspoon baking powder

¼ teaspoon baking soda

½ cup/71 g dark chocolate chips or chunks chopped from a block (60 to 70% cacao)

1 large egg

¼ cup/56 g unsalted butter, melted and cooled slightly

½ cup/114 g packed dark brown sugar

¼ cup/62 g granulated sugar

1 teaspoon vanilla extract

Preheat the oven to 375°F/190°C/Gas 5. Line two baking sheets with parchment paper or a silicone baking mat. Set two oven racks at the lower and middle positions.

Put the oats, pecans, walnuts, salt, baking powder, and baking soda in the bowl of a food processor and process for 15 seconds, or until the mixture grinds down to a fine meal but not a flour. Dump everything into a large mixing bowl along with the chocolate and set aside.

Crack the egg into the food processor and process it until uniformly yellow, about 30 seconds. Add the butter, brown sugar, granulated sugar, and vanilla and blend for another 30 seconds until a smooth, thick liquid forms. Scrape this out into the large bowl of dry ingredients. Fold everything together using a large rubber spatula until the dry ingredients are completely coated by the wet ingredients, forming a sticky, mealy batter.

Scoop a tablespoon of the batter and roll it into a ball. Repeat to make two dozen cookies and set the balls 2 inches/5 cm apart on the parchment-lined baking sheets. Bake for 12 to 15 minutes, or until they spread flat and the edges are lightly browned. Let the cookies rest on the baking sheets for 2 minutes after they come out of the oven and then use a spatula to transfer them to a rack. Steal one or two while still warm and let the others cool completely.

Store in an airtight container up to 1 week.

{Recipe continues on next page}

BELLY BONUS: Yes, you're having a cookie (or two), but you can feel better knowing that these have redeeming nutrients such as fiber, folate, iron, and calcium that overly processed packaged ones simply don't have. And don't forget about the beneficial flavanols in the dark chocolate, which can help increase blood flow to the brain and heart and lower blood pressure. Nuts may be high in calories, but they're also packed with nutrients like fiber, protein, and omega-3 fatty acids, which can help lower blood pressure and protect our brains. Walnuts are the only nuts that contain a significant source of alpha-linolenic acid (ALA), a type of omega-3 fatty acid.

NUTRITION PER SERVING (1 COOKIE)

Calories 124 | Total fat 7 g (Saturated 2 g, Poly 2 g, Omega-3 0.25 g, DHA 0.00 g, EPA 0.00 g, Mono 2 g) | Cholesterol 13 mg | Protein 2 g | Sodium 72 mg | Carbohydrates 14 g | Fiber 1 g | Sugars 8 g | Vitamin A 20 mcg | Vitamin B6 0 mg | Vitamin B12 0 mcg | Vitamin C 0 mg | Vitamin D 3 IU | Choline 8 mg | Folate 4 mcg | Calcium 14 mg | Iron 1 mg

Belly-to-Belly

Memories of Pregnancy . . .

Tara H: "By the time I was free to eat after delivering my son, it was after midnight, the hospital cafeteria was closed, and I was absolutely ravenous. My parents forgot their restaurant leftovers in the nurse's fridge when they went home, so my first post-delivery meal was cold eggplant rollatini, chicken picatta, and linguini marinara, eaten with my fingers at 2 in the morning. And honestly, it was the best meal of my life."

Carrie P: "The place where I bought my daily muffin would ask me each day what kind of muffin 'she' wanted. And they would always ask if I wanted two: one for me, and one for the baby."

Christine R: "I liked finding out I was pregnant. I liked feeling the first kick. I liked the final push. Everything else for me was a means to an end."

Dina V: "I drank Italian sodas cut with club and a lot of ice, in my favorite wine or cocktail glass to replace a happy hour drink."

Laurie F: "Chocolate chip cookies on the way to my glucose tolerance test didn't do me well. I had to beg my doctor not to label me a gestational diabetes patient. Thankfully, he listened."

Jess T: "I was on bed rest in the hospital for two weeks for preeclampsia. On the night of what was to be my baby shower, a friend called the local cupcake company and ordered six cupcakes to be delivered to my room. The cupcake place was closing for the night and thought it was a sweet gesture, so they sent all their leftovers to the nurses on the antenatal floor. I ate two or three that night . . . and promptly went into labor. The nurses laughed. Apparently it wasn't such an unusual thing for preggo ladies to gorge on sugar and start contracting."

Lauren B: "While I was pregnant, my husband was dieting and lost twenty pounds as I gained forty. We ended up weighing the same when I was nine months pregnant and I was horrified."

Carita G: "I never felt more important in my life. Pregnancy was the greatest job I had ever taken on, and I promised myself, my baby, and my husband I would do everything and anything possible to take care. That included watching my nutrition."

References and Resources

Annie Murphy Paul: What We Learn Before We're Born. 2011. TED. http://www.ted.com/talks/ annie_murphy_paul_what_we_learn_before_we_re_born.html.

Brady, Michael T., Carrie L. Byington, H. Dele Davies, Kathryn M. Edwards, Mary P. Glode, Mary Anne Jackson, Harry L. Keyserling, et al. 2014. "Consumption of Raw or Unpasteurized Milk and Milk Products by Pregnant Women and Children." *Pediatrics* 133 (1): 175–79. doi:10.1542/ peds.2013–3502.

Brown, Lisa. "Nutritional Requirements During Pregnancy and Lactation" edited by Sari Edelstein and Judith Sharlin. *Life Cycle Nutrition: An Evidence-Based Approach.* Sudbury, MA: Jones and Bartlett. 2010.

Coletta, Jaclyn M., Stacey J. Bell, and Ashley S. Roman. 2010. "Omega-3 Fatty Acids and Pregnancy." *Reviews in Obstetrics and Gynecology* 3 (4): 163–71.

Curtis, Glade B., and Judith Schuler. *Your Pregnancy Week by Week.* Cambridge, MA: Da Capo Press. 2004.

"Dietary Reference Intakes and Adequate Intakes, Total Water and Macronutrients." 2014. Institute of Medicine of the National Academies. Accessed January 1. http://www.iom.edu/ Activities/Nutrition/SummaryDRIs/~/media/Files/Activity%20Files/Nutrition/DRIs/New%20 Material/3_RDA%20AI%20AMDR%20Values_Total%20Water%20and%20Macronutr.pdf.

"Dietary Reference Intakes and Adequate Intakes, Vitamins and Elements." 2014. Institute of Medicine of the National Academies. Accessed January 1. http://iom.edu/Activities/Nutrition/ SummaryDRIs/~/media/Files/Activity%20Files/Nutrition/DRIs/RDA%20and%20AIs _Vitamin%20and%20Elements.pdf.

Duyff, Roberta L., and American Dietetic Association. *American Dietetic Association Complete Food and Nutrition Guide.* New York: John Wiley & Sons. 2006.

Fackler, Martin, and Hiroko Tabuchi. 2013. "With a Plant's Tainted Water Still Flowing, No End to Environmental Fears." *The New York Times*, October 24, sec. World / Asia Pacific. http://www .nytimes.com/2013/10/25/world/asia/with-a-plants-tainted-water-still-flowing-no-end-to -environmental-fears.html.

Fisher, Nicholas S., Karine Beaugelin-Seiller, Thomas G. Hinton, Zofia Baumann, Daniel J. Madigan, and Jacqueline Garnier-Laplace. 2013. "Evaluation of Radiation Doses and Associated Risk from the Fukushima Nuclear Accident to Marine Biota and Human Consumers of Seafood." *Proceedings of the National Academy of Sciences* 110 (26): 10670–75. doi:10.1073/ pnas.1221834110.

Frazier, A. Lindsay, Carlos A. Camargo, Susan Malspeis, Walter C. Willett, and Michael C. Young. 2014. "Prospective Study of Peripregnancy Consumption of Peanuts or Tree Nuts by Mothers and the Risk of Peanut or Tree Nut Allergy in Their Offspring." *JAMA Pediatrics* 168 (2): 156–62. doi:10.1001/jamapediatrics.2013.4139.

Friedlander, Blaine. 2013. "More Choline for Mom Decreases Down Syndrome Effects." *Cornell Chronicle Website*. September 11. http://www.news.cornell.edu/stories/2013/09/more-choline -mom-decreases-down-syndrome-effects.

Gerendasy, Rebecca, and Fred Gerendasy. 2012. *Are You Worried about Mercury Levels in Tuna?* Cooking Up A Story. http://cookingupastory.com/are-you-worried-about-mercury-levels-in-tuna.

Howatson, Glyn, Phillip G. Bell, Jamie Tallent, Benita Middleton, Malachy P. McHugh, and Jason Ellis. 2012. "Effect of Tart Cherry Juice (Prunus Cerasus) on Melatonin Levels and Enhanced Sleep Quality." *European Journal of Nutrition* 51 (8): 909–16. doi:10.1007/s00394–011–0263–7.

Jones, Sandy, Marcie Jones, Peter S. Bernstein, and Claire M. Westdahl. *Great Expectations: Your All-in-One Resource for Pregnancy & Childbirth*. New York: Sterling Pub. 2004.

Koletzko, Berthold, Eric Lien, Carlo Agostoni, Hansjosef Böhles, Cristina Campoy, Irene Cetin, Tamas Decsi, et al. 2008. "The Roles of Long-Chain Polyunsaturated Fatty Acids in Pregnancy, Lactation and Infancy: Review of Current Knowledge and Consensus Recommendations." *Journal of Perinatal Medicine* 36 (1). doi:10.1515/JPM.2008.001. http://www.degruyter.com/view/j/jpme.2008.36.issue-1/jpm.2008.001/jpm.2008.001.xml.

Largeman-Roth, Frances. *Feed the Belly: The Pregnant Mom's Healthy Eating Guide*. Naperville, Ill.: Sourcebooks. 2009.

Luke, Barbara, and Tamara Eberlein. *When You're Expecting Twins, Triplets, or Quads: Proven Guidelines for a Healthy Multiple Pregnancy*. New York: HarperResource. 2004.

Martini, Kim. 2013. "True Facts about Ocean Radiation and the Fukushima Disaster." *Deep Sea News*. http://deepseanews.com/2013/11/true-facts-about-ocean-radiation-and-the-fukushima-disaster/.

Murkoff, Heidi Eisenberg, and Sharon Mazel. *What to Expect When You're Expecting*. New York: Workman Pub. 2008.

Oster, Emily. *Expecting Better: Why the Conventional Pregnancy Wisdom Is Wrong—and What You Really Need to Know*. New York: Penguin. 2013

Paul, Annie Murphy. *Origins: How the Nine Months before Birth Shape the Rest of Our Lives*. New York: Free Press. 2010.

Physicians for Social Responsibility, USA, Physicians for Global Survival, Canada, MedAct-Health professionals for a safer, fairer & better world, UK, Dutch Association for Medical Polemology, The Netherlands, International Physicians for the Prevention of Nuclear War, Germany, Physicians for Social Responsibility / IPPNW, Switzerland, Association of Doctors for the Prevention of Nuclear War, France, et al. 2013. "Annotated Critique of United Nations Scientific Committee on the Effects of Atomic Radiation (UNSCEAR) October 2013 Fukushima Report to the UN General Assembly." http://www.psr.org/assets/pdfs/critique-of-unscear-fukushima.pdf.

Planck, Nina. *Real Food for Mother and Baby: The Fertility Diet, Eating for Two, and Baby's First Foods*. New York: Bloomsbury USA. 2009.

Roizen, Michael F., and Mehmet Oz. *You: Having a Baby: The Owner's Manual to a Happy and Healthy Pregnancy*. New York: Free Press. 2009.

Simopoulos, Artemis P., Alexander Leaf, and Norman Salem. 1999. "Workshop on the Essentiality of and Recommended Dietary Intakes for Omega-6 and Omega-3 Fatty Acids." *Journal of the American College of Nutrition* 18 (5): 487–89. doi:10.1080/07315724.1999.10718888.

Index

NOTE: PAGE REFERENCES IN *ITALICS* INDICATE RECIPE PHOTOGRAPHS.

Q

Quinoa
  Baby Bundle Burritos, 188–89
  and Salmon Two Ways, 133–34, *135*

R

Raisin(s)
  Cinnamon Bread, 42–43
  Mama Nature's Candy Bars, 96, *97*
  Trail Mix (Bars), 103–5, *104*
  Yogurt Muesli Parfait with Strawberry Sauce,
    71–73, *72*

Ratatouille, Lentil, with Baked Polenta, 211–12, *213*

Registered dieticians, 41

Relish, Celery Avocado, Smoky Turkey Tacos with,
  144–46, *145*

Rice
  Black, Salad with Roasted Asparagus and Tuna,
    157–59, *158*
  Brown, and Escarole Minestrone, 160–61
  Pudding, Brown Butter Fig, 245
  Sushi-Fix Veggie Hand Roll with Scallion Mayo,
    139–41, *140*

S

Salads
  Alaskan Niçoise, with Lemon Vinaigrette, *150*,
    151–52
  Apple, with Pepitas and Honey Cider Vinaigrette,
    153
  Black Rice, with Roasted Asparagus and Tuna,
    157–59, *158*
  Cranberry Pistachio, with Chive Vinaigrette,
    162
  Green Grape and Avocado, with Lime Yogurt
    Dressing, 166
  Kale and White Bean, Everlasting, 167
  Rainbow Farro, 171
  Red and Orange Sunflower, 172, *173*
  Spicy Cabbage Crunch, 176
  Spring Mix with Strawberries, Pine Nuts,
    and Goat Cheese, 177
  Steak and Orange, with Sesame Dressing,
    178, 179–80

Vinegar Slaw, 225–26
  Watermelon, with Muddled Mint Vinaigrette, 184

Salmon
  Alaskan Niçoise Salad with Lemon Vinaigrette,
    150, 151–52
  and Quinoa Two Ways, 133–34, *135*
  wild Alaskan, buying, 131

Salsa
  Lime, with Giant Chips, 91
  Pineapple, Kickin' Chicken with, 124, *125*

Sandwiches
  Beefy Chopped Veggie Sloppy Joes, 191–92
  Chive Fried Egg and Bacon, 40–41
  Grilled Tomato, Red Onion, and Mozzarella Cheese,
    120–21
  Quinoa and Salmon Salad, 134

Sausage
  Kale, and Mushrooms, Bulgur with, 136–37
  Sweet Potato Black Bean Hash, 142–43

Scones, Lemon-Berry Barley, 51–52

Seafood. *See* Fish; Shellfish

Shellfish
  One-Pot Pearl Couscous with Shrimp and Tomatoes,
    122–23
  raw or uncooked, avoiding, 31, 141
  Simple Fish Stew, 221–22

Shrimp
  Simple Fish Stew, 221–22
  and Tomatoes, One-Pot Pearl Couscous with,
    122–23

Slaw, Vinegar, 225–26

Sloppy Joes, Beefy Chopped Veggie, 191–92

Smoothies
  Blueberry Kefir, 36, *37*
  Honeydew Kiwi, 88
  Peaches and Creamsicle, 98
  Strawberry Mango, 102

Snacks. *See also* Dips
  Citrus Ginger Pops, *80*, 81
  grab-and-go, ideas for, 82
  Mama Nature's Candy Bars, 96, *97*
  Maple Pecan Popcorn, *92*, 93–94
  Olive Oil Parmesan Popcorn, 95